Computing Concepts
for Information Technology
How computers really work

Computing Concepts
for Information Technology
How computers really work

Bob Brown

Campers' Press

Atlanta

ISBN: 979-8-9887530-0-1 (Paperback)
         979-8-9887530-1-8 (ePub)

Bob Brown: https://isni.org/isni/0000000491573348

Cover design by Andrea Vom Ende Thoma, Cover photograph by nexusplexus/123RF. Back cover author photo by Ali Laipple Photography.

The photograph of John von Neumann, Figure 3-1, is courtesy of Los Alamos National Laboratory. Unless otherwise indicated, this information has been authored by an employee or employees of the Los Alamos National Security, LLC (LANS), operator of the Los Alamos National Laboratory under Contract No. DE-AC52-06NA25396 with the U.S. Department of Energy. The U.S. Government has rights to use, reproduce, and distribute this information. The public may copy and use this information without charge, provided that this Notice and any statement of authorship are reproduced on all copies. Neither the Government nor LANS makes any warranty, express or implied, or assumes any liability or responsibility for the use of this information.

Algorhyme by Radia Perlman, Figure 5-8, appeared in "An Algorithm for Distributed Computation of a Spanning Tree in an Extended LAN," *ACM SIGCOMM Computer Communication Review Volume 15 Issue 4 Sept. 1985,* copyright © 1985 by the Association for Computing Machinery and is used by permission.

The image of Blaise de Vigenère, Figure 7-1, is © Trustees of the British Museum. Re-use of the image requires a license from the British Museum.

Publisher's Cataloging-in-Publication
Provided by Cassidy Cataloguing Services, Inc.

Names:	Brown, Bob (Robert L.) (professor), author.
Title:	Computing concepts for information technology : how computers really work / Bob Brown.
Description:	Atlanta : Campers' Press, [2023] | Audience: University and high school students; professors; general audience interested in how computers work. | Includes bibliographical references and index.
Identifiers:	ISBN: 979-8-9887530-0-1 (Paperback) | 979-8-9887530-1-8 (ePub) | LCCN: 2023912874
Subjects:	LCSH: Computers. | Information technology. | Computer science. | Computer architecture. | Computer systems. | Binary system (Mathematics) | Computer arithmetic. | Digital electronics. | Logic circuits. | Input design, Computer. | Computer input-output equipment. | Data transmission systems. | Computer networks. | Computer programming. | Computer software. | Computer security. | Electronic information resources--Security measures. | BISAC: COMPUTERS / Information Technology. | COMPUTERS / Computer Architecture. | COMPUTERS / Hardware / General.
Classification:	LCC: QA76.5 .B76 2023 | DDC: 621.39--dc23

Printed and bound in the United States of America
Fourth printing: February 1 2024.

To the hundreds of
Southern Polytechnic State University
students who helped me refine
my approach to this material,
thank you!

Table of Contents

Chapter 2   Digital Logic   49

Chapter 3 The CPU and Memory   69

Chapter 4 Input and Output   107

Chapter 7 Information Security   215

Foreword

Why study this book? To understand the importance of this type of book, one needs to look at the topics in the book and their relevance to students studying a computing discipline in the 21st century. These topics are crucial to understanding the foundations for information technology, computer science, and the other computing disciplines. Why are the topics included in this book important to you?

If you were building a house, you would not start putting walls up without first preparing a foundation. A foundation serves to keep the house stable. When a foundation is unstable, the whole house becomes unstable. How does this relate to computing? The concepts in this book are the foundation for the computing disciplines.

The diagram shows the hierarchy of the interaction between a computing user, application software, operating systems, and hardware. Notice that hardware is at the bottom of the hierarchy. It is our computing foundation. Hardware interacts with software, both operating systems and application software and all of these interact with users. Each one of these levels has many components. To get to each higher level we need to understand the levels below it. To build and use an operating system correctly, we need to understand all components that make up computing hardware and how they interface with the operating systems. To understand the use and need for application software, we should know the basics of operating systems so we can write software application code to work efficiently and accurately with the operating system and hardware. The application software must support the needs of the users.

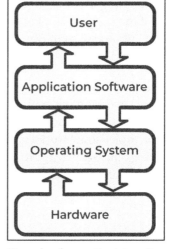

Hierarchy of computing interactions
Wikipedia /McGeddon

Most computing disciplines concentrate on the "soft" side of computing – primarily operating systems and computer applications. Computer engineers are more concerned with computer hardware – in other words, their discipline teaches how to design and build the hardware components. However, this does not mean that computing majors don't need to know anything about hardware and how it interfaces with the operating system and application software. Practitioners of information technology, computer science, and other computing disciplines need to know what components make up the hardware of a computer system, but not how to design and manufacture the actual hardware.

Many computer programmers believe they don't really need to understand operating systems or hardware because they are just working with computer programs. A computer programmer who uses, writes, and updates application software needs the knowledge of how operating systems work, and how the hardware components interface with the operating system. This knowledge is crucial in writing complete, efficient, and usable software applications. However, most programmers feel very removed from the operating systems and hardware. As shown in the hierarchy diagram, the interfacing of hardware, operating systems, application software and users is both "up" and "down". Computing professionals need to be able to move both up and down in the hierarchy. Our primary study in information technology and computer science is the operating system and application software, but many information technology and computer science students go into networking where they work with the physical network and the software that controls it. They also go into cloud computing or web programming where they interface with physical and virtual networks. Computer security is a huge area of study in computing the practitioners of which need to have a good understanding of hardware and operating systems and their interaction with application software in order to protect all parts of a system.

This book is dedicated to helping students in the computing disciplines master the basics of computing hardware and how it interfaces with the operating system, application software, and the users. It supplies some fundamental information on how information is represented and processed in computer systems and surveys some areas you will study more deeply in later classes.

Dr. Bob Brown has been teaching hardware and software concepts to undergraduate students majoring in computing disciplines for many years. He also worked for 30 years in the information technology industry, dealing with hardware, software, and operating systems. His professional work experience has given him a unique knowledge of these areas and he brings this knowledge to this textbook. Learning these important concepts will give you a solid foundation for your computing career.

Rebecca H. Rutherfoord
Professor Emerita of Information Technology
former Information Technology Department Chair
June, 2023

Preface

About this book

In more than twenty years of university teaching, I spent countless hours translating textbook information into language comfortable to students who were engaged with the material. Prior to my career in academia, I spent nearly thirty years managing information technology in the healthcare industry. The person who recommended me for my first university teaching position told the department chair that the basics of computing hardware and software "made sense" to me. After fifty years of the material making sense to me and helping others make sense of it, and after I had retired from teaching, I convinced myself that I could explain it in writing in a way that would be clear to university students.

This book is suitable for those with no prior study of computer systems, although it may be helpful to have had prior experience with a high-level programming language such as Java or Python.

The careful reader will notice that the level of detail in this book is highly variable. That is the result of a conscious decision to delve into those parts that are likely to be mysterious to students and treat more lightly the parts with which most students are comfortable and those they are likely to study in more detail in later classes. This book principally addresses students of information technology. They will have full semester classes in subjects like operating systems and information security, but almost none will have a course in computer architecture. The chapters on digital logic and how the CPU and memory work have enough detail to stand alone. Subjects like information security are written to provide a starting point for further study.

The careful reader will also notice frequent references to people, their contributions to computing, and the dates of those contributions. Students who may read this book have never known a world without iPhones. I believe it is important that they know that the inventions that make 21st century computing possible did not spring fully formed from some Silicon Valley corporate campus.

This is an open access, that is, free[*] book. I've tried to achieve the same level of quality as books costing hundreds of dollars. Every chapter has been reviewed by a peer and at least one subject matter expert, then proofread by a colleague who is an absolute stickler for detail. I hope you won't judge the value of this book by its cost.

---

[*] Unless you want a "real book," printed on dead trees, or a formatted EPUB book. Those necessarily cost money, but in this case, not very much.

To the reader

This book tells a story. It's a story with characters and events, and a plot line that leads from the earliest attempts at automatic computation to the ubiquitous, seamless, always-connected world of computing in the 21st century. I urge you to read it like a story, beginning at Chapter 0 and continuing to the end. If you do that and put effort into seeing how the pieces fit together, you will come away with a conceptual model of computing hardware and software that, one hopes, has just the right amount of detail in every part to prepare you for your future studies.

One of the reviewers of this book remarked that we should not allow students to graduate until they know enough about what makes computers work to understand that they don't contain little green Martians using calculators. *Computing Concepts for Information Technology* will allow you to meet that obligation; the only Martian in this book is in .

Conventions

Boldface indicates defined words and important concepts.
Italics are for emphasis, for foreign words and abbreviations, publication titles, and to highlight proper names in the index.
SMALL CAPS are function names, operators, logic signals, and instruction mnemonics.
`Monospaced text` is used for code, of which this book has very little.

Acknowledgments

This book would not have been possible without the help and encouragement of Bob Harbort, Emeritus Professor of Computer Science, Kennesaw State University. He read every word of this book, many of them more than once, and provided advice and discussion that vastly improved the original draft.

The subject matter expert reviewers checked the details, spotted my mistakes, and kept me on track. Their help was essential to success. Thank you to James Cannady, Georgia Tech Research Institute, Sumit Chakravarty, Lance Crimm, Bill Forsyth, Dan Lo, Douglas Malcolm, and Liang Zhao of Kennesaw State University.

Thanks to Becky Rutherfoord for help, encouragement, and for the Foreword to this book.

Thanks also to Betty Abbott, Cindy Neck, and Anthony Trauring for their painstaking and careful reading and for their helpful suggestions.

The cover design and the Martian in Figure 3-3 are by Andrea Vom Ende Thoma.

Thanks to Ken Saladin, author of *Anatomy & Physiology–The Unity of Form and Function*, for advice on the structure of the chapter summaries of learning objectives.

Errata

I had an enormous amount of help with this book, but any errors that remain are mine alone. As errors are discovered and reported, I will maintain a list of errata here: https://computingconcepts.net/errata.html

Remarks and corrections

If you have remarks on this material, and especially if you find errors, please write to me: Bob.Brown@Kennesaw.edu.

The latest information about the book is available here: https://computingconcepts.net/

Emory Village, Georgia
August, 2023

Chapter 0
Where We Are – How We Got Here

"…a device in which an individual stores all his books, records, and communications, and which…may be consulted with exceeding speed and flexibility."

—Vannevar Bush

This book will be in the hands of students in the third decade of the 21st century. Although there were early attempts at mechanical computing machines, electronic, programmable, digital computers have been around for only about 80 years.

In the twenty-first century, digital computers are everywhere. You almost certainly have one with you now, although you may call it a "phone." You are more likely to read this book on a digital device than on paper.

Figure 0-1
Vannevar Bush
U.S. Library of Congress

An electronic digital computer is a machine. It has mechanisms for receiving input of information, for processing and storing information, and for producing and communicating results. You will find computers in all kinds of specialized devices, but the computer itself is one of the most general-purpose machines ever devised.

The more general a technology, the more and more varied are the uses to which it will be put. We use computers for everything from preparing tax returns and processing them to landing airplanes, generating medical images, and displaying pictures of cats.

0.1 Computing in the 21st Century

As we begin the 21st century, those ubiquitous "phones" are the most numerous computers. We use them to communicate with both voice and text, but each one also has more computing power than all of NASA during the first manned moon landing in the summer of 1969. Although phones are the most numerous computers, they aren't the only ones. Many individuals and nearly all businesses also have larger personal-use computers, from tablets like the iPad to laptop computers and desktop computers. People use more powerful personal-use computers called workstations for graphic arts and scientific computing.

Huge data centers house thousands of pizza-box size computers and power enterprises like Google, Facebook, and Amazon along with many others. Similar data centers offer "cloud" computing and storage to individuals and to businesses of all sizes from tiny to Fortune 10.

Mainframe computers, machines with very large memories and enormous input and output capabilities, once called "dinosaurs," still power about two thirds of the Fortune 100 businesses. The principal reasons are outstanding ability to perform input and output, which we will cover in more detail in Chapter 4, and the ability to handle hundreds or thousands of transactions per second while maintaining database consistency. Database technology is covered in Chapter 6.

Supercomputers, computing machines vastly more powerful than those used by most people, perform such jobs as weather forecasting and complex simulations. We now call the use of supercomputers **high performance computing**.

Tiny computers embedded in machinery from microwave ovens to automobiles, ships, and airplanes perform control functions formerly handled by special-purpose mechanical or electronic devices. Using programmable controllers in this way makes the functions they perform both more flexible and less expensive than the custom components they replaced. They may, however, make the devices in which they are embedded more difficult to repair because repairs might require software changes. Making those changes may be complex, and manufacturers often consider their embedded software to be proprietary and a trade secret.

Not only are computers everywhere, nearly all are also interconnected. Most of the students reading this book cannot remember a time when Internet access was not available to nearly everyone. Today Internet access is available with our phones, in our homes and places of work, and in our cars in most parts of the United States. The 5G cellular technology being widely deployed as this is written and the 6G technology coming next promise to make speeds in the billions of bits per second available nearly everywhere.

We use computers primarily for communication, from text messages and phone conversations to surfing web sites and streaming sound and video. We also use computers for storage of very rapidly growing amounts of data, for control functions, and for computational tasks like simulations. Making computing machines "intelligent," for some definition of intelligence, has been a goal of computer scientists for nearly as long as there have been computers. The 21st century has seen remarkable progress in machine learning and artificial intelligence. As storage, processing speed, and input and output capabilities have improved, it has become possible to analyze truly huge quantities of data. The ability to process "big data" has spawned the new discipline of **data science and analytics**. Those increases in storage capacity and processing speed have also enabled what is called **generative artificial intelligence**, the technology of programs like ChatGPT.

None of this will seem new to most readers of this book, but the way we got here is a fascinating story. It probably began in pre-history when people first began to count their possessions and to trade with one another. Advances in mathematics from the 17th century onward laid some of the foundations. Although there have been mechanical counting and computing devices since ancient times, the foundation for today's electronic computing machines was laid much later.

0.2 Early Ideas

Computers operate on numbers, and the development of systems of numbers suitable for use as the internal representation of data in a computer is a story of its own. That story appears in the next chapter.

A fundamental characteristic of computers is that they are **programmable**. Different programs allow the computer to do different things; computers are general purpose machines. Possibly the first programmable machine was invented in the years just after 1801 by French weaver Joseph Marie Jacquard. Jacquard invented a weaving loom that could be programmed by punching holes in cards. Once a set of cards was prepared, the same fabric design could be woven over and over, error-free. Different cards wove a different design. The Jacquard loom was programmable. In the 1960s and 1970s, punched cards similar to Jacquard's were used as input for electronic computers. Jacquard looms are still used in the 21st century, but the programs are stored in electronic memory, not on punched cards.

Celestial navigation – navigation using the positions of the sun, moon, planets, and stars – was important to the British Navy, merchant shipping, and military forces everywhere until the development of radio navigation systems in the 20th century. Celestial navigation used a sighting instrument called a sextant to measure angles to celestial objects and a book of tables called an ephemeris to determine the position of that celestial object at that time. Preparation of the tables was time-consuming, and calculation, transcription, or typesetting errors could result in lost ships.

About 1822 Charles Babbage, a British mathematician and philosopher, proposed to automate the production of such tables, including the automation of printing plates, to eliminate sources of error. With funding by the British government, Babbage designed and began construction of a mechanical computing machine called the Difference Engine. He and the craftsman hired to build the Difference Engine disagreed over costs and the project was never completed. Babbage designed an improved version but was not able to get funding to complete it.

The Difference Engine was a special-purpose mechanical computer. Confident that his design was correct,[1] Babbage went on to design a general-purpose mechanical computing machine, the Analytical Engine, that was remarkably similar to a modern computer. The part Babbage called the mill corresponds to the central processing unit of a modern computer, and the part Babbage called the store corresponds to the memory.

Lord Byron's[2] daughter, Augusta Ada King, Countess of Lovelace, had corresponded with Babbage because of her interest in mathematics. She was fascinated by the Analytical En-

---

1   It was. Near the end of the 20th century, the Science Museum in London built two Difference Engines from Babbage's plans and to the manufacturing tolerances of the 19th century. The Difference Engines worked as intended.

2   The same Lord Byron you met or will meet in English classes.

gine, and in her *Notes* included programs to be run on the Analytical Engine, possibly making Lady Ada the first computer programmer.

In 1854, George Boole, another British mathematician and philosopher, published *An Investigation of the Laws of Thought* in which he expanded on his earlier idea of an algebra over finite sets of discrete values. We now call that Boolean algebra. It was not until 1937 that Claude Shannon, an American mathematician and electrical engineer, wrote in his master's thesis that, if the discrete values of Boolean algebra were zero and one, or on and off, they could describe switching systems, and that Boolean algebra could be used to optimize switching systems. We'll meet Boole and Shannon again in Chapter Three.

0.3 The World War II Era

During the World War II era, several important inventions were made at about the same time by different people or groups in different places. Simultaneous invention occurred at other times in history, too. Some historians say these inventions were possible "because it's time." That is, the necessary knowledge and technology had been developed to allow invention to occur. By the 1930s electricity was widely available in cities and towns, electrical engineering was an established discipline, and electronic components like vacuum tubes were being mass-produced. Babbage's idea of a programmable computing device was over a hundred years old, as was George Boole's algebra. The Boolean algebra was applied to switching by Shannon in 1937. Alan Turing's 1936 doctoral dissertation described what Alonzo Church later called a Turing machine.

The World War itself provided incentive to complete quickly anything related to the war effort and provided liberal funding for research and development.

Howard Aiken of Harvard conceived the Harvard Mark I computing machine, which IBM called the Automatic Sequence Controlled Calculator. Aiken presented the concept to IBM in 1937 and IBM funded and built it. The Mark I included and improved upon many of the features of Babbage's Analytical Engine. One of the uses of the Mark I was the production of mathematical tables, Babbage's original intention over a hundred years earlier.

Also in 1937, John Vincent Atanasoff of Iowa State College and graduate student Clifford Berry conceived and began work on the Atanasoff-Berry Computer, or ABC. The ABC used binary numbers internally and had an electronic arithmetic and logic unit. World War II interrupted Atanasoff's work on the ABC and it fell into obscurity.

Artillery in World War II was aimed using firing tables much like the tables of an ephemeris. Each kind of artillery piece needed its own firing tables, and the tables included such factors as kind of shell, kind of propellant, distance to the target, and wind direction and velocity. They were computed by hand by women whose job title was "computer." The process was slow, and new artillery pieces were being developed faster than firing tables could be prepared for them. Army Lieutenant Herman Goldstine convinced his superiors that electronic computation of firing tables would get them into the field faster. That was the beginning of the ENIAC[3] project. J. Presper Eckert, John Mauchly, and many others were involved in the design and construction of ENIAC at the University of Pennsylvania. ENIAC began solving operational problems in December 1945. The first real problem was a calculation for the Los Alamos National Laboratory related to the development of the hydrogen bomb, World War II having ended in September.

ENIAC was entirely electronic, having no mechanical parts. However, it did not yet have the capability to store programs. A mechanism to allow for stored programs, and eventually an electronic memory, were added later. ENIAC used vacuum tubes as its computing elements. ENIAC remained in operation until 1956.

Those building the ENIAC learned quite a lot about the design of electronic computers, much of it too late to be implemented in ENIAC itself. Eckert and Mauchly proposed to the Army's Ballistic Research Laboratory another computer to be called EDVAC.[4] John

Figure 0-2
ENIAC

U.S. Army

von Neumann,[5] then at the Los Alamos National Laboratory, was serving as a consultant on the ENIAC project. In June, 1945 while returning by train to Los Alamos from the Moore School of Electrical Engineering in Philadelphia, von Neumann compiled a set of design notes which he called *First Draft of a Report on the EDVAC*.[6] Von Neumann mailed the handwritten notes to Herman Goldstine, who was the Army's project manager for the construction of computers at the Moore School. Although von Neumann's notes were a distillation of the work of many people, Goldstine had the notes typed and circulated listing von Neumann as the sole author.

Von Neumann's *First Draft* described what came to be known as the **von Neumann architecture** and is a description of how computers are still designed. He described a computer with an arithmetic and logic unit, a control unit, a memory, input and output, and storage. Programs and data were to be stored in the same memory, instructions to be executed in

---

3   Electronic Numerical Integrator and Computer

4   Electronic Discrete Variable Automatic Computer

5   Pronounced "von NOY-man."

6   If you are curious about what a description of how computers are still designed looks like, you can find copies of the *First Draft* on line or buy a typeset copy of all 47 pages!

sequence, and data represented as binary numbers.

There were significant developments in computing in the United Kingdom during World War II as well, but, because of the British Official Secrets Act, most were not revealed until the 1970s. A key figure was Alan Turing, who designed a code-breaking machine called a Bombe based on an earlier design from Poland. Turing also contributed to the design of the Colossus electronic computers. Probably Turing's most important contribution was the description, in his 1936 doctoral dissertation of what we now call a Turing machine. The **Turing machine** is a mathematical model of computation that can be used to prove that there exist problems that "look computational" but cannot be solved.

Eckert and Mauchly, having built ENIAC and EDVAC, formed the Eckert–Mauchly Computer Corporation to design, build, and sell electronic computers. Their first product was called UNIVAC.[7] It is important as the first computer design of which multiple units were sold commercially.

0.4 Vannevar Bush and the Memex

…a device in which an individual stores all his books, records, and communications, and which is mechanized so that it may be consulted with exceeding speed and flexibility. It is an enlarged intimate supplement to his memory. (Bush, 1945).

Apart from the somewhat outdated language and the citation date at the end, which is a dead giveaway, you might think this was a description of a 21st century smartphone. This remarkable description is from Vannevar[8] Bush's essay, "As We May Think," published in the *Atlantic Monthly* in July, 1945.

Dr. Bush was describing, not a smartphone, but a hypothetical device he called a **memex**. The size of an office desk, the memex was for information storage and retrieval. Bush was not trying to predict future technology. The memex was based on technology available at the time or likely to be available in the five- to ten-year future. For example, Bush discussed a camera that could take pictures that would be instantly available without development needing chemicals and a darkroom. The first Polaroid instant camera was sold in 1948; the first digital camera was not made until 1975, thirty years after Bush's article.

Bush's memex addressed the information storage and retrieval needs of that time, 1945. He was concerned by what we now call information overload. An important part of the memex was enough storage to hold all the documents an individual might need and the ability to connect documents with associative links, which we now call hyperlinks. Bush's description included the ability to respond to voice commands and even to take dictation automatically. He envisioned a head-mounted camera that would allow the user to photograph whatever

---

7   Universal Automatic Computer

8   Pronounced "va-NEE-var," to rhyme with achiever.

was being seen. That was realized in 2013 as Google Glass.[9] In short, Bush was describing using technology to manage information in ways that were impossible for an unaided human. In doing so, he foresaw much of the technology which we take for granted in the 21st century.

0.5 Transistors, Chips and Moore's Law

The ENIAC was an important advance in electronic computing, but it had a serious physical limitation: its computational elements were vacuum tubes. Vacuum tubes are made of glass, and so relatively delicate to begin with. If the vacuum is lost, the tube will not function. Vacuum tubes work on the principle of thermionic emission. The cathode (negative element) was heated by a heater similar to the filament in an incandescent light bulb. Like the filaments in incandescent light bulbs, those heaters eventually failed; the tube burned out. At first several tubes a day failed. By running the tubes at a slightly lower voltage, they reduced the failure rate to one every two or so days (Randall, 2006). Doubling the computing power by doubling the number of tubes would lead to a crash a day.

Figure 0-3
A vacuum tube.
Anucha Par-
brohm/123RF

An other problem was heat. The ENIAC consumed about 150 kW of power, the equivalent of 1,500 100-watt incandescent bulbs and produced as much heat as 1,500 incandescent bulbs. It required two twelve-horsepower blowers to conduct that heat away (Williams, 1985).

The transistor, invented at Bell Laboratories in 1947 and independently by Herbert Mataré in 1948, could perform the same switching functions as vacuum tubes. That solved both problems. Transistors are solid-state devices, so do not need a vacuum or glass envelope. There is no heater, so transistors consume much less power than vacuum tubes and produce much less heat. A transistor as a discrete electronic component is about the size of a pencil eraser, while a vacuum tube is about the size of a human thumb.

The next step was the invention in 1958 of the integrated circuit "chip" nearly simultaneously by Robert Noyce, Jack Kilby, and Kurt Lehovec. An integrated circuit packages many transistors and other electronic devices on a single semiconductor chip. The first commercial chips had tens of transistors. Modern chips can have billions.

In 1965, Gordon Moore, then director of research and development at Fairchild Semiconductor, wrote in the *Electronics* magazine that the density of devices on integrated circuits doubles about every year, and that he expected this trend to continue at least until 1975

---

9   For those who may not remember, Google Glass was mounted on a frame like eyeglasses. It could take pictures or video, respond to voice commands, and display information in the wearer's field of vision. Google Glass Enterprise Edition 2 was intended for workers in industrial, medical, or similar settings. Google discontinued Google Glass Enterprise Edition in March, 2023.

(Moore, 1965). Moore later revised his estimate to doubling about every two years. This came to be known as Moore's Law, although it is an empirical observation, not a physical law. Moore died in March, 2023 at the age of 94.

The significance of Moore's Law is this: the cost of a semiconductor chip is roughly proportional to the area and the computational power is roughly proportional to the number of devices. If the density doubles every 12 to 24 months, in two years or less, we can get the same computational power at half the cost or twice the power at the same cost.

People have predicted the end of Moore's Law several times in the last decade. In Chapter 3 you will meet Chenming Hu, whose invention of the FinFET transistor probably extends the life of Moore's Law to 2030 or later. (Perry, 2020) Following the FinFET will be Gate All Around and 3D complementary transistors that will further extend Moore's Law. (Radosavljevic & Kavalieros, 2022)

0.6 Computing Grows Up

The field of computing did not leap directly from 1950 to 2023. There was a lot of growing up, and it was not without growing pains.

Computers probably first came to the attention of the general public when CBS television and Remington Univac arranged to use a UNIVAC computer to attempt to predict the outcome of the U.S. presidential election of 1952 from early returns. News staff, including Walter Cronkite and Charles Collingsworth, described the computer as a "giant electronic brain" in television news programs. Programming correctly predicted the outcome of the election very early in the evening, but CBS held the prediction for several hours because they didn't trust it.

In 1957 the Soviet Union launched Sputnik, the first artificial Earth satellite. That feat convinced the American public and policy-makers that the Soviet Union was far ahead of the United States scientifically and began an effort to increase science education in the U.S.

As you saw in Section 0.5, the integrated circuit "chip" was invented in 1958. It is impossible to overstate the importance of this invention. Without integrated circuits, the other advances in computing would have been impossible.

Beginning about 1959, IBM and other computer manufacturers introduced computers that mid-sized companies could afford. In the same year, Digital Equipment Corporation released the first minicomputer, the PDP-1.

In 1969, ARPA, the U.S. Advanced Research Projects Agency began work on what would become the Internet.

Also in 1969, the Nippon Calculating Machine Corporation approached Intel with a request to design a chip set for an electronic calculator. The result was the Intel 4004, a complete four-bit CPU on a single chip, introduced in 1971. It was quickly followed by the Intel 8008, an eight-bit CPU. (That pocket calculator cost nearly $400, the equivalent of almost $3,000 in 2023 dollars.)

The first microcomputer, the Datapoint 2200, was introduced in 1971 at a price of $7,800 and equipped with 8 K bytes of memory. The first microcomputer that an individual could reasonably afford was the MITS Altair in 1975. It came as a $200 kit and included 256 bytes of memory. Paul Allen and Bill Gates wrote a version of the Basic programming language for the Altair and that was the beginning of Microsoft. Apple Computer didn't come along until 1976 and the IBM PC wasn't released until 1981.

Figure 0-4
Datapoint 2200.
Ken Shirriff

Commercial access to the Internet was available in 1989 and that same year Sir Tim Berners-Lee invented the World Wide Web. Bill Gates and Microsoft thought the Internet would be a passing fad, and so were very late to adapt to the idea of ubiquitous connectivity. Microsoft did eventually adjust to the fact that the Internet is here to stay.

Vannevar Bush's memex was realized as a pocket device with the introduction in the mid-1990s of the Palm Pilot, a personal digital assistant small enough to be carried in a pocket. Cellular phones were available then, too, but they only made phone calls. The Blackberry could send two-way text messages.

From about 1995, everyone was concerned with the so-called Y2K problem. Programmers had represented dates using only two digits for the year, and suddenly four would be needed. That caused high anxiety and the expenditure of hundreds of millions of dollars to remediate millions of computer programs amid dire predictions of disaster. About the worst that happened was that, in the early morning of January 1, 2000, the U.S. Naval Observatory briefly reported the date as "January 1, 19100." (Oops!)

Smart Phones combine the functions of that personal digital assistant and the cellular telephone. The Handspring Treo 180, in 2002, was the first fully-integrated smart phone. Now we have smart phone operating systems from Apple and Google, among others.

Remote job entry facilities allowed the use of distant computers in the 1960s, and timesharing systems were available before 1970. Cloud computing was first visualized by J.C.R. Licklider as "the Intergalactic Network" in about 1969. What we call cloud computing – self-provisioned and scalable computing – didn't arrive until the first decade of the 21st century.

We continue to make huge advances in both hardware and software. The "big thing" as this is being written is generative artificial intelligence, such as ChatGPT. Other advances, like fully autonomous automobiles, seem relatively far away despite decades of work. And, we still have to live with Wirth's Law: "software is getting slower more rapidly than hardware is becoming faster."[10]

0.7 The Internet and the World Wide Web

Most of the people reading this book are accustomed to sending a message to a friend or acquaintance anywhere in the world and having it delivered in seconds or less. An observation called Metcalfe's Law states that the value of a network to a user is proportional to the number of people one can contact. The *total* value is $n \times (n-1) / 2$, the number of connections. (Shapiro & Varian, 1998)[11] According to the Pew Research Center (2021), as of February, 2021, 77% of U.S. households had broadband Internet access at home and another 15% did not have broadband access but use smartphones as their primary means of Internet access at home. An astonishing 92% of Americans have Internet access at home or via a personal device. Of those who don't, poverty or geography explain some. There are even some Americans who choose not to have Internet access.

The Internet is an *Inter*net to emphasize that it is not a simple network, it is a network of networks. Your home or apartment router acts as a gateway to a connection to any other Internet-connected network in the world. It is *The* Internet because there's only one, connecting nearly all the world's networks. Metcalf's Law shows the enormous utility of having a single internetwork to connect all the world's networks.

The Internet had its beginnings in 1966 at ARPA, the U.S. Defense Advanced Research Projects Agency. A design based on the work of J. C. R. Licklider resulted, by 1969, in a packet-switched network of four nodes. Packet switching and the Transmission Control Protocol, TCP, both of which are integral to the modern Internet, were developed at ARPA. We will visit those fundamental concepts in detail in Chapter 5.

A very large number of standards, called RFCs, came out of the research funded by ARPA. A few of those are still in use, and many are direct ancestors of today's standards.

ARPANet was primarily a military network with universities and other sites connected under contract to ARPA. Military sites were later segregated onto their own network, with work completed in 1984. In 1986 the U.S. National Science Foundation founded a network using packet switching and the TCP protocol. The NSFNet was eventually opened to commercial access and finally operated entirely by commercial organizations since 1995.

The Internet of the 1980s was limited to electronic mail and file transfers. The University of Minnesota's Gopher[12] protocol provided a mechanism for indexing and searching Internet resources. There are still Gopher servers running, and Gopher clients are available for Win-

---

10   You will meet Dr. Wirth, whose name is pronounced "veert," in Chapter 6.

11   According to Shapiro and Varian, this observation was formulated by George Gilder and attributed to Metcalfe.

12   The University of Minnesota's athletic teams are the Golden Gophers.

dows, MacOS, Linux and Android.

The invention of the World Wide Web in 1989 by Tim Berners-Lee at CERN[13] changed the way most people access information, goods, and services. The Web protocols alone were not enough. The Mosaic Web browser was the first browser to be able to render pictures, and one of the first graphical browsers. Mosaic was developed at the National Center for Supercomputer Applications at the University of Illinois at Urbana-Champaign and released in 1993. The other missing piece was the search engine. Digital Equipment Corporation's AltaVista search engine, available to the public at the end of 1995, was among the earliest attempts to index all the World Wide Web.

To put the magnitude of this change into perspective, in 1985 Delta Air Lines had over 20 city ticket offices in the Atlanta area and hundreds throughout the United States. Today there are no city ticket offices in Atlanta, and only one in the entire United States. It's in Manhattan on East 45th Street.

0.8 Convergence

By 1990 the telephone system in the United States was nearly all digital apart from the "first mile" from telephone subscriber to the telephone office or multiplexing point. Invention of the compact disc in 1982 and the digital video disk[14] about 1995 meant that nearly all recorded audio and video were in digital formats by the end of the 20th century. The invention of the World Wide Web in 1989 and the transition of the Internet from a U.S. government funded network to the commercial Internet beginning in 1993 fundamentally changed the way most people get access to information, goods, and services.

Nearly every kind of information is now transmitted using the Internet Protocol. These changes led to the realization that all information, not just numbers and symbols, could be received, transformed, stored, and retrieved using computing and communication technology. That realization came to be called technological convergence, digital convergence, or just *convergence*. Convergence broadens the scope of practice of information technology. That means a broader scope of technology must be mastered by the student.

0.9 Systems and Architecture

We talk routinely about systems: computer systems, operating systems, sound systems, alarm systems, and many others. A major part of information technology is **systems integration**, that is, making multiple systems work together to achieve some purpose. Given that *systems* are so important in the profession of information technology, it makes sense to have a definition.

---

13 *Conseil Européen pour la Recherche Nucléaire*, or European Council for Nuclear Research

14 Later called "digital versatile disk," and still later, just DVD.

We can define **system** as a collection of components linked together to perform specific functions, and recognizable from the outside as a unit. Everything outside the system is its **environment,** and systems communicate with their environments through **interfaces.**

For example, a sound system might have a CD player, an amplifier, and speakers. The CD player is an interface; recorded music is communicated to the sound system through the interface. The speakers are also an interface, changing electrical signals into acoustic waves that we can hear.

In information technology, systems provide computation or communication, or some other service such a projecting media on a screen. Such systems consist of hardware, at least two layers of software: operating system and application software, and interfaces.

There are several ways to design information technology systems. These design paradigms are called architectures. Common architectures include monolithic, client-server, and multi-tier.

In a monolithic architecture, a single computing subsystem performs all the system's functions. A desktop computer not connected to a network is a simple example of a monolithic architecture. Everything that happens within that desktop computing system happens within a single computing subsystem.

The World Wide Web is an example of a client-server architecture. The web server receives requests from the client, a web browser, and responds by serving web pages. Client and server nearly always run on separate computing subsystems and communicate through a network.

Web mail is an example of a multi-tier architecture. There would be a browser client and web server, but the web server might communicate with both the browser and a "back end" mail server running in a different computing subsystem.

0.10 The Importance of Standards

Every day we use computing and communication equipment made by myriad companies and we expect it all to work together. Usually, it does. No one is surprised when a Samsung smart phone connects to a network operated by AT&T. We aren't even surprised when we place a voice call to a friend on another continent and have a perfect connection. That music CD made in Germany plays flawlessly on a player made in Japan. The pieces all fit together seamlessly because of thousands of standards published by more than a dozen standard-setting organizations.

Absence or incompatibility of standards can range from an annoyance to a serious problem. The three wireless devices on the author's desk have three different chargers with three different connectors. In the early days of the World Wide Web, browser makers competed in part by inventing their own HTML tags. Writing complex HTML that displayed identically across multiple browsers was effectively impossible before the World Wide Web Consortium took over the maintenance of standards. Even after the publication of standards it was many years before browser-makers implemented the official standards at least mostly uniformly.

Standards come from two types of organizations: official standards development organizations and standards development interest groups. The defining characteristic of standards development organizations is government authority or recognition. In the United States, it is the standards themselves, and not necessarily the standards development organizations, that receive government recognition. Interest groups have a less formal authority and are often formed as contractual organizations among companies that want to make their products interoperable (Biddle et al, 2012).

In the United States, the American National Standards Institute (ANSI) accredits standards-setting organizations. ANSI is a non-profit organization, not a government agency (Biddle et al, 2012).

The difference between a standards development organization and an interest group is illustrated by the wireless local area communication standards. The standard for short-range wireless Ethernet is established by the Institute for Electrical and Electronics Engineers, IEEE. IEEE acts as a standards development organization. The Wi-Fi Alliance, a group of over 400 manufacturers that provides testing, compliance certification and the "Wi-Fi Certified" logo is an interest group.

You will meet many important standards development organizations and interest groups as you work through this book.

0.11 No Such Thing as a Free Lunch

A recurring theme in Robert A. Heinlein's 1966 novel *The Moon is a Harsh Mistress* is TAN-STAAFL, "There ain't no such thing as a free lunch." As you go through this book, and as you go through a career in computing, you will find that TANSTAAFL is a recurring theme in computing as well. The rapid progress described by Moore's Law can sometimes fool us into thinking we're getting something for nothing; technology that was prohibitively expensive even five years ago is suddenly within reach of almost anyone. As you dig deeper, you will find that all of computing is a study in trade-offs.

The design of computing hardware is full of such trade-offs. It's possible to add circuitry to memory that will allow memory errors to be detected and even corrected. Doing so not only increases the cost of memory modules, it also slows the memory down slightly. Most of the slowdown can be avoided with a technique called triple modular redundancy, but avoiding the slowdown increases the cost by nearly three times and also increases the power consumption and the physical space required. Chapter 2 introduces the ripple-carry adder. It is simple to design, easy to understand, but very slow if numbers of more than a few bits are to be added. There are other adder designs, not considered in this book, that are much faster, but also more complex and consequently more expensive. In Chapter 3, you will learn that there are two approaches to designing a control unit for a CPU. One approach is fast but relatively expensive; the other approach is less expensive, but also slower. In the field of software, there are whole classes of algorithms that can be replaced by others that are much faster, but only if sufficient memory is available. This circumstance is so common that it has a name: space-time trade-off.

0.12 Information Technology

The term information technology was coined in 1958 in an article in the *Harvard Business Review*. Although electronic computers were barely ten years old, the authors predicted coming major changes not only in how information was processed but also in how it would be used, with the result of major changes in organizational structures (Leavitt & Whisler, 1958).

We define the *practice* of information technology as the integration, operation, and maintenance of computing hardware, software, communication facilities, services, and infrastructure to receive, transform, store, and retrieve information of all types in an efficient, effective, and secure manner.[15]

The Association for Computing Machinery defines the *academic discipline* of information technology this way: "Information Technology is the study of systemic approaches to select, develop, apply, integrate, and administer secure computing technologies to enable users to accomplish their personal, organizational, and societal goals" (Task Group on Information Technology Curricula, 2017). Information technology is the applied discipline of the field of computing.

A look at the breadth of the ACM definition explains why information technology is such an engaging and fun profession: of the computing disciplines, it is the one requiring the most breadth of knowledge. Sometimes it's enough to know that a particular area of knowledge exists so that you can recognize when you need it and look it up. Sometimes knowledge at the conceptual level is sufficient. In other cases, substantial depth of knowledge is needed. Your information technology curriculum will prepare you with the knowledge you need. This book is a step in that direction.

0.13 Professionalism

This book focuses on the *computing* concepts for information technology, that is, a high-lev-

---

15 This is the kind of long-winded sentence that gets a D– from English teachers, yet you will encounter sentences like this in another definition immediately below and in all manner of disclaimers, software contracts, and the like. See the endnote of this chapter for advice on making sense of such a sentence.

el look at the technology itself, with more detail in some areas. Other courses will provide even more technical detail. Not covered here is the broad area of skills, knowledge and behaviors generally called professionalism.

Information technology is increasingly a strategic asset and a customer-facing function for organizations. The obvious example is Amazon, but consider an airline trying to operate without information technology, and even the pharmacy that lets patients request refills online.

When information technology is a strategic asset, its practitioners must work within the organization, not performing an isolated back-office function. That means practitioners need excellent communication and teamwork skills. They must also know the business of the organization as well as the details of the technology.

When information is customer-facing, errors and defects are highly visible and not well tolerated. In the batch processing environment of 60 years ago, if there was an error, one could fix it and start over. Now errors and defects cause dissatisfaction, loss of business, and even major news stories. These can be what is euphemistically known as career-limiting events.

"Ethics" means doing the right thing (Baase 2008). Sometimes the "right thing" is obvious, sometimes less so. For example, is it ethical for your spouse or partner to bid on a contract at your organization? Professionals make a concerted effort to understand what is right in varying circumstances, and then to do what is right. The incredible power of information technology makes ethical decisions far more reaching than they were in the past. Professional associations such as the Association of Information Technology Professionals and the Association for Computing Machinery have codes of ethics to which members subscribe and which provide help in discerning what is right in difficult situations.

The practice of information technology is also influenced by local, national, and sometimes international law. Often such laws address the operation of types of organizations and not the information technology directly. Professionals will know the laws that affect their industry and how those laws constrain the operation of the organization.

You will see as you work through this book that the face of information technology changes incredibly rapidly. The nature of the world in which organizations operate also changes, sometimes very rapidly. The practitioner of information technology must stay current with both the technology and with the organization's business. That requires a conscious effort at lifelong learning.

If you are using this book as part of a formal curriculum of study, you will find that the curriculum includes the elements of professionalism. If you are studying on your own, be careful not to neglect the elements of professionalism.

0.14 Summary of Learning Objectives

*This section of the chapter tells you the things you should know about, but not **what** you should know about them. To test your knowledge, discuss the following concepts and topics with a study partner or in writing, ideally from memory.*

Charles Babbage's work, especially his work on the Analytical Engine, was of importance in the development of computing, as was his collaboration with Augusta Ada King, Countess of Lovelace. Babbage's work emphasized a fundamental difference between computers and other machines.

Development of computing machines was extremely rapid during the World War II era for at least two reasons. There were several important advances during that period. Of particular importance was Von Neumann's *First Draft of a Report on the EDVAC*.

The invention of the transistor and, a decade later, of the integrated circuit made a large difference in the development of computer hardware. Gordon Moore made an empirical observation later to be called Moore's Law that emphasized the importance and also made a prediction.

The Internet and the World Wide Web developed in the period between the World War II era and the 1990s. Those two technologies made a profound difference in both commerce and society.

Beginning around the turn of the 21st century, the effect of Moore's law changed who had computers and how they were used. New uses seemed to emerge daily. One such use was the convergence of computing and communications.

Information Technology began to be recognized as a profession with a specific definition and specific knowledge requirements early in the 21st century. It emerged as an academic discipline during that time.

Robert A. Heinlein's novel *The Moon is a Harsh Mistress* included a running theme particularly applicable to information technology.

0.15 References

Baase, S. (2008). *A Gift of Fire* (Third ed.). Upper Saddle River, NJ: Pearson Education.

Biddle, Brad, Frank X. Curci, Timothy Haslach, Gary E. Marchant, Andrew Askland, and Lyn Gaudet (2012). The Expanding Role and Importance of Standards in the Information and Communications Technology Industry, *Jurimetrics Journal*. 52(2), 177-208 (2012).

Bush, V. (1945). As We May Think. *Atlantic Monthly, 176*, pp. 101-108.

Leavitt, H. J., & Whisler, T. L. (1958). Management in the 1980's. *Harvard Business Review, 36*(6), 41-48.

Perry, T. S. (2020, May). How the Father of FinFETs Helped Save Moore's Law. *IEEE Spectrum, 57*(5), pp. 46-52.

Radosavljevic, Marko and Jack Kavalieros, (2022). Taking Moore's Law to New Heights. *IEEE Spectrum 50* (12), pp. 32-37, December 2022.

0.16 Endnote

This chapter includes the following horrible sentence: "We define the *practice* of information technology as the integration, operation, and maintenance of computing hardware, software, communication facilities, services, and infrastructure to receive, transform, store, and retrieve information of all types in an efficient, effective, and secure manner."

To make sense of such a thing, you must deconstruct it. Often you can do this mentally, but here is an example in print. Try it on the other definition in this chapter.

=====We define
the practice of information technology
===== as
the integration,
operation,
and maintenance
===== of
computing hardware,
software,
communication facilities,
services,
and infrastructure|

===== to
receive,
transform,
store, and retrieve
information
===== of
all types
===== in
an efficient,
effective,
and secure manner.

Chapter 1
Representing Information

"A picture may be worth a thousand words; a formula is worth a thousand pictures."

—Edsger Dijkstra

We do so many things with our digital devices that we may forget the original purpose: computation. When Dr. Howard Aiken was in charge of the huge, mechanical, Harvard Mark I calculator during World War II, he wasn't happy unless the machine was "making numbers," that is, completing the numerical calculations needed for the war effort. We still use computers for purely computational tasks, to make numbers. It may be less obvious, but the other things for which we use computers today are, underneath, also computational tasks. To make that phone call, your phone, really a computer, converts an electrical signal that's an analog of your voice to numbers, encodes and compresses them, and passes them onward to a cellular radio which is itself is controlled by numbers. Numbers are fundamental to our digital devic-

Figure 1-1

Howard Aiken, center, and Grace Murray Hopper, on Aiken's left, with other members of the Bureau of Ordnance Computation Project, in front of the Harvard Mark I computer at Harvard University, 1944.

Defense Visual Information Center

es, and so to understand those digital devices, we have to understand the numbers that flow through them.

1.1 Numbers as Abstractions

It is easy to suppose that as soon as humans began to accumulate possessions, they wanted to count them and make a record of the count. Someone's wealth might be told by the answer to "How many dogs do you have?" It is equally easy to suppose that such a question might be answered this way: ⲔⲎ ‖. Those tally marks, which could be scratched into stone or "written" on wood with charcoal, are an abstraction for some number of things, in the example, seven dogs.

Tally marks don't lend themselves well to representing large quantities, nor even to simple arithmetic, but they *do* serve as abstractions for physical quantities. Many civilizations invented systems of numbers more complex, and more useful, than tally marks. You are likely to be familiar with Roman numerals; we would represent those seven dogs as VII, which looks suspiciously like tally marks. It's easy to represent numbers of up to several thousand with Roman numerals and addition is easy. Subtraction, multiplication, and even division are possible.

In every case, numbers served as abstractions of physical quantities: dogs, sheep, hectares of land, gold pieces, and on and on. As you progress through the book, you will see that we can use numbers to represent symbols, sounds, pictures, video, and things like gestures on a touch screen. To do so, we need something more tractable than tally marks, or even Roman numerals.

1.2 Positional Number Systems

To get that something more tractable, number systems needed two things: a symbol for the null or empty value, which we now call zero, and the idea that the value of a symbol should depend not only on the symbol itself, but also on its position within a number. A symbol for the null value, or additive identity, was invented in India, and separately by the Mayans and Babylonians. There are ancient examples of positional notation, but without a symbol for the null value, it was hard to tell an empty space from sloppy writing.

The breakthrough came in the year 498 CE when Indian mathematician and astronomer Āryabhaṭa described a system of numbers in which each position had a value ten times its predecessor and which used a special symbol as a placeholder. You learned this in grade school. The teacher told you that numbers have a ones place on the right, then tens place, hundreds place, and so on.

The word zero started out in India as *śūnya*, translated by the Arabs as *sifr* (empty) and transliterated into Italian as *zefiro*. The word "zero" didn't appear in English until 1598. English-speakers still sometimes use the word *cipher* to mean something worthless and *ciphering* to mean arithmetic.[16]

Combining those breakthrough ideas of a symbol for the additive identity and positional notation for the value of symbols in a number gave us the modern decimal system of numbers. Let's look at an example. The number 1,037 is $1 \times 1000 + 0 \times 100 + 3 \times 10 + 7 \times 1$. Starting from the right, that's the ones place, tens place, hundreds place and thousands place we learned about in grade school. It's called the **decimal** system because it is based on powers of ten. Another word for "decimal" system is **base ten** system.

To examine the decimal system further we need two rules of mathematics.

Rule: Any number to the power zero is one.
Rule: Any number to the power one is itself.

With those two rules, we can express the ones place, tens place, hundreds place, and so on as powers of ten. Let us look at our example again:

$$1,037 = 1 \times 10^3 + 0 \times 10^2 + 3 \times 10^1 + 7 \times 10^0.$$

---

16 In the 21ˢᵗ century, "cipher" is much more likely to be related to cryptography than to arithmetic.

In decimal numbers, and in all positional number systems, zero serves as a placeholder. In the example, it tells us that there is nothing in the hundreds place. It is that placeholder zero that pushes the one into the thousands place.

Using just the digits zero through nine, the decimal number system can express any non-negative integer, however large. The value of an n-digit decimal integer is

$$a_{n-1}\times10^{n-1} + a_{n-2}\times10^{n-2} + \ldots + a_1\times10^1 + a_0\times10^0$$

This can be written more compactly as[17]:

$$\sum_{i=0}^{n-1} a_i \times 10^i$$

Adding a minus sign to the available symbols lets us express any integer, positive or negative. To express fractions, we use the period symbol as a decimal point. The digit immediately to the right of the period represents 10^{-1} or $1/10$ the next digit 10^{-2} or $1/100$ and so on. Although we can represent any integer with decimal numbers, the same is not true of fractions. For example, the fraction $1/3$ cannot be exactly represented as a decimal fraction. However, we can make an arbitrarily precise approximation; if 0.33 isn't close enough, we can write 0.333, or even 0.3333333333.

1.3 Other Bases

The discussion so far has been limited to base ten or decimal numbers because they are familiar to us. It is possible to represent numbers in positional notation using bases other than ten. An n-digit non-negative integer in base B would be represented as

$$\sum_{i=0}^{n-1} a_i \times B^i$$

The only difference between this expression and the one above is that we have substituted some base B for ten. The choice of a base isn't entirely arbitrary; we'd like it to be an integer, greater than one, and relatively small. These constraints are because a base B number system requires B symbols. We need at least two symbols so that we can have a zero to serve as a placeholder. We don't want so many symbols that reading and writing numbers becomes unwieldy. In computing, it is common to deal with numbers expressed as base two, base eight, and base 16 in addition to the decimal numbers.

---

17 The Greek capital Σ (sigma) means summation; the expression below the Σ shows the index and starting value, the expression above shows the ending value.

1.4 Binary Numbers

Numbers in base two are called binary numbers. A binary number system requires two symbols; we choose 0 and 1. The positions within a binary number have values based on the powers of two, starting with 2^0 in the rightmost position. The digits of a binary number are called bits; **bit** is a contraction of *binary digit*. A binary number is expressed this way:

$$\sum_{i=0}^{n-1} a_i \times 2^i$$

Which is the same as $a_{n-1} \times 2^{n-1} + a_{n-2} \times 2^{n-2} + \ldots + a_1 \times 2^1 + a_0 \times 2^0$.

1.4.1 Binary Integers

Consider the binary number 10101. This represents the value

$1 \times 2^4 + 0 \times 2^3 + 1 \times 2^2 + 0 \times 2^1 + 1 \times 2^0$, or $1 \times 16 + 0 \times 8 + 1 \times 4 + 0 \times 2 + 1 \times 1$,

or $16 + 4 + 1$, or 21.

Let's look at the same thing a different way:

Binary number	1	0	1	0	1
Powers of two	2^4	2^3	2^2	2^1	2^0
Decimal values of powers of two	16	8	4	2	1
Add values where binary digits are one	16		+ 4		+ 1 = 21

The first row is the binary number we want to examine. On the second row starting at the right, we write the power of two that corresponds to each position. The rightmost position is 2^0 and the power increases by one with each position to the left.

The third row is the decimal value of each of the powers of two. Notice that each of the numbers is twice the value of its predecessor. You simply start with one in the rightmost position and double each time you move left.

The decimal value of each digit is the digit itself, zero or one, multiplied by the power of two indicated by the digit's position. If the digit is a one, we copy the power of two to the fourth row; if the digit is a zero, we do not. This is equivalent to multiplying each positional value by the associated binary digit, one or zero. Finally, we add across the bottom row to get the decimal value of the binary number.

Students of computing will find it convenient to memorize the values of the first several powers of two, plus certain other values like 2^{10}, 2^{16}, and 2^{20}. You can easily find the value of any small power of two by starting with one you know and doubling until you reach the desired value. For example, if you know 2^{16}, you can find 2^{18} by doubling twice. If necessary, you can start with $2^0 = 1$ and double until you reach the value you need.

Usually, the base of a number will be clear from the context; if necessary, the base is indicated by a subscript following the number, so we could write, for example, $1010_2 = 10_{10}$.

Units for powers of two

Earlier in the history of computing it was common to use the prefixes kilo, mega, and giga to refer to larger powers of two. Strictly speaking, kilo is 1,000, but the difference between 1,000 and $2^{10} = 1,024$ is small. However, by the time one reaches giga, the difference is significant. One giga is 1,000,000,000, but 2^{30} is 1,073,741,824. The difference caused confusion, particularly in describing storage devices. To resolve the confusion, in 1999 the International Electrotechnical Commission (IEC) adopted a standard set of names for powers of two similar to kilo, mega, and giga, but including the syllable *bi* for binary.

IEC Units for Powers of Two		
Unit	**Abbrev**	**Value**
kibibyte	KiB	$2^{10} = 1,024$
mebibyte	MiB	$2^{20} = 1,024^2$
gibibyte	GiB	$2^{30} = 1,024^3$
tebibyte	TiB	$2^{40} = 1,024^4$
pebibyte	PiB	$2^{50} = 1,024^5$

Figure 1-2
Units for Powers of Two

Values are defined up to yobibyte, $1,024^8$. Sadly, consistent use of these standard units hasn't been widely adopted. Worse, units are used confusingly. A gigabyte might be 1,073,741,824 when referring to memory but 1,000,000,000 when referring to a disk[18]. The implication is that you should use the IEC units when precision is important and you must be sure you understand the meaning of units used by others.[19]

---

18 It doesn't make sense to use powers of ten to specify memory sizes because memory addresses are binary numbers and one wants every bit combination to be a valid address.

19 This book uses the IEC powers of two units for storage and memory, and the mega-, giga-, and tera- units for data transfer and communication speeds.

1.4.2 Why Binary?

We've gone to some length to describe a number system based only on zero and one. It is appropriate to digress briefly to explain why we choose to use binary numbers instead of the familiar decimal system when building computers. Part of the answer is **reliability**. It is relatively easy to design electronic circuits that can reliably distinguish between on and off, or between positive and negative. It is much harder to build circuits that can reliably discriminate among several levels. Seemingly identical electronic components will be slightly different even when new because of manufacturing tolerances. These differences are magnified with age and with differences in operating environment.

Consider a decimal computing machine in which we choose to represent the digits zero through nine with signals of zero through nine volts. We design the machine so that an actual signal of 6.8 volts is interpreted as the digit seven, allowing some tolerance for error. We might also decide that 6.4 volts represents the digit six. What do we do with a voltage of 6.5? Does this represent seven or six? With this scheme, a difference of 0.5 volts, or five percent, causes an error that cannot be resolved.

With binary circuits, we need only the symbols zero and one. If we say that zero volts represents a zero and five volts represents a one, we can interpret anything less than 2.5 volts as zero and anything greater as one. This design can tolerate an error of nearly 50% and still produce correct results.

It is possible to use binary circuits to represent decimal numbers. For example, ENIAC[20] used ten binary elements, only one of which was on at any given time, to represent the each decimal digit. John von Neumann, in his *First Draft of a Report on the EDVAC*, observed binary circuit elements used in that way can represent values from zero to nine; if the same ten elements are used as a ten-digit binary number, they can represent values from zero to 1,023. The second part of the reason is that the use of binary numbers **maximizes the expressive power of binary circuits**.

1.4.3 Converting Decimal to Binary

Converting binary numbers to decimal is easy. Just write down the powers of two which correspond to each digit in the binary number, then add those for which the binary digit is a one. To convert a decimal number to binary, we express the decimal number as a sum of powers of two. These indicate which binary digits are ones; the rest will be zeros.

One approach to converting decimal to binary is repeated division by two. In the example at Figure 1-3, we convert 141_{10} to binary. In the example, the *remainders* are the binary digits.

---

20 "Electronic Numerical Integrator and Computer." ENIAC and EDVAC were early electronic computers.

The remainder from the first division in Figure 1-3 tells whether the number is even or odd; in other words, whether the 2^0 place is zero or one. In the example, it is one. The second division determines the value of the 2^1 place, then the 2^2 place, and so on. The algorithm terminates when the quotient is zero. The digits of the binary number are read from bottom to top, and 141_{10} is equal to 10001101_2.

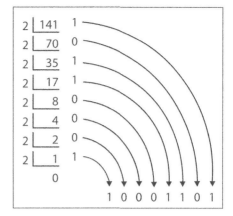

Figure 1-3
141 converted to binary using
repeated division by two

1.4.4 Finite Precision Arithmetic – How High Can We Count?

With pencil and paper, we can write down any number we can imagine, using either the decimal or binary number systems. If we need more digits, we just write them. With computing machinery, the number of bits available for a number is likely to be fixed by the architecture. So, the question, "How high can we count given a fixed number of bits?" becomes an important one. Fortunately, it's easy to answer.

An n-bit binary number has 2^n possible values. This is easy to see. A single bit has two possible values, zero and one. With two bits, you get four values: 00, 01, 10, and 11. Three bits can generate eight distinct combinations, and so on. Of the 2^n possible values of an n-bit number, one will be all zeros and represent the value zero. So, the largest value that can be represented using an n-bit number is $2^n - 1$. An eight-bit binary number has 2^8 (256) possible values, but since one of those values represents zero, the largest possible eight-bit number is $2^8 - 1$ or 255. It is even smaller if a signed number is needed, as discussed below.

There's another implication to the fact that in computers, binary numbers are stored in fixed-size areas. It is that each binary number must be the same number of bits. For unsigned integers, this is accomplished by padding on the left with zeros. We cover signed numbers in Section 1.4.6.

Computers perform arithmetic on fixed-size numbers, called **words**. The arithmetic of fixed-size numbers is called **finite-precision arithmetic**. The rules for finite-precision arithmetic are different from the rules of ordinary arithmetic.

The sizes of numbers which can be arithmetic operands are determined when the architecture of the computer is designed. Common sizes for integer arithmetic are 16, 32, and 64 bits. It is possible for the programmer to perform arithmetic on larger numbers or on sizes which are not directly implemented in the architecture. However, this usually requires multiple steps. Often the programmer picks the most appropriate size implemented by the architecture.

This puts a burden on computer architects and computer language designers to select appropriate sizes for integers, and on the programmer to be aware of the limitations of the size he has chosen and the limitations of finite-precision arithmetic in general.

Consider what it would be like to perform arithmetic if one were limited to three-digit decimal numbers. Neither negative numbers nor fractions could be expressed directly, and the largest possible number that could be expressed is 999. This is the circumstance in which we find ourselves when we perform computer arithmetic because the number of bits is fixed by the computer's architecture. Although we can usually express numbers larger than 999, the limits are real and small enough to be of practical concern. Working with unsigned 16-bit binary integers, the largest number we can express is $2^{16}-1$, or 65,535. If we assume a signed number, the largest number is 32,767.

There are other limitations. Consider again the example of three-digit numbers. We can add 200 + 300, but not 600 + 700 because the latter sum is too large to fit in three digits. Such a condition is called **overflow** and it is of concern to architects of computer systems. Because not all operations which will cause overflow can be predicted when a computer program is written, the computer system itself should check whether overflow has occurred and, if so, provide some indication of that fact.

The algebra of finite-precision is different from ordinary algebra. Neither the associative law nor the distributive law applies. Two examples from Tanenbaum (1990) illustrate this. If we evaluate the expression

$$a + (b - c) = (a + b) - c$$

using $a = 700$, $b = 400$, and $c = 300$ and three digits of precision, the left-hand side evaluates to 800, but overflow occurs when evaluating $a + b$ in the right-hand side. The associative law does not hold.

Similarly, if we evaluate

$$a \times (b - c) = a \times b - a \times c$$

using $a = 5$, $b = 210$, and $c = 195$, the left-hand side produces 75, but in the right-hand side, $a \times b$ overflows and distributive law does not hold.

1.4.5 Binary Arithmetic – Addition

Since we've talked about binary numbers as the basis for the electronic circuits for computers, it won't surprise you that we can do arithmetic on binary numbers. All the operations of ordinary arithmetic are defined for binary numbers, and they work much the same as you are used to. Let's look at the rules for binary addition in Figure 1-4.

The first three of those don't require any explanation, but rules (d) and (e) might. In rule (d), the result is a binary number, so 10_2 represents one two and no ones, and in binary one plus one is two, exactly as you would expect. The rule says that $1+1=0$, with one to carry to the next place. This is the same principle as carrying numbers in decimal addition, except that we carry when the partial sum is greater than one. Rule (e) adds three ones to get a one as the partial sum and another one to carry. We've written $1+1+1=3$, which

```
                    1
  0    0    1    1    +1
 +0   +1   +0   +1    +1
 ─────────────────────────
  0    1    1   10    11
 (a)  (b)  (c)  (d)   (e)
```

Figure 1-4
Rules for Binary Addition

is what we expect.

Now we will add two binary numbers with more than one bit each so you can see how the carries "ripple" left, just as they do in decimal addition as shown in .

The three carries are shown on the top row. Normally, you would write these down as you complete the partial sum for each column. Adding the rightmost column produces a one with no carry; adding the next column produces a zero with one to carry. Work your way through the entire example from right to left. Then convert the addends and sum to decimal to verify that you got the right answer.

```
      1  1  1
   0  0  1  1  0
 + 0  1  1  1  1
 ──────────────
   1  0  1  0  1
```

Figure 1-5
Addition showing carry

One can also express the rules of binary addition with a truth table. This is important because there are techniques for designing electronic circuits which compute functions expressed by truth tables. The fact that we can express the rules of binary addition as a truth table implies that we can design a circuit which will perform addition on binary numbers, and that turns out to be true. We will examine such a circuit in Chapter 2.

We only need to write the rules for one column of bits; we start at the right and apply the rules to each column in succession until the final sum is formed. Binary addition is remarkably similar to decimal addition. As you would expect, the other arithmetic operations are also defined for binary numbers.

1.4.6 Negative Numbers – Two's Complement

So far we have dealt only with non-negative integers – whole numbers zero or greater. For a computer to be useful, it must be able to handle binary negative numbers and fractions. For pencil-and-paper arithmetic we could represent signed binary numbers with plus and minus signs, just as we do with decimal numbers. With computer circuits, our only symbols are zero and one. We must have a way of representing negative numbers using only zeros and ones. There are four possible approaches: signed magnitude, ones' complement, two's complement, and excess n.[21] In the first three of these, the leftmost bit is considered the sign bit. A zero in the sign bit indicates a positive number and a one indicates a negative number. The ones' complement is formed by complementing each bit of the binary number. Signed-magnitude and excess-n numbers are used in floating-point operations and will be discussed there. Ones' complement arithmetic is obsolete in computer design.

In signed-magnitude representation, a zero in the sign bit indicates a positive number, and a one indicates a negative number. There is a problem with signed magnitude: it has two representations for zero. Consider an eight-bit word. 00000000 is "plus zero" and 10000000 is "minus zero." Since testing for zero is something that's done very frequently in computer programming, we would like to develop a better idea.

The better idea is something called **two's complement**. Two's complement numbers are used almost universally for integer representation of numbers in computers. The sign still resides in the leftmost bit, and positive numbers are treated just like the unsigned integers we've already used except that results are never allowed to flow over into the sign bit.

Let's go back to the basic idea of a binary number. In the binary number system, we can express any non-negative integer as the sum of powers of two where the bits of the binary number are the coefficients:

$$a_{n-1} \times 2^{n-1} + a_{n-2} \times 2^{n-2} + \ldots + a_1 \times 2^1 + a_0 \times 2^0 = \sum_{i=0}^{n-1} a_i \times 2^i$$

In two's complement numbers, the leftmost bit, or sign bit, represents a negative coefficient of a power of two and the remaining bits represent positive coefficients which are added back. So, an n-bit two's complement number has the form:

$$-2^{n-1} + \sum_{i=0}^{n-2} a_i \times 2^i$$

Consider 10000000, an eight-bit two's complement number. Since the sign bit is a one, it represents -2^7 or -128. The remaining digits are zeros, so 10000000 = -128, a minus 128 with nothing added back. The number 10000001 is $-128+1$ or -127. The number 10000010 is -126, and so on. 11111111 is $-128 +127$ or -1.

Now consider 01111111, also an eight-digit two's complement number. The sign bit still represents -2^7 or -128, but the coefficient is zero, and this is a positive number, $+127$.

The two's complement representation has its own drawback. Notice that in eight bits we can represent -128 by writing 10000000. The largest positive number we can represent is 01111111 or $+127$. Two's complement is *asymmetric about zero*. For any size binary number, there is one more negative number than there are positive numbers. This is because, for

---

21 The apostrophes are in the right places. "… a two's complement number is complemented with respect to a single power of 2, whereas a ones' complement number is complemented with respect to a long sequence of 1s." (Knuth, 1969)

any binary number, the number of possible bit combinations is even. We use one of those combinations for zero, leaving an odd number of values to be split between positive and negative. Since we want zero to be represented by all binary zeros and we want the sign of positive numbers to be zero, there's no way to escape from having one more negative number than positive.

If you think of a two's complement number as a large negative number with positive numbers added back, you could conclude that it would be difficult to form the two's complement. It turns out that there's a method of forming the two's complement that is very easy to do with either a pencil or a computer:

- Take the complement [22] of each bit in the number to be negated. That is, if a bit is a zero, make it a one, and vice-versa.
- To the result of the first step, add one as though doing unsigned arithmetic.

Let's do an example: we will find the two's complement of 87, so –87 in two's complement binary.

0	1	0	1	0	1	1	1	original number
1	0	1	0	1	0	0	0	each bit complemented, or "flipped"
+							1	add 1 to 10101000
1	0	1	0	1	0	0	1	this is the two's complement, or –87

Figure 1-6

Forming the two's complement of 87_{10}

We start with the binary value for 87, or 01010111. That leading zero is necessary because it is in the leftmost, or sign bit, position. If it were one, that would indicate a negative number. Here are the steps:

We can check this out. The leftmost bit represents –128, and the remaining bits have positive values which are added back. We have –128 + 32 + 8 + 1, or –128 + 41 = –87. There's another way to check this. If you add equivalent negative and positive numbers, the result is zero, so –87 + 87 = 0. Does 01010111 + 10101001 = 0? Perform the addition and see.

A shortcut for forming the two's complement

There is an even easier way to form the two's complement of a binary number:

- Copy bits from the right until you have copied a one bit
- Complement (flip) the remaining bits.

---

22   In the discussion of two's complement, *complement*, *invert*, and *flip* all mean change zero to one and one to zero.

Why does this work? You can add one to a binary number by flipping bits from the right until a zero is reached, flip the zero to a one, and copy the remaining bits. That trick for adding one flips all the bits to the right of the first zero-bit and also the first zero-bit itself. The shortcut for forming the two's complement effectively flips all bits, then flips the first 1 (now 0) and the bits to the right of it back, thus inverting all the bits and adding one.

Sign Extension

In working with two's complement numbers, you will often find it necessary to adjust the length of the number, the number of bits, to some fixed size. Clearly, you can expand the size of a positive (or unsigned) number by adding zeros on the left, and you can reduce its size by removing zeros from the left. If the number is to be considered a two's complement positive number, you must leave at least one zero on the left in the sign bit's position.

It's also possible to expand the size of a two's complement negative number by supplying one-bits on the left. That is, if 1010 is a two's complement number, 1010 and 11111010 are equal. 1010 is −8 + 2 or −6. 11111010 is −128+64+32+16+8+2 or −6. Similarly, you can shorten a negative number by removing ones from the left so long as at least one one-bit remains.

We can generalize this notion. A two's complement number can be expanded by replicating the sign bit on the left. This process is called **sign extension**. We can also shorten a two's complement number by deleting digits from the left so long as at least one digit identical to the original sign bit remains.

Addition of signed numbers

We have already considered addition of unsigned binary numbers. Binary addition of two's complement signed numbers can be performed using the same rules given above for unsigned addition. If there is a carry out of the sign bit, it is ignored. Why? Although not precisely correct mathematically[23], it is easiest to think of a two's complement number as having a sign bit on the left and value bits elsewhere. A problem occurs only if the carry-in to the sign bit is different from the carry-out of the sign bit. That causes an incorrect sign bit, which is an overflow condition.

Since we are dealing with finite-precision arithmetic, it is possible for the result of an addition to be too large to fit in the available space. The answer will be truncated and will be incorrect. This is the overflow condition discussed above. The **overflow rule** for determining whether overflow has occurred in two's complement numbers is:

- Overflow cannot occur if two numbers of opposite signs are added.
- If two numbers of the same sign are added and the result is of the opposite sign, overflow has occurred.

---

23   A precise explanation requires the use of modulus arithmetic, which would make the author's hair hurt.

The first part says if we add a positive and a negative number, the result is necessarily of smaller magnitude than the larger of the two addends and overflow is impossible. The second part says if we add two positive numbers and get a negative answer, *something is wrong!* The same is true of adding two negative numbers and getting a positive answer. The something that is wrong is that overflow has occurred.

With pencil-and-paper arithmetic, it is usual to ignore a carry-out on the left and verify the sign of the result. In a digital logic circuit, the easy way is to feed the carry-in to the leftmost bit and the carry-out from it into an XOR gate. If the result is a logic 1, overflow has occurred. The carry out is not otherwise used nor stored. See the ALU diagram in Figure 1-10.

Subtraction

Addition has the property of being commutative, that is, $a+b = b+a$. That is not true of subtraction. 5 − 3 is not the same as 3 − 5. For this reason, we must be careful of the order of the operands when subtracting. We call the first operand, the number that is being diminished, the minuend; the second operand, the amount to be subtracted from the minuend, is the subtrahend. The result is called the difference.

$$
\begin{array}{rl}
51 & \text{minuend} \\
-22 & \text{subtrahend} \\
\hline
29 & \text{difference}
\end{array}
$$

Since we can form the complement of a binary number easily and can add signed numbers easily, the obvious answer to the problem of subtraction is the **subtraction rule**: *take the two's complement of the subtrahend and add it to the minuend.* We don't have to build special circuits to perform subtraction. All we need are a circuit which can form the bitwise complement of a number and an adder.

1.4.7 Binary Fractions

In ordinary decimal numbers, we represent fractions as negative powers of ten, and we mark the division between the integer and fraction parts with a "decimal point." The same principle applies to binary numbers. 0.1_2 is 2^{-1} or 1/2; 0.11_2 is $2^{-1} + 2^{-2}$ or 1/2 + 1/4 = 3/4. As with decimal fractions, not all fractional values can be represented exactly, but we can get arbitrarily close by using more fraction bits.

With pencil and paper, we can use a period as a "binary point" to separate the fractional part of a binary number from the integer part. Within a computer, we don't have a symbol we can use for the "binary point." A programmer who wants to use binary fractions directly must pick a location for the implied binary point and scale all numbers to maintain binary point alignment. There is an easier way, and that is to use floating-point numbers, which are discussed in Section 1.5.

1.4.8 Hexadecimal Numbers as Shorthand

The **hexadecimal**, or base 16 number system is a positional number system. It needs 16 symbols; we choose 0...9 and A, B, C, D, E, and F.[24] The place values are powers of 16. However, the principal use of hexadecimal numbers in computing is as shorthand for binary numbers. Copying long strings of ones and zeros is error prone. Using hexadecimal notation let us write one hex symbol to represent four binary digits as shown in Figure 1-7.

Binary	Hex	Binary	Hex	Binary	Hex	Binary	Hex
0000	0	0100	4	1000	8	1100	C
0001	1	0101	5	1001	9	1101	D
0010	2	0110	6	1010	A	1110	E
0011	3	0111	7	1011	B	1111	F

Figure 1-7
Correspondence of binary numbers to hexadecimal digits

It is common to use indications other than a subscript 16 to identify numbers as hexadecimal when it is not clear from the context. The following are all examples of indicators of hexadecimal numbers: $7A_{16}$, x'7A', 0x7A, and 7Ax.

1.5 Very Large and Very Small Numbers

The natural arithmetic operand in a computer is the binary integer. However, the range of numbers that can be represented is limited by the computer's word size. We cannot represent very large or very small numbers. For example, in a computer with a 32-bit word, the largest signed number is $2^{31} - 1$. The range is further diminished if some bits of the word are used for fractions. There are techniques for performing integer arithmetic on groups of two or more words, but these are both painful for the programmer and consuming of CPU time.

It is not uncommon for very large and very small numbers to occur in the kinds of problems for which computers are used. These numbers do not lend themselves to representation in integer form, or integer and fraction form. Another approach is needed for problems whose variables are not small integers.

1.5.1 Scientific Notation

Scientists and engineers have developed a compact notation for writing very large or very small numbers. If we wrote it out, the mass of the sun in grams would be a two followed by

---

24   In general, the letters used for the last six symbols are not considered to be case-sensitive, so *a* and *A* are equivalent.

33 zeros. The speed of light in meters per second would be a three followed by eight zeros. These same numbers, when expressed in scientific notation, are 2×10^{33} and 3×10^8. Any number n can be expressed as

$$n = f \times 10^c$$

where f is a fraction and c is an exponent. Both f and c may be negative. If f is negative the number n is negative. If c is negative, the number is less than one.

The essential idea of scientific notation is to *separate the significant digits of a number from its magnitude*. The number of significant digits is determined by the size of f and the range of magnitude is determined by the size of c.

We wrote the speed of light as 3×10^8 meters per second. If that is not precise enough, we can write 2.997×10^8 to express the same number with four digits of precision. Numbers expressed in this way can be made as precise as necessary by increasing the number of digits, the precision, of the fractional part. The range can be increased by increasing the size of the exponent. Finite precision arithmetic in computers means that exponent and fraction are of fixed size for a given floating-point format.

1.5.2 Floating-Point Numbers

Floating-point number systems apply this same idea – separating the significant digits of a number from its magnitude – to representing numbers in computer systems. Relatively small numbers for the fraction and exponent part provide a way to represent a very wide range with acceptable precision.

In the early days of computers, each manufacturer developed their own floating-point representation. These were incompatible. In some cases, they even produced wrong answers. Floating-point arithmetic has some subtleties that are beyond the scope of this book.

In 1985, the Institute of Electrical and Electronic Engineers published IEEE Standard 754 for floating-point arithmetic. Virtually all general purpose processors built today have floating-point units which conform to IEEE 754. The examples in this chapter describe IEEE 754 single precision floating-point number format. There are other standard formats with greater precision and range.

Instead of using base ten and powers of ten like scientific notation, IEEE 754 floating-point uses a binary fraction and an exponent that is interpreted as a power of two. The format of a single-precision floating-point number is shown in Figure 1-8. The leftmost bit indicates the sign of the number, with a zero indicating positive and a one indicating negative. The exponent occupies eight bits and is also signed. A negative exponent indicates that the fraction is multiplied by a negative power of two, that is, that the number is less than one. The fraction part, called the significand, occupies 23 bits in the single precision format. The name **significand** was chosen to emphasize that the size of the significand determines the maximum number of significant digits, the precision, or the number represented.

The exponent is stored as an excess-n number.[25] For the single precision format, it is excess 127. That means that the value stored is 127 more than the true value. A stored value of one indicates a true value of −126. A stored value of 254 indicates a true value of +127. Exponent values of zero and 255 (all ones) are used for special purposes described later. The excess-n form is used because it allows for bitwise comparison for greater-than or less-than.

The significand is a 23-bit binary fraction with the binary point assumed to be to the left of the first bit of the fraction. The approximate range of such a number is ± 10^{-38} to ±10^{38} for the single-precision format. This is substantially more than we can express using a 32-bit binary integer. How-

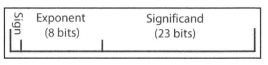

Figure 1-8

IEEE 754 single-precision format

ever, *floating-point gives up precision for range*; the precision of a single-precision floating-point number is a little more than seven decimal digits.

In addition to the single precision format, IEEE 754 defines several other formats. The double precision format occupies 64 bits with an 11-bit exponent and a 52-bit significand. That gives a precision of almost 16 decimal digits and a range of ± 10^{-308} to ±10^{308}. The extended precision format is 80 bits, and the quad precision format is 128 bits. Spreadsheet programs and languages like JavaScript frequently use the double precision format. The extended precision format was developed for hardware floating-point units to avoid loss of precision on internal operations when using 64-bit operands. Extended precision is supported by many programming languages as a "long double" type.

1.5.3 Normalized Numbers

We represented the speed of light as 2.997×10^8. We could also have written 0.2997×10^9 or 0.02997×10^{10}. We can move the decimal point to the left, adding zeros as necessary, by increasing the exponent by one for each place the decimal point is moved. Similarly, we can compensate for moving the decimal point to the right by decreasing the exponent. However, if we are dealing with a fixed-size fraction part, as in a computer implementation, leading zeros in the fraction part cost precision. If we were limited to four digits of fraction, the last example would become 0.0299×10^{10}, a cost of one digit of precision. The same problem occurs in binary fractions.

In order to preserve as many significant digits as possible, floating-point numbers are stored such that the leftmost digit of the fraction part is non-zero. If, after a calculation, the leftmost digit is not significant (*i.e.* it is zero), the fraction is shifted left and the exponent

---

25 Excess-n is also called offset binary.

decreased by one until a significant digit – for binary numbers, a one – is present in the leftmost place. A floating-point number in that form is called a **normalized number**. There are many possible unnormalized forms for a number, but only one normalized form.

Storing numbers in normalized form provides an opportunity to gain one more significant binary digit in the fraction. If the leftmost digit is known to be one, there is no need to store it; it can be assumed to be present. IEEE 754 takes advantage of this; there is an implied one bit and an implied binary point to the left of the fraction. To emphasize this difference, IEEE 754 refers to the fractional part of a floating-point number as a **significand**. Did we get a free lunch with this extra bit of precision? No, because computing time is used to normalize numbers.

1.5.4 Precision of Floating-Point Numbers

Although the range of a single-precision floating-point number is about $\pm 10^{-38}$ to $\pm 10^{38}$, it is important to remember that there are still only 2^{32} distinct values. The floating-point system cannot represent every possible real number. Instead, it approximates the real numbers by a series of points. If the result of a calculation is not one of the numbers that can be represented exactly, what is stored is the nearest number that can be represented. This process is called **rounding**, and it introduces error in floating-point calculations. Since rounding down is as likely as rounding up, the cumulative effect of rounding error is generally negligible.

The spacing between floating-point numbers is not constant. Clearly, the difference between 0.10×2^1 and 0.11×2^1 is far less than the difference between 0.10×2^{127} and 0.11×2^{127}. However, if the difference between numbers is expressed as a percentage of the number, the distances are similar throughout the range, and the relative error due to rounding is about the same for small numbers as for large.

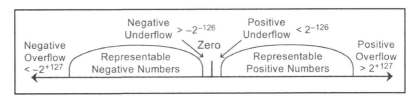

Figure 1-9
Representable floating-point numbers

Not only are there real numbers that cannot be expressed exactly, there are whole ranges of numbers that cannot be represented at all. Consider the real number line as shown in Figure 1-9. The number zero can be represented exactly because it is defined by the standard. The positive numbers that can be represented fall approximately in the range 2^{-126} to 2^{+127} for single-precision floating-point; the longer formats have more exponent bits, and so larger range. Numbers greater than 2^{+127} cannot be represented in single-precision format; this is called **positive overflow**. A similar range of negative numbers can be represented. Numbers to the left of that range cannot be represented; this is **negative overflow**. There is also a range of numbers near zero that cannot be represented. The smallest positive number that can be represented in normalized form is 1.0×2^{-126}. The condition of trying to represent smaller numbers is called **positive underflow**. The same condition on the negative side of zero is called **negative underflow**. Prior to IEEE 754, manufacturers just set such results to zero or signaled an error exception. The IEEE standard provides a more graceful way of handling such conditions: the requirement that numbers be normalized is relaxed near zero. The exponent is allowed to become zero, representing 2^{-127}, the implicit one at the left of the binary point becomes a zero, and the fraction part is allowed to have leading zeros. Such a number approaches zero with increasing loss of significant digits.

A caution about loss of precision

The floating-point standard is designed to be robust, that is, to give reasonable results for most computations. There are two areas where caution is required. One is addition or subtraction of numbers of significantly different sizes. That is because one of the numbers must be denormalized to make their exponents the same. The process of denormalizing causes loss of precision. For a concrete example, consider calculating the average height of 50 million people. The straightforward approach is to add all the heights, then divide by 50 million. That will give an incorrect answer with single precision numbers because, as the sum gets large enough that its exponent is greater than that of the individual observations, loss of precision occurs. The last additions are likely to increase the sum very little if at all. There are techniques for handling such a situation. (Kahan, 1965)

When two nearly equal numbers are subtracted, the difference is formed of the lowest-order parts of the numbers. If the two values are exact, then no error is introduced by the subtraction. However, if the low-order parts are imprecise as a result of rounding, the difference after subtraction may consist only of the parts in error. Goldberg (1991) calls this catastrophic cancellation.

1.5.5   Special Values in IEEE 754

Each of the IEEE 754 formats provides a way to represent special numbers in addition to the regular normalized floating-point format. An exponent of zero with a non-zero fraction is the denormalized[26] form discussed above to handle positive and negative underflow. A number with both exponent and fraction of zero represents the number zero. Both positive and negative representations of zero are possible.

Positive and negative overflow are handled by providing a representation for infinity. This

---

26   Numbers in denormalized format are sometimes called subnormal.

is a positive or negative sign bit, an exponent of all ones, and a fraction of zero. This representation is also used for the result of division by zero. Arithmetic operations on infinity behave in a predictable way.

Finally, all ones in the exponent and a non-zero fraction represents **Not a Number**, also called **NaN**. Arithmetic on NaNs also behaves in a predictable fashion.

1.6 Representing Symbols – Encoding Systems

Humans communicate using not only numbers, but also languages, alphabets, symbolic notation, sounds, images, and gestures. Computers deal only with binary numbers; everything stored or processed by a computer must be represented as a binary number. Alphabets and symbols are represented in computers as codes; that is, the representable graphemes[27] in a symbol set are represented by binary numbers.[28] In addition to the printable, or visible symbols, a code set needs control characters like the ENTER character that completes a unit of text. Such an encoding system is called an **alphanumeric code**.

There are two important considerations in designing an alphanumeric code system: the number of code points and the collating sequence. The number of code points possible in any coding system is determined by the number of bits used for the code. If an alphanumeric code uses eight bits, it is limited to 2^8, or 256 characters. In the 21st century, a coding scheme, UTF-8, with a variable number of bits is in common use. UTF-8 is described below.

The **collating sequence** defines the order of characters within the coding scheme. In early coding schemes, it was sufficient to assign a larger code number to the letter B than to A, for example, and sort using the binary values. As encoding schemes became more complex, sorting programs needed rules for such things as handling upper- and lowercase letters.

1.6.1 ASCII and ISO 8859

At first, computer manufacturers invented their own encoding schemes for alphanumeric data. One of the first widely-adopted standard code sets was the American Standard Code for Information Interchange, or ASCII.[29] The first ASCII standard was published in 1963. ASCII had its roots in encoding schemes for electromechanical teletypewriters. Because data transmission was slow and therefore expensive, teletypewriters, and ASCII, used a seven-bit code, the fewest bits to represent English text without the use of shift codes[30]. That allowed for 2^7 or 128 characters. There were 95 printable characters, including the up-

---

27 A grapheme is the smallest unit of the writing system of a language, a character or character-like symbol.

28 Not every grapheme is necessarily representable in a given alphanumeric code; some early code sets did not include lowercase Latin letters, for example.

29 Pronounced "ASS-key."

30 A shift code is a transmitted code roughly analogous to the CAPS LOCK key on a computer keyboard. Shift codes are undesirable because an error in receiving a shift code garbles the rest of the message.

per and lowercase Latin letters, the ten digits, punctuation, special symbols and diacritical marks, and 32 control characters. Even though seven bit characters were distinctly awkward for computers even at the time, ASCII was widely adopted.

Led by IBM's System 360, computer manufacturers settled on eight bits as the smallest addressable unit of memory. This eight-bit unit was called a **byte** or **octet**, and it became common to store one seven-bit ASCII character per octet. Since each octet can hold one of 256 values and ASCII needed only 128 of them, computer manufacturers and operating system developers used the remaining 128 positions for things like line-drawing characters and smiley faces. Different ways of assigning the 128 extra characters were called code pages, and data written using one code page but read using another would be garbled. The Japanese word *mojibake*[31] is used to describe that condition. In modern computer systems, an unrecognized character is likely to be presented as a vertical box with an X, ⊠ , a white square or a vertical box with question mark, the "not defined character" of the operating system. The Unicode replacement character, �, is used to replace an invalid Unicode value.

Not only did code page problems lead to *mojibake*, the 52 upper and lowercase Latin letters are not enough even for Western languages. Some languages have additional letters, and most use diacritical marks far more extensively than does American English. Computer manufacturers wanted to sell their products internationally, so code pages proliferated until there were hundreds of them, not all of which were the same even in the first 128 positions.

The ISO 8859 standard, developed in the mid-1980s, standardized the "upper half" of the available eight-bit characters by adding another 96 printable characters. The "lower half" was identical to ASCII to make the transition from ASCII to ISO 8859 easier. Programs and data that used *only* the 128 ASCII characters could use ISO 8859 transparently. However, an extra 96 characters do not come close to covering even Western languages, so ISO-8859 standardized 15 "parts" that are equivalent to code pages, and which have the same potential to cause *mojibake*. The ISO 8859 part best suited to U.S. English is ISO 8859-1 Western Latin. A document composed using ISO 8859-8 Latin/Hebrew would have all characters above 128 garbled if interpreted as ISO 8859-1. East Asian scripts and many other languages were not covered at all.

1.6.2 Unicode

Even before the ISO 8859 standard was complete it was clear that no set of 256 characters could solve the problem of multilingual representation, nor were 256 characters sufficient for East Asian languages. In 1980 the Xerox Corporation had developed a 16-bit character coding system, XCCS, with the symbols required for many languages, including the Chinese, Japanese, and Korean (CJK) writing systems. Joe Becker from Xerox, along with others from other computer companies, began work on a coding system that could represent

---

31 *Mojibake* (文字化け) means "character transformation" in Japanese.

the symbols used for all modern languages in a single code set that came to be called Unicode.[32] That group was incorporated as the *UNICODE Consortium* in 1991 and published their first standard in two volumes, in 1991 and 1992.

Unicode defines numeric code points, each of which represents an abstract character[33] without reference to how that character will be rendered when displayed and connected only indirectly with how it will be represented in computer storage. Code points are referred to by the letter U, a plus sign, and the hexadecimal number of the code point, like U+0041 for the Latin uppercase A. For ease in conversion, the first 256 UNICODE code points are identical to ISO 8859-1.

Each code point has several properties that are defined in the standard, such as a name, guaranteed to be invariant since Unicode 2.0, direction[34] of script, case value, whitespace characteristics, and punctuation characteristics. These properties are intended to be used when deciding how to render each code point.

Unicode code points are just numbers. How they are represented in computer storage is called a **transformation format**. Unicode characters were at first represented in storage as 16 bit numbers using two bytes per character in a coding scheme called UCS-2.[35] Unicode does not specify the physical appearance of a character, the glyph. That is left to designers of type fonts.

The Unicode Consortium's members had estimated that there were fewer than 214 (16,384) frequently used symbols in all the languages in current use, and so each Unicode code point could be stored in 16 bits, two octets. They soon found that "rarely used" did not mean inessential. Moreover, people who studied ancient languages wanted to represent them in computer files. The number of code points soon exceeded the capacity of a 16-bit value. The successor to the USC-2 format, UTF-16 (16-bit Unicode Transformation Format) defines a set of surrogate code points that signal a second 16-bit value follows. By using 32 bits in those cases, it is possible to represent the more than 1.1 million possible code points in Unicode.

Unicode code points are divided into 17 planes, numbered zero to 16, each of which could potentially hold 2^{16} (65,536) code points, for a total of over 1.1 million code points. Plane zero, the basic multilingual plane, has 55,444 of the possible 65,536 code points defined. The remainder are surrogate code points, code points reserved for private use, and a small number of unallocated code points. Plane zero defines code points for most of the characters used in modern languages.

---

32 The Remington-Rand Corporation developed a computer language called UNICODE for UNIVAC computers in the 1950s. The coding system describe here is entirely different.

33 Graphemes or grapheme-like language units

34 Some languages, like Arabic and Hebrew, are written from right to left.

35 Strictly speaking, UCS-2 was a part of ISO standard 10646.

Plane one, the supplemental multilingual plane, defines code points for historic scripts, musical, mathematical, and other notations, game symbols, emoji, and some modern scripts. Plane two, the supplemental ideographic plane, defines code points for CJK ideographs not included in plane one. The remaining planes are unassigned, reserved for private use, or define CJK points for non-graphical characters.

Problems with double-byte character sets

An obvious problem is that, for information which could be represented in ASCII or ISO 8859, everything takes twice as much space with 16-bit characters. A more serious problem is that different computer hardware architectures handle 16-bit values differently. Some store the most significant byte, the "big end," at the first (lowest) address and the least significant byte following, an architecture called big-endian.[36] Little-endian architectures store the least significant byte at the lowest address. A file written on a machine with big-endian architecture would be unreadable if opened on a machine with little-endian architecture and vice-versa. To address this problem, UTF-16 defines a **byte order mark**, hexadecimal FEFF, that may appear as a "magic number" at the beginning of files written using UTF-16. If the byte order mark is found to be reversed, there is an architecture incompatibility, and the byte order mark and everything following must have its octets reversed. Scanning a character string or finding a particular position within the string is complicated by having some 16-bit characters and some 32-bit characters.

1.6.3   UTF-8

The difficulties with multi-byte coding systems led to a search for a suitable byte-stream encoding of Unicode. In 1992, David Prosser of Unix Systems Laboratories submitted a proposal for a byte-stream encoding. Two more people with background in the Unix operating system at Bell Labs, Ken Thompson and Rob Pike, designed an improved Unicode transformation format for Unicode, **UTF-8**. UTF-8 uses one to four octets per character as shown in Figure 1-10. If the first bit of the leading octet is a zero, the character is encoded in the remaining seven bits and only one octet is used to encode the character. If the first bit of the leading octet is a one, the number of ones prior to the first zero is the total number of bytes, including the leading byte. The remaining bits of the leading byte encode a part of the character. The remaining bits of the character are encoded in continuation bytes, each of which starts with a 10 bit pattern and encodes six bits of the code point.

The first 128 code points of Unicode are identical to ASCII. That means that an ASCII-encoded file is also valid UTF-8. That accounts for a huge amount of existing data. Two octets, eleven bits, cover the European languages, including the Greek, Cyrillic, and Hebrew alphabets. UTF-8 is self-synchronizing; it is never possible to confuse a leading octet with a con-

---

36   The terms big-endian and little-endian were introduced by Danny Cohen in 1980 and were drawn from Jonathan Swift's *Gulliver's Travels.*

tinuation octet or vice-versa. At any point in a UTF-8 octet stream, a leading octet can be found by moving at most three octets forward or backward. However, many Asian scripts that can be represented in 16 bits with UTF-16 required three octets when represented in UTF-8. That is a serious problem because far more people use Asian scripts than European.

Bits	Last Code Point	Leading Octet	Byte 2	Byte 3	Byte 4
7	U+007F	0xxxxxxx			
11	U+07FF	110xxxxx	10xxxxxx		
16	U+FFFF	1110xxxx	10xxxxxx	10xxxxxx	
21	U+10FFFF	11110xxx	10xxxxxx	10xxxxxx	10xxxxxx

Figure 1-10
Structure of UTF-8

1.7 Sounds, Images, and Video

Humans communicate using numbers and symbols, but also using sound, images, and moving images. In computer storage, only binary values are available to represent data, so sound, images, and video are stored as numbers. Often the representations are approximate, but, as with any numbers, we can achieve arbitrarily high precision by using more storage.

1.7.1 Sounds

Sounds are inherently analog, that is continuously varying. When sounds are captured with a microphone, the resulting electrical signal is also continuously varying; it is *analogous* to the pressure waves that are the sound. Such signals are called **analog** signals. If you captured a fraction of a second of speech using a microphone and displayed the electrical signal on an oscilloscope, it might look like the waveform in Figure 1-11. Sound waves and their electrical analogs have two dimensions, frequency (pitch) and amplitude (loudness), each of which can vary independently over time. Frequency is measured in Hertz (Hz), cycles per second. Amplitude is measured in decibels; the scale is logarithmic.[37]

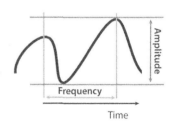

Figure 1-11
Amplitude and frequency of a sound wave

To store or process sounds with a computer, the sound signals must be encoded as digital data. Encoding is done by sampling the amplitude of the sound waveform at regular inter-

---

37 You may see units of dBA, A-weighted decibels, reflecting an adjustment for how the human ear responds. Units of dBA are used to indicate how loud a sound must be to damage hearing.

vals. The number of bits in each sample, the **bit-depth**, determines the precision with which the sample is encoded. More bits per sample means smaller sampling error and so higher quality sound.

The maximum frequency that can be reproduced is determined by the number of samples per second. The **Nyquist-Shannon sampling theorem** states that one must sample at twice the maximum frequency to be reproduced. Figure 1-12 shows how a sound signal is encoded. Horizontal lines on the grid represent the bit-depth; vertical lines represent the sampling interval. The original signal is the smooth waveform, and the reproduced signal is the stair-step of samples taken. Increasing the bit-depth or decreasing the sampling interval, or both, makes the reproduced signal closer to the original. However, increasing either or both also increases the number of bits stored and the bit rate of playback. The bit-depth and sampling rate are different for different applications.

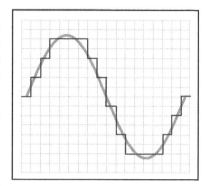

Figure 1-12
Encoding a sound signal

A healthy human ear can hear sounds up to about 20,000 Hz. To reproduce those sounds, the original signal must be sampled at least 40,000 times each second. That's why, for CDs, the sampling rate is 44,100 samples per second. A CD uses a depth of 16 bits and two stereo channels. The number of bits per second is $44,100 \times 16 \times 2 = 1,411,200$ bits/second for storage and playback. About an hour of uncompressed music can be stored on a CD.

For a telephone call, it is necessary that voices be understandable and recognizable. Reproducing frequencies up to 4,000 Hz with a bit-depth of 8 bits is sufficient. Telephone channels are engineered for 8,000 samples of eight bits per second, so 64,000 bits per second for storage or playback.

Compression

The storage required for audio data can be reduced by compressing the data. There are two major categories of compression algorithms. **Lossless compression** takes advantage of similarities in the data to compress in such a way that, when decompressed, produces an exact duplicate of the data before compression. **Lossy compression** takes advantage of the way the human ear perceives sound to discard the less critical parts of the original signal. In computer systems, compression and decompression are accomplished by software or hardware modules called coder-decoders or **codecs**. The mathematical details of compression are beyond the scope of this book

1.7.2 Images

Images are stored as collections of numbers that specify what a display device or printer will produce. Images are stored as bitmap images or vector images.

Bitmap images

If you look closely at a computer screen, you will see that the images on the screen are composed of a matrix of tiny dots. This matrix is called a **bitmap**,[38] and each dot is called a picture element, or **pixel**. The number of pixels per unit area is the **resolution** of an image, and the number of bits per pixel is called the **color depth**. Resolution is generally specified as dots per inch, or DPI. Although image files can contain resolution information, when the image is displayed on a screen, it is the resolution of the screen that controls how images are displayed. If one displays an image with a resolution of 300 DPI on a monitor with 96 DPI resolution, one will get a really big image displayed at 96 DPI. To the monitor, a pixel is a pixel, and the resolution of the monitor is determined by its design.

(a)   *(b)*

Figure 1-13

(a) High-resolution image
(b) Low-resolution image showing pixilation.

Conversely, if a bitmap image is expanded without additional processing, the individual pixels become prominent, an effect known as pixilation. Figure 1-13 (b) is an example of pixilation.

Apple's "retina" displays and high-resolution displays from other manufacturers have high enough resolution that one generally cannot see the dots at normal viewing distance.

Color

If each pixel is represented by a single bit, one has a black and white image. That is inadequate for most uses. For monochrome images, it is more common to use eight bits per pixel to produce a **gray scale image** with 256 levels from white to black.

Color images are more common than gray scale. The most common model for color images on displays the **RGB color model**, in which red, green, and blue are represented using eight bits each. That allows for 16,777,216

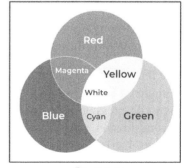

Figure 1-14
The RGB Color Model

---

38   Bitmap images are sometimes called raster images in reference to the scan lines on a display. "Bitmap" is a general term for an array of bits. A bitmap *image* is an image represented as a bitmap.

distinct colors. Humans can distinguish more colors, particularly in hues of green, but the RGB color model is sufficient for photo-realistic images.

A combination of red and blue produces magenta; red and green produce yellow, blue and green, cyan, and all three together produce white. By varying the intensity of the three colors, any of the 16 million possible colors can be produced.

An extension to the RGB color model adds a fourth eight-bit quantity, the **alpha channel**, which describes the transparency of the pixel, from fully transparent to fully opaque. That makes each pixel 32 bits, which is convenient for 32- and 64-bit computer architectures.

The RGB color model is an additive color model, suited to emitted light such as one finds with display screens, but not to reflected light. Color printing on paper depends on reflected light and needs a subtractive color model. The complementary colors to red, green, and blue are cyan, magenta, and yellow. Printed images use a CMYK color model, cyan, magenta, and yellow, with a separate color for black. The black ink is necessary because equal parts of cyan, magenta, and yellow do not produce a true black color.

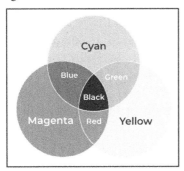

Figure 1-15
The CMYK color model

The **gamut** of a color model refers to the number of colors that can be displayed. The gamut of the RGB color model is larger than that of the CMYK model, which means that not every color that can be displayed can also be printed. Some color printers expand the gamut of printable colors by using additional inks that are lighter shades of cyan and magenta. In commercial printing, it is common to use non-primary "spot" colors.

Bitmap Image formats

There are many ways of arranging bitmaps for processing and display. These are called file formats. Among the most common are JPEG, GIF, and PNG.

The JPEG format and name come from the name Joint Photographic Experts Group, who designed a file format that considered the characteristics of the human eye. It allows for lossy compression with minimal degradation of the visible image. However, at high levels of compression, wave-like artifacts can appear in what should be areas of a single color. The JPEG format is best suited to photographs; it should be avoided in artwork with large areas of one color. The JPEG standard is still under active development.

The GIF[39] format was developed by Steve Wilhite and team at CompuServe in 1987 to allow

---

39 "Graphics Interchange Format." According to the inventors of the format, it's pronounced "Jif," like the brand of peanut butter.

for color images on the CompuServe platform. In its basic form, a GIF file contains a palette of 256 24-bit colors, one of which could be transparent, with each pixel in the file selecting one color of the 256. That meant each pixel needed only eight bits, but also limited the number of colors in an image to 256. Extensions to the format allowed for more colors, and for storing animations. The GIF format produces small files and is useful for simple artwork and animations.

The GIF format employed a patented compression algorithm, although CompuServe was apparently unaware of the patent at the time. There was controversy when the patent owner, Unisys Corporation, decided to enforce the patent and collect license fees. The United States patent expired in 2003. Patents in other countries have also expired.

The PNG[40] format was developed in part because of the patent problems affecting GIF images. Files in the PNG format can be formatted with a color palette and indices into the color palette, similar to the GIF format, or with color information for each pixel. The format provides for both color and gray scale files, with or without an alpha (transparency) channel.

The WebP file format is a derivative of the WebM format for video, discussed below.

Vector images

Vector images are stored very differently from bitmap images. Instead of storing information about individual pixels, vector images store a mathematical description of the image. For example, a line is represented by the locations of the two endpoints, the stroke width, and the color. Very complex images can be represented as vector images using mathematical functions called **splines**. Vector images must be "rasterized," that is, converted to an array of pixels, for printing or display.

Figure 1-16
Vector graphic example
Wikimedia Commons/Tonchino

One of the most useful features of vector images is that they can be scaled larger or smaller without loss of quality. Curves and lines do not exhibit the aliasing[41] effect seen in parts of bitmap images. In addition to scalability, vector graphics files can be smaller than similar bitmap images. The example in Figure 1-16 is in the scalable vector graphics format and is less than seven KiB. The same image in PNG format is 172 KiB. The advantage diminishes as images become more complex.

There are dozens of vector image file formats, many of them proprietary to makers of graphic software. The most common open format is scalable vector graphics, or SVG. The scalable vector graphics format is a World Wide Web Consortium standard. The W3C began devel-

---

40   "Portable Network Graphics."

41   Aliasing is the stair step effect seen on curves and on lines that are not horizontal or vertical.

opment of the standard in 1999. An SVG file encodes image objects using XML[42] text, which means SVG files can be compressed using the same techniques as other text files. The SVG standard includes provision for interactivity by defining events like "onmouseover," and for animated images.

1.7.3 Video

The appearance of motion in images is achieved by showing a rapidly-changing series of static images, each of which is slightly different from its predecessor. These images are called "frames." Human **persistence of vision** converts this into an illusion of continuous motion. Motion pictures on film show 24 frames per second, with each frame being displayed for about 41 milliseconds. In the United States and Japan, television shows 30 frames per second; elsewhere television is 25 FPS. Other frame rates are possible and used in special cases. The quality of a video image is determined by the number of frames per second and the number of scan lines. A 1080P television will have 1,080 scan lines and progressive scan. The width of each line is determined by the aspect ratio, commonly 16:9, so a horizontal resolution of 1,920 pixels. Newer televisions typically have higher resolution.

As with sound, the images that make up video are encoded and compressed for storage with codec software, or sometimes with specialized hardware. There are many video codecs, some of which use proprietary or patented technology.

A video file is a container that holds images, sound, possibly metadata like subtitles, and possibly information for digital rights management. It is the job of the media container to assure synchronization of sound and image.

There are several current and important video container formats. The MPEG-4 format is the most widely used format for content delivered over the Internet. The WebM format is an open format developed by Google specifically for delivery of video content over the Internet. Its compression formats were designed to decompress with low computational requirements, permitting video on mobile devices.

1.8 Summary of Learning Objectives

*This section of the chapter tells you the things you should know about, but not **what** you should know about them. To test your knowledge, discuss the following concepts and topics with a study partner or in writing, ideally from memory.*

Everything that happens inside a modern digital computer consists of operations on binary numbers. The binary number system is a positional number system based on powers of two. Digits of a binary number are called bits. Binary circuits are used in computers for reliability, and binary numbers are used to maximize the expressive power of binary circuits.

---

42   Extensible Markup Language.

Computers do arithmetic on fixed size words and follow the rules of finite-precision arithmetic. Overflow is the condition that a result will not fit in the intended space. In binary addition, a carry occurs whenever a partial sum is greater than one. Negative numbers are represented in two's complement form. Subtraction is covered by the subtraction rule.

Floating-point numbers are used to represent very large and very small numbers. The essential idea of floating-point is separating the precision and magnitude of numbers. Except in special cases, floating-point numbers are stored in normalized form. Floating-point numbers are rounded to the nearest representable number. Numbers too large to represent are called overflow; positive overflow for positive numbers and negative overflow for negative numbers. Underflow is the case that a number is too close to zero to represent. There are both positive underflow and negative underflow.

Certain operations that require one operand to be denormalized can cause loss of precision in floating-point operations.

The IEEE 754 standard defines special values for zero, positive and negative overflow, and not a number. Arithmetic on these special values behaves in a predictable way.

Symbols such as alphabets are stored by encoding each symbol as a number. Such a code is called an alphanumeric code. The alphanumeric code in modern use is Unicode. There is a huge amount of data stored in earlier formats, including ASCII and ISO 8859. Incompatibilities between code sets caused *mojibake*. The first 256 Unicode code points were assigned in such a way as to be compatible with those earlier files. Storing Unicode code points in 16-bit numbers causes difficulty because of the incompatible storage of different computer architectures. The UTF-8 transformation format uses a variable number of bytes to store any of the more than 1.1. million Unicode code points.

Sounds are stored by sampling analog signals. The maximum frequency that can be reproduced is determined by the sampling rate, as given in the Nyquist-Shannon sampling theorem. For a given frequency range, the quality of sound is determined by the number of bits per sample, called the bit-depth. Sound signals can be compressed using a number of different algorithms. Codecs are software and sometimes hardware that compress and decompress sound.

Images can be stored in bitmap or vector format. Bitmap images store a number of bits for each pixel in the image. Color images fir display store numbers for the red, green, and blue components of each color, and sometimes a fourth value that tells the degree of transparency. High quality images require high resolution, that is, many pixels per inch, and 24 or 32 bits per pixel. Like sounds, bitmap images can be compressed and decompressed using codecs. Printed images use the CMYK color model.

Vector images describe the components of the image mathematically instead of representing each pixel. As a result, vector images can be scaled up or down without loss of resolution. A widely used format for vector images is Scalable Vector Graphics.

Moving images take advantage of human persistence of vision by showing a rapidly changing sequence of static images. Each static image is called a frame. A video file is a container for image files, synchronized sound files, and possibly metadata. The MPEG-4 format is widely used.

1.9 References

Goldberg, D. (1991). What every computer scientist should know about floating-point arithmetic. *ACM Computing Surveys*, 23(1), 5–48. https://doi.org/10.1145/103162.103163

Kahan, W. (1965). Pracniques: Further remarks on reducing truncation errors. *Communications of the ACM*, 8(1), 40. https://doi.org/10.1145/363707.363723

Knuth, Donald E. (1969). *The Art of Computer Programming: Seminumerical Algorithms* (Vol. 2). Addison-Wesley.

Tanenbaum, A. S. (1990). *Structured Computer Organization* (3rd ed.). Prentice-Hall.

Chapter 2
Digital Logic

"Any sufficiently advanced technology is indistinguishable from magic."

— Arthur C. Clarke.

The work of computation is performed by millions of tiny electronic devices called **digital logic gates**, or just "gates," each made of several transistors. These gates take binary inputs and produce binary outputs, zero or one, depending on the function the gate computes and the inputs applied to the gate. This chapter explores digital logic gates and shows how they are used for computation.

2.1 Boolean Algebra: The Logic of True and False

George Boole (1815 – 1864) was a British mathematician and philosopher. He made a number of important contributions to mathematics. The most important to those who study computing was the **Boolean algebra**, an algebra over finite sets of discrete values. Boole studied and wrote about propositions – statements which may be true or false – and operators like AND, OR, and NOT that connect them.

Figure 2-1
George Boole

Think about two propositions:

>   *a*: it is midnight in the southern United States.
>   *b*: the sun is not visible.

We can write the proposition as $a \Rightarrow b$ which is read "*a* implies *b*." Note that the reverse is not true in this case. The fact that the sun is not visible does not mean it is midnight.

Propositions can be combined with logical operators. Consider these propositions

>   *a*: A graduating grade point average of greater than 3.7 earns honors.
>   *b*: Bill's graduating GPA was 3.96.
>   *f*: Bill has graduated with honors.

We can write $f = a \wedge b$ where $\wedge$ is the AND operator. Both *a* (the criterion for earning honors) and *b* (Bill's graduating GPA being greater than 3.7) must be true for Bill to have graduated with honors. If Bill's graduating GPA were 3.5, then *f* would be false; Bill did not graduate with honors.

A special case of Boolean algebra is the **switching algebra**, introduced by Claude Shannon in the late 1930s. In the switching algebra, variables can have only two possible values, true or false; the result of a function in the switching algebra can therefore only be true or false. Those involved with computing often refer to the switching algebra as Boolean algebra, and so does this book. By considering true to be one and false to be zero, Boolean algebra, specifically the switching algebra, becomes an algebra over finite sets of binary numbers.

We can express the AND operator as $f(a,b) = a \cdot b$ where $a \cdot b$ is the Boolean product, or conjunction. This says that $f(a,b)$ is one if and only if both a and b are one. We will use the center-dot, $a \cdot b$, in place of $\wedge$ as the AND operator.

2.2 Truth Tables

A more visual way of thinking about Boolean functions is to use the **truth table**. The use of truth tables was probably first published by C. S. Peirce in the 1880s. Truth tables were used extensively by Polish mathematician Jan Łukasiewicz.[43] The truth table for the AND function is shown as Figure 2-2.

The left side of the table lists the two variables, a and b. The right side shows the function value.

a	b	f
0	0	0
0	1	0
1	0	0
1	1	1

Figure 2-2
Truth table for the AND function

There are two important things to notice about this. The first is that there are $2^2 = 4$ rows in the table when there are two variables, a and b. If there were three variables, there would be $2^3 = 8$ rows, and for four variables, $2^4 = 16$ rows. A truth table has 2^n rows where n is the number of variables. Truth tables are most useful when the number of variables is small.

The other thing to notice is that if a and b are considered as bits of a binary number, they are written in ascending order in the truth table: zero, one, two, three. We will always use the convention that the variables of a truth table are written in ascending order. We will also refer to the function result being zero or one.[44]

If the variables of truth tables are always written in the same order, then we do not really need the left side at all; we know what it must be. A Boolean function is completely defined by the f column of the truth table. For the AND function, reading from the top, that is 0001. That is called the **characteristic number** of the function.

By looking at the truth table, and especially at the characteristic number, it should be clear that there are only 16 possible Boolean functions of two variables. The characteristic num-

---

43   Pronounced "yahn woo-ka-SHAY-vitch," give or take some North American ideas of how Latin letters sound.

44   When using T and F in truth tables, it is customary to start with all T the first row and proceed in descending order, which necessarily changes the result. We will not write truth tables in that way here.

ber is four bits because there are four rows in the truth table, and there are only 16 combinations of four bits. Each combination represents one Boolean function of two variables.

In the general case of a Boolean function of n variables, the truth table will have $2^n = r$ rows and there will be 2^r such functions possible. Combining, we see that there are 2^{2^n} possible Boolean functions of n variables.

2.3 Functions of One Variable and the NOT Function

We expect there to be 2^{2^1} or four possible Boolean functions of a single variable. We can enumerate them as shown in Figure 2-3.

Only one of these functions, $\bar{a}$, is useful. The TRUE and FALSE functions always produce the same result regardless of the variable value, and the IDENTITY function is always equal to the

a	$\bar{a}$	TRUE	FALSE	IDENTITY
0	1	1	0	0
1	0	1	0	1

Figure 2-3

*Truth table for NOT
and the other functions of one variable*

variable. The function $\bar{a}$, pronounced "not a" is the Boolean inverse, or NOT function. When used in this way, the overbar is the unary negation operator.

2.4 Functions of Two Variables

There are 2^{2^2} or 16 Boolean functions of two variables. As with functions of a single variable, not all of them are useful. Among those that are not useful are TRUE and FALSE, as above. There are two identity functions, IDENTITY(a) where the result is always equal to a and IDENTITY(b) where the result is always b. For functions of two variables, $\bar{a}$ and $\bar{b}$ are not useful; we have the NOT function for that purpose. Those six functions are not useful either because the result is independent of the combinations of the variables or because a function of a single variable produces the same result. Let us look at the ten remaining functions. In computing, the six most frequently used functions of two variables are AND, OR, XOR, EQUIV, NAND, and NOR. They are shown in truth table form in Figure 2-4.

a	b	AND $a \cdot b$	OR $a + b$	XOR $a \oplus b$	EQUIV $a \Leftrightarrow b$	NAND $\overline{a \cdot b}$	NOR $\overline{a + b}$
0	0	0	0	0	1	1	1
0	1	0	1	1	0	1	0
1	0	0	1	1	0	1	0
1	1	1	1	0	1	0	0

Figure 2-4

Truth tables for frequently-used digital logic functions

51

The AND function has the value one when both *a* and *b* are one and zero otherwise. It is also called the Boolean product. This book uses the center-dot, *a•b*, to indicate AND. It is sometimes written as $a \wedge b$ or as implicit multiplication: *ab*.

The OR function results in a one when either *a* or *b*, or both, are one. It is called the Boolean sum and is written $a + b$, or sometimes $a \vee b$, and pronounced "or." It is important to remember that the + symbol when used in a Boolean expression is not the arithmetic plus.

The XOR function is **exclusive or**. It results in a one when either *a* or *b*, but *not both*, is one. The "not both" part is what makes it exclusive. It is written $a \oplus b$. It is also called the not-equal function; when there are two variables, it is one when $a \neq b$. In the case of two, and also three or more variables, exclusive or produces a one when the number of one-variables is odd, and so XOR can also be called the odd function.

The equivalence function, EQUIV, is one when *a* and *b* are equal. It is sometimes called the XNOR function because its characteristic number, 1001, is the inverse of that for XOR in the same way that OR is the inverse of NOR.

NAND is a contraction of "not and." It is the inverse of the AND function, that is, $\overline{a \cdot b}$. From the truth table, you can see that the characteristic number for AND is 0001 and that for NAND is 1110.

NOR is a contraction of "not or" and is the Boolean inverse of the OR function, that is, $\overline{a + b}$. Check the two columns of the truth table to see that NOR is the inverse of OR.

Both NAND and NOR have the important property that they are **functionally complete**. Functional completeness is discussed in Section 2.6.

Each of the functions described above can be extended in an intuitive way to apply to three or more variables.

For completeness, the remaining four functions are $a \Rightarrow b$, $\overline{a \Rightarrow b}$, $b \Rightarrow a$, and $\overline{b \Rightarrow a}$. Recall that $\Rightarrow$ is the implication symbol, so a $\Rightarrow$ b is read "*a* implies *b*." These functions are used infrequently if at all in digital logic.

That covers all 16 possible functions of two variables.

2.5 Boolean Algebra, Switches, and Claude Shannon's Master's Thesis

Claude Shannon (1916 – 2001), an American mathematician and electrical engineer, made many contributions to the science of computing. One of the most important was his 1937 MIT master's thesis, in which he showed that switching circuits could solve any problem that switching algebra could solve. In other words, we can build a switching circuit that can compute any switching algebra function. Since we can represent such functions as truth tables, we can build a switching circuit that can compute the function values given in the truth table.[45]

2.5.1 Electric Circuits, Switches, and Transistors

In electrical engineering, a **circuit** is an arrangement that provides for a complete path from a power source like a battery, through a load like a lamp, and back to the power source. The connection back to the power source is often called "ground" by electrical engineers. Switches can be used to open the circuit, which removes power from the load.

In the circuit of Figure 2-5, the power source is a battery and the load is a lamp. Power can flow to light the lamp only if both switches are closed. Such a circuit forms the AND function. Power can flow only when switch A AND switch B are closed.

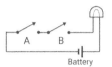

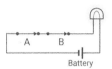

Figure 2-5

Electric circuit forming the AND function

Shannon worked with electromechanical relays, where a relatively low powered electrical signal could switch circuits of much higher power. Such a relay is an electrically controlled switch. Because these devices had a mechanical component, switching speeds were on the order of tens of milliseconds. Computers like the IBM Automatic Sequence Controlled Calculator, also called the Harvard Mark I and first used in 1944, used electromechanical relays to perform computations.

Vacuum tubes can also work as controlled switches, and can operate at electronic speeds, more than 1,000 times faster than relays. The first electronic computers, like ENIAC[46], used vacuum tubes as their switching elements. Vacuum tubes are bulky, fragile because of their glass enclosures, and have a limited lifetime because they have a heating element that operates at around a thousand degrees Celsius. As the number of tubes in a computer increases, the frequency of failures caused by tubes "burning out" increases. That puts an upper limit on the number of tubes that could be used in a computer, and so a limit on the computational power of tube-based computers. Even so, a number of interesting and important vacuum tube computers were built in the 1940s and 1950s.

One of the most historically important machines of the vacuum tube era was *EDVAC*, Electronic Discrete Variable Automatic Computer. The principal importance of EDVAC was John von Neumann's *First Draft of a Report on the EDVAC* in June, 1945. In that document, von Neumann described a binary, sequential, stored program computer. That design has come to be called the von Neumann architecture, and is the basis for design of modern computers.

---

45   We will not go further into that here, but for reading on your own, a web search on "sum of products" will show how it is done.

46   Electronic Numerical Integrator and Computer, the first programmable general purpose electronic computer, built during the World War II era and used from 1945 to 1955.

The invention of the **transistor** at Bell Laboratories by John Bardeen, Walter Brattain, and William Shockley in 1947 allowed designers of computing machines to replace vacuum tubes with transistors. Transistors were small, rugged, consumed little power, generated comparatively little heat, and could act as controlled switches just like vacuum tubes. The transistor was possibly the most important invention of the 20th century.

Almost simultaneous inventions by Robert Noyce, Jack Kilby, and Kurt Lehovec in 1958 led to the development of the **integrated circuit**, which combined multiple transistors and other electronic components on a single piece, or **chip,** of silicon. Transistors in modern computer chips have switching speeds of nanoseconds or faster, more than a million times faster than relays. The earliest commercial chips had dozens of transistors; modern CPU chips have up to tens of billions of transistors. The inventions of the transistor and integrated circuit effectively removed power consumption and heat dissipation as limitations to the number of devices in a computing machine for most of the rest of the 20th century.[47] The remaining limit was that of size. The size of objects on a chip is limited by the wavelength of the light used to project the image, or mask, onto the chip. Modern integrated circuit fabrication uses frequencies far higher than visible light. There is also a physical limit to how small a transistor can be made before quantum effects overwhelm classical semiconductor physics. That limit is likely to be reached in the third decade of the 21st century. See the discussion of Moore's Law in Chapter 0.

2.5.2 Digital Logic Gates

You saw in the previous section that the AND function can be computed using switches. Transistors can function as switches, so we could draw circuit diagrams with a bunch of transistors showing how each of the Boolean functions of two inputs could be computed. Doing that belongs in a course in electronic engineering. Instead, we will abstract away the internal details of how such functions are computed, and also abstract away the details of power supply and return. We will use a set of stylized symbols to represent **digital logic gates**, electronic devices that can compute Boolean functions. The commonly used symbols their truth tables are shown in Figure 2-6.[48] The truth tables are identical to those in Figure 2-3 and Figure 2-4.

To save space, the inputs and outputs are not labeled in Figure 2-6. We will refer to the inputs as *a* and *b*, and the output as either *f* or with the appropriate Boolean expression. The first symbol in Figure 2-6 is the NOT gate symbol; the result is the inverse of the input. For this symbol and all the others in the table, the input is on the left and the output is on the

---

47   As the density of transistors in integrated circuits increased according to Moore's law, heat dissipation again became a limiting factor late in the 20th century.

48   These are the **distinctive shape** symbols. Another way of drawing digital logic gates is to use the same rectangular symbol for every type of gate and to label each rectangle with the appropriate function. The distinctive shape standard is based on a U.S. Air Force standard, formalized by American Institute of Electrical Engineers and American Society of Mechanical Engineers in 1960. When the distinctive shape symbols are used, the output is always on the "pointy end."

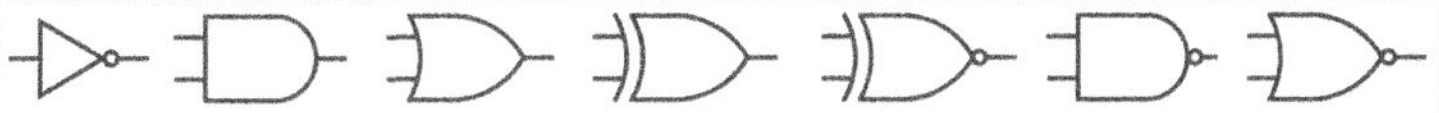

NOT	AND	OR	XOR	EQUIV	NAND	NOR
0 │ 1	0 0 │ 0	0 0 │ 0	0 0 │ 0	0 0 │ 1	0 0 │ 1	0 0 │ 1
1 │ 0	0 1 │ 0	0 1 │ 1	0 1 │ 1	0 1 │ 0	0 1 │ 1	0 1 │ 0
	1 0 │ 0	1 0 │ 1	1 0 │ 1	1 0 │ 0	1 0 │ 1	1 0 │ 0
	1 1 │ 1	1 1 │ 1	1 1 │ 0	1 1 │ 1	1 1 │ 0	1 1 │ 0

Figure 2-6
Symbols and truth tables for important digital logic gates

right. As a function of one variable, its truth table has two rows. They are the same as the *a* and $\bar{a}$ columns in Figure 2-3. The symbol is a triangle with a circle at the output end. The triangle is the symbol for an amplifier. The ability of one gate to drive the inputs of several others, the fan-out, is an important property when designing digital logic circuits. The circle is called a negation bubble, and indicates that the output signal is inverted. The NOT gate is also called an inverter.

The AND symbol is a bullet shape. It computes the Boolean product. Its truth table is that of the AND column in Figure 2-4. In addition to computing the Boolean product, the AND gate can serve to perform an enable function. If *ena* is zero, the output of AND is always zero regardless of the value of *in*. However, if *ena* is one, the output of AND is equal to *in*; the AND gate has served to **enable** the value of *in* at its output when *ena* is one and to produce a zero otherwise. We will use AND gates this way in Chapter 3.

ena	*in*	*out*
0	0	0
0	1	0
1	0	0
1	1	1

Figure 2-7
AND as enable

The OR symbol is the shield shape, and computes the Boolean sum: $a + b$. As mentioned above, the plus symbol is pronounced "or." It is *not* the same as the arithmetic plus. Its truth table is that of the OR column in Figure 2-4.

The XOR symbol, exclusive or, is an OR symbol with a curved chevron across the inputs. Unlike the OR gate, XOR is not one when both *a* and *b* are one; the output is one when *a*, exclusively, is one and when *b*, exclusively, is one. The XOR function is sometimes called the "odd function" because it produces a one at the output when the number of ones at the input is odd. Similarly, it can be considered a "not equal" function since it produces a one when the inputs are not equal. Another way to look at it is that xor computes even **parity**. Count the number of one-bits in the two inputs and the result; it will always be even. Parity is used for error-checking as described in Section 3.5.3

Inv	*in*	*out*
0	0	0
0	1	1
1	0	1
1	1	0

Figure 2-8
XOR as controlled inverter

The XOR gate can be used as a **controlled inverter** as shown in Figure 2-8. When *inv* is zero, the output of XOR is the same as *in*. When *inv* is one, the output is $\overline{in}$, the inverse of the input. We will use it that way in Chapter 3.

The EQUIV or XNOR symbol is an XOR gate with a negation bubble at the output. The characteristic number of the result is the inverse of XOR. The principal use of EQUIV is as a comparator; it produces a one when *a* and *b* are equal, a zero otherwise.

All digital logic gates require connections for power and return or ground. Those connections are abstracted away in logic diagrams, but are present in the physical circuits.

2.6 NAND and NOR: Circuit Equivalence and Functional Completeness

There is frequently more than one way to design a digital logic circuit. Two circuits which produce the same result for all combinations of inputs are **equivalent**.

There is an important property of NAND and NOR: each, by itself, is **functionally complete**. The property of functional completeness means that any Boolean expression can be rewritten so that it can be computed using only NAND or only NOR gates in correct arrangement. It follows that one can design circuits using only NAND or only NOR that are equivalent to

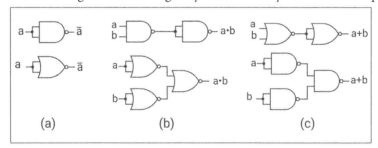

Figure 2-9

Circuit equivalence and functional completeness (a) NAND and NOR as inverters (b)computation of the AND function (c) computation of the OR function

circuits using any other gates. Figure 2-9(a) shows that both NAND and NOR can compute the NOT function, or Boolean inverse. If signal *a* is connected to both inputs of a NAND gate, then both inputs will be identical, either zero or one, depending on the value of *a*. From Figure 2-4 we see that if both inputs to a NAND gate are zero, the result is a one, and if both inputs are one, the result is zero. The NAND gate of Figure 2-9(a) computes the NOT function.

Also from Figure 2-4 we see that if both inputs to a NOR gate are zero, the result is a one, and if both inputs are one, the result is zero. The NOR gate of Figure 2-9(a) *also* computes the NOT function.

Showing equivalence using Boolean algebra

Figure 2-9(b) shows the computation of AND using only NAND and using only NOR. Recall that the characteristic number of NAND is 1110, and that is computed by the leftmost NAND gate. The second NAND gate is wired as an inverter, and so transforms 1110 to 0001, the characteristic number of AND. The upper circuit of Figure 2-9(b) computes the AND function using only NAND gates.

The lower diagram of Figure 2-9(b) shows computation of and using only nor gates. We can show that the circuit is equivalent to and using Boolean algebra. The first two nor gates compute $\overline{a}$ and $\overline{b}$. The rightmost nor gate computes $\overline{\overline{a} + \overline{b}}$. By De Morgan's theorem,[49] that is $\overline{\overline{a}} \cdot \overline{\overline{b}}$; the double negations cancel, leaving $a \cdot b$.

The leftmost NOR gate of Figure 2-9(c) computes the NOR of the inputs, a characteristic number of 1000. The second NOR gate inverts that, giving 0111, the characteristic number of the OR function.

Showing equivalence using truth tables

We showed that the second circuit in Figure 2-9(b) was equivalent to the AND function using Boolean algebra. It is also possible to show that two circuits are equivalent using truth tables, and we will show using a truth table that the lower circuit of Figure 2-9(c) computes the OR function. The left column of Figure 2-10 enumerates all possible values of the two inputs, a and b.

$a\ b$	$\overline{a}\ \overline{b}$	f
0 0	1 1	0
0 1	1 0	1
1 0	0 1	1
1 1	0 0	1

Figure 2-10

Computation of OR using NAND gates

The leftmost NAND gates of the lower circuit of Figure 2-9(c) function as inverters. The middle column of Figure 2-10 shows the inverse values as computed by those NAND gates. The middle column is no longer in ascending binary order.

The two values in the center column are inputs to the rightmost NAND gate in the lower circuit of Figure 2-9(c). Using the truth table for NAND, we see that an input of 1 1 produces an output of 0; an input of 1 0 produces an output of 1, and so on. Column f, the result of the circuit, has the value 0111, which is the characteristic number of the OR gate. We have shown that the lower circuit of Figure 2-9(c) computes the OR function.

Equivalence of more complex circuits can be shown using Boolean algebra or, for small numbers of inputs, with truth tables.

There are other combinations of gates that, together, are functionally complete. For example, the set {AND, OR} is functionally complete. NAND and NOR are important because they are the only two that are, alone, functionally complete. NAND gates are particularly

---

49 De Morgan's theorem is one of the fundamental theorems of Boolean algebra. It has both an AND form and an OR form. The AND form is $\overline{a \cdot b} \equiv \overline{a} + \overline{b}$. The OR form, used above, is $\overline{a + b} \equiv \overline{a} \cdot \overline{b}$. You may find DeMorgan's theorem useful in developing programming logic to sort out the effect of combining AND, OR, and NOT, as well as in analyzing digital logic. The mnemonic to help you remember it is, "Break the line, change the sign."

important in chip design because they have better propagation performance and take up less silicon area than NOR gates. Recall the space / computational power / cost trade-offs discussed in Chapter 0.

2.7 Digital Logic Building Blocks: Combinational Circuits

Digital logic gates become much more interesting when we do things with them. There are a few digital logic building blocks that occur frequently in the construction of computing equipment. We'll look at two of them, adders and decoders, in detail, and mention some others. These are **combinational circuits**. When the input to a combinational circuit changes, the output changes correspondingly. Combinational circuits have no memory.

2.7.1 Adders

A prolific writer on computing has remarked, "a computer that cannot add integers is unthinkable"[50] (Tanenbaum, 1990) so it will not surprise you that one can build a digital logic circuit that can perform addition. Recall from Figure 1-4, that the rules of binary addition are as shown in Figure 2-11.

The rightmost column says one plus one is two. In binary, that's a zero in the units' place, with one to carry. Leaving the carry aside for a moment, the characteristic number for binary addition of two bits is 0110, the XOR function.

$$
\begin{array}{cccc}
0 & 0 & 1 & 1 \\
+0 & +1 & +0 & +1 \\
\hline
0 & 1 & 1 & 1\,0 \\
(a) & (b) & (c) & (d)
\end{array}
$$

Figure 2-11
Rules of binary addition

The carry is a one when both addends are one, and zero otherwise. That is the and function. So, it is possible to build a digital logic circuit that will add two bits using an xor gate and an and gate. Such a circuit is called a half adder and is shown in Figure 2-12(a).

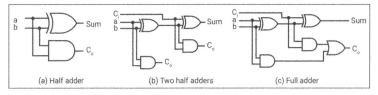

(a) Half adder   (b) Two half adders   (c) Full adder

Figure 2-12
Half adder and full adder

In this circuit, and the others in this book, the lines represent conductors, or wires. Connections are indicated by a heavy dot. Lines that cross without a dot are not connected. So, in the circuit of Figure 2-12(a), input *a* is connected to the upper input of the XOR gate and

---

50 In fact, the IBM Model 1620, a scientific computer of the 1960s, could not add. Instead, it used a table lookup to find sums. It was said that IBM's code name for the 1620, CADET, meant "Can't Add, Doesn't Even Try."

the lower input of the AND gate, but not to input b.

The half adder has a drawback: it can produce a carry-out, but it has no provision for a carry-in. Without a carry-in, one cannot add numbers larger than two single-digit binary numbers, a serious limitation.

We can use a second half adder to compute the sum of the first result and a carry-in, giving a total sum of three bits. That is shown in Figure 2-12(b). The and gate of the leftmost half adder has been moved down a little to keep wires from crossing, but the logic is the same.

We've solved the problem of having a carry-in, but now there are two carry-outs. They cannot both be one. The carry-out from the first half adder is one only if a and b are both one. In that case, the intermediate sum will be zero and so the second carry-out will be zero. If carry-in and either a or b, but not both, are one, then the intermediate sum will be one and the carry-out from the second half-adder will be one. So, if the carry-out from either half adder is one, the carry-out of the total sum will be one. We can connect the two carry-outs with an OR gate to compute the carry-out of the result. That circuit is called a full adder and is shown in Figure 2-12(c).

A full adder adds two bits and a carry-in to produce a one-bit sum and a carry-out. We can use multiple full adders to add binary numbers more than one bit wide. Given a design for a full adder, we can abstract away the details and just draw a box labeled "full adder." Figure 2-13 shows an adder capable of adding two four-bit binary integers, A and B, to produce a sum, S, and a carry out.

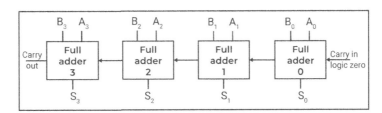

Figure 2-13
Four-bit ripple-carry adder

The carry-in input of the low order (rightmost) full adder is permanently wired to logic zero. The carry-out of the low order adder is connected to the carry-in of the next one, and so on. We could make an adder capable of adding integers larger than four bits by adding more full adders on the left.

2.7.2 Combinational Circuits and Gate Delay

The adder circuits developed above, and the other circuits discussed in this section, are

combinational circuits. The output of a combinational circuit depends only on its input at the time; if the input changes, the output will change accordingly. In other words, combinational circuits have no memory of previous states.

Modern transistors can change state from on to off or vice versa very fast; some transistors used in integrated circuits have switching speeds measured in picoseconds.[51] However, there is always some delay between the time the input to a gate changes and the time the output reflects the changed input. The time required for the output of a gate to change state after the input has changed state is the **propagation time** or **gate delay**. It also takes time for a signal to move from one device to another. Designers of computing equipment must take this delay into consideration.

Consider the adder in Figure 2-13. If the total delay through one full adder is two nanoseconds, then the carry-out from adder zero will not be correct until two nanoseconds after the inputs are applied to the adder. That means that the carry-in to the next full adder, numbered one, will not be correct until two nanoseconds after the inputs are applied. The carry-in to adder two will not be correct for another two nanoseconds, and so on. The carry value "ripples" from the low order digit to the higher order digits, with each successive carry taking the time for a full adder to complete its computation. That is why the circuit of Figure 2-13 is called a **ripple carry adder**.

For a four-bit ripple carry adder made of full adders with two nanosecond add time, the result will not be correct until eight nanoseconds after the inputs have been applied. A 32-bit adder built in this way will take 64 nanoseconds to produce correct output. To improve speed, we need more sophisticated circuits, faster transistors, or both. The adder circuit in a modern computer is much more sophisticated than our ripple carry adder and much faster. It is also much more expensive in terms of number of gates and chip area occupied. One of the basic trade-offs in computing is speed *vs.* cost. There is no such thing as a free lunch.

2.7.3 Decoders, Multiplexors, and other Building Blocks

Suppose we have a signal with which we want to activate one of two outputs, perhaps a green LED when the signal is on, or asserted, and a red one when it is off. We can do that with a single NOT gate. In the circuit of Figure 2-14, if the input at *a* is on, the input will drive the upper LED and turn it on. The output of the NOT gate will be a zero, or off, and the lower LED will be off. Conversely, if *a* is zero or off, the upper LED will be off, but the NOT gate will produce a one and the lower LED will be on.

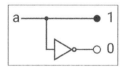

Figure 2-14
A one-bit decoder controls two outputs with one input.

---

51 A picosecond is one trillionth of a second, or 1/1000 of a nanosecond.

It is possible to extend this idea to an arbitrary number of inputs. Such a circuit is called a **decoder**. It receives a binary number at its inputs and activates exactly one of 2^n outputs, where n is the number of bits of the input. In the circuit of Figure 2-14, there's a one-bit number at a and one of two possible outputs is activated. In Figure 2-15, there are two inputs. The high-order digit is a and the low-order digit is b. If the input is 01, as shown, output 1 will be high and the others will be low. Other values at the input will select exactly one of the four possible outputs.

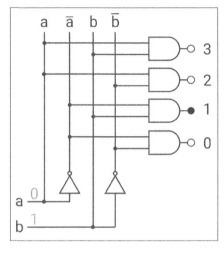

Figure 2-15

A two-to-four decoder..

The complementary circuit to the decoder is the **encoder**. It has 2^n inputs and generates an n-bit binary number at its output, depending on which input is high. (Only one input is allowed to be high at any time.)

Another digital logic building block is the **multiplexor**, which picks one of 2^n signals to transmit. It has n selector inputs, 2^n data inputs, and one data output. One of the data inputs is connected to the data output. Which one? It is determined by the binary number supplied at the selector inputs. The complementary circuit is the **demultiplexor**. It has one data input, n selector inputs, and 2^n data outputs. The value on the data input line is directed to one of the 2^n data outputs depending on the value of the selector inputs.

2.7.4 Shifters

A **shifter** is a combinational circuit that can shift the bits of a word one or more places to the right or left. Shifters are used for both logical operations on data and for arithmetic.

To see how a shifter can be used for arithmetic, consider that we can multiply a decimal number by ten by adding a zero on the right, like this: $13 \times 10 = 130$. What has actually happened is that the original digits are shifted left one place so that the one is shifted from the tens place to the hundreds place and the three is shifted from the units place to the tens place. The added zero occupies the units place. Removing a digit on the right of a decimal number has the effect of dividing by ten; the digit removed is the remainder.

Shifting binary numbers left one place multiplies by two. Shifting right divides by two. The bit shifted out is the remainder.

When shifting numbers with pencil and paper, it is not necessary to consider what happens at the left end of a number, but computers represent numbers in fixed sizes. Adding a digit at the right means discarding a digit at the left. If a significant digit is shifted out on the left, the result is no longer correct multiplication by two. Some shifter circuits preserve the digit shifted out so that it can be tested for significance.

When shifting right, we must supply a digit on the left. When shifting unsigned or positive numbers, supplying a zero on the left produces the expected result. Such a shift is called a **logical right shift**.

A problem arises when right-shifting signed numbers because the leftmost bit represents the sign. When shifting signed numbers, we want to replicate the sign bit, supplying a zero for positive numbers and a one for negative numbers. Such a shift is called an **arithmetic right shift**. When shifting left, there is no distinction between logical and arithmetic shifts.

It is not uncommon for shifters to have a control signal for "no shift" that passes the input value through the shifter unchanged. Allowing the shifter to be present even when shifting isn't needed simplifies the design of some kinds of circuits.

Modern computer designs depend in large part on relatively few digital logic building blocks like these in the same way that modern buildings depend on a few standard sizes for things like lumber, bricks, and doors. The existence of these building blocks helps explain why it is easier to build complex hardware that works reliably than to build software of equal complexity that works equally reliably.

2.8 Sequential Circuits and Memory

So far, we have considered combinational circuits. If the input to a combinational circuit changes, the output changes correspondingly. Combinational circuits have no memory of past inputs or states. There are several ways to implement circuits with memory. One way is to use digital logic gates, but arrange them differently. In the circuits we have considered so far, signals flow from input to output. Circuits with memory can be achieved by connecting the output of a circuit back to its input, a mechanism called **feedback**. Circuits that employ feedback to achieve memory are called **sequential circuits**.

2.8.1 The S-R Latch

The circuit of Figure 2-16 is one of the simplest memory circuits, the S-R latch. Applying a one to input S turns Q on and $\overline{Q}$ off. They will remain in that state even when S returns to zero. Applying a one to R turns $\overline{Q}$ off and Q on. The S-R latch remembers, or **latches**, which of S or R was seen last, even after the input is removed. We can think of S and R as *set* and *reset*, respectively. A circuit like this one that has two stable states is called **bistable**. The condition of

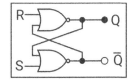

Figure 2-16

S-R latch.

$S=R=1$ is not allowed; the behavior of the circuit is unpredictable .

Because the S-R latch has memory, it cannot be described with a truth table. Instead, one needs a **state table**, which has Q, the output, on both the input and output sides. We will not consider state tables here, but if you'd like to make one for the S-R latch, you will need columns for S, R, and Q on the input side of the table and *NextQ*, often written as Q', on the output side. Since there are three inputs, the table will have $2^3 =$ eight rows. You will not need a column for $\overline{Q}$ because it is always the inverse of Q.

2.8.2 The Clocked D-latch

The S-R latch will store one bit of data, but it's not as convenient as we might like because we need separate signals for storing zero and one. What is really needed is one data input bit, which we call D. Recall that one-bit decoder of Figure 2-14. The one-bit decoder can generate the S signal when D is a one and the R signal when D is a zero. That is accomplished with a single NOT gate.

In addition to a single input, we need a way to control when the input is stored. The ripple-carry adder of Figure 2-13 takes eight nanoseconds after the inputs are applied to produce a correct sum. Because combinational circuits compute continuously, the output bits are always present, but they're not correct until after the longest propagation delay, in this case eight nanoseconds, have passed. The **clocked D-latch** provides a way to signal when the result should be stored.

The right side of Figure 2-17 is an S-R latch. Ignoring the two AND gates for a moment, if the input at D is zero, a one will be sent to the R input of the S-R latch and a zero to the S input. If the input at D is one, a zero will be sent to R and a one to S. Now we consider those AND gates. An AND gate can be used to control whether the input is passed to the output or the output is zero regardless of the input, as shown in Figure 2-7. Notice that when *ena* is zero, the output is always zero. When *ena* is one, the output is the value of *in*. When used this way, the AND gate performs an **enable** function; that is, the input is enabled to propagate to the output.

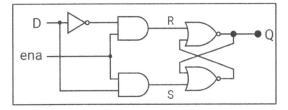

Figure 2-17
Clocked D-latch

That is the function of the AND gates. The value of D is stored in Q only when the *ena* signal is high or true. The enable signal is often called a **clock** signal.

The clocked D-latch and similar circuits are **level-triggered** memories. The input, at D in the diagram, is stored any time the enable signal is true. Level-triggered devices are also **transparent** when the enable signal is high. If the value at D changes when the enable signal is true, the value at the output, Q, will also change.

2.8.3 Edge-Triggered Devices

If we think about computing systems rather than individual circuits, it is easy to see that the output of one step of a calculation is frequently the input to the next step of the calculation. Even in simple circuits, if there are two or more paths through the circuit, signals will likely not propagate through all paths at exactly the same time. Conditions that can cause an unwanted change in the output of a circuit are called **hazards**, and cause erroneous results if they occur.

To overcome these problems, designers use **edge-triggered memory devices**. In an edge-triggered device, it is the transition of the clock signal that causes the input value to be stored. The clock period must be long enough for all circuits to settle to correct values. Since the clock transition happens very quickly, result values are captured quickly, before other changes can occur. Edge-triggered devices can be built to capture the value to be stored on either the rising edge of a clock pulse or the falling edge, or both.

2.9 Clocks and Synchronous Circuits

The diagram at Figure 2-18 shows how edge-triggered memory devices use a clock signal to store the results of a computational circuit, often a CPU, without causing hazards.

The clock cycle begins at the start of one peak and ends at the same point on the following peak. The time taken by one cycle is called the **period** of the clock. The number of clock cycles per second[52] is the **clock speed** of a computer. The clock speed is the inverse of the period. A clock with a speed of one gigahertz completes one billion clock cycles each second, so each cycle is one nanosecond, the inverse of one billion.

The clock in Figure 2-18 is **asymmetric**; the time during which the clock signal is high is less than the time when the clock signal is low. The transitions from high to low and low to high are sloped in the diagram, showing that the transitions are not instantaneous.

In our hypothetical computer, data are sent from storage to the computing element on a high-to-low transition signal from the clock. Control signals describing the computation are generated at the same time.

Computation takes place using combinational logic conceptually similar to the ripple carry adder of Figure 2-13, but more complex. The time required to complete the computation is the time for the data signals to propagate through the computational unit. In the four-bit ripple carry adder, if each full adder takes two nanoseconds, the data at the outputs will not be correct until eight nanoseconds after the inputs are stable. Designers of computers know

---

52 Strictly speaking, the correct unit of measurement for clock speed is Hertz (Hz), which is the inverse of the period.

that it will take some time to set up the input signals and that all gates are not identical; some may be slightly slower than others. So, the clock period for the ripple carry adder would need to be slightly longer than eight nanoseconds. How much longer can be calculated if the characteristics of the circuits are known. Data are stored on the transition of the clock from low to high.

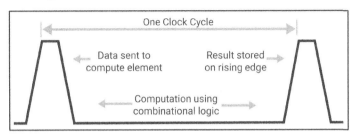

Figure 2-18
One clock cycle, showing use of edge-triggered data storage
Adapted from Tanenbaum (1999)

It is likely that the result of a computation will be stored in the same memory that supplied the input. However, edge-triggered memory devices will store the data far faster than the time for a signal to propagate through the computational unit, so the fact that the input changes does not cause an incorrect result.

2.10 Registers

Figure 2-19 is a clocked latch that can send its output to two destinations. The input to the latch is connected to an input bus, which may also connect to other storage devices. There will always be one bit of data at the input to the latch, but it may not always be valid. The triangle at the clock input indicates that the latch is edge triggered on the rising edge of the signal. A negation bubble at the base of the triangle would indicate that the latch is triggered on the falling edge. The AND gate that drives the clock input of the latch receives two signals, CLOCK and WRITE. The CLOCK signal is the system clock; it produces a regular train of pulses, similar to Figure 2-18. The WRITE signal is generated by a control unit. This latch will store one bit of data, whatever is on the input bus, on the rising edge of the system clock pulse, but only if the WRITE signal is also asserted.

The latch has a single output line that is always on, and is the bit that was most recently stored. The two triangular symbols on the right side of the latch are **tristate buffers**. A tristate buffer provides a mechanism to pass a signal or no output at all. In the on state, the input, either zero or one, is copied to the output; in the off state, it is as though there were no

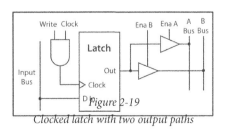

Figure 2-19
Clocked latch with two output paths

65

connection at all. Electrical engineers call this a high impedance state. If the *ena A* signal is asserted, that tristate buffer passes the latch output to the A bus. Similar, *ena B* passes the output to the B bus. Both buses can be driven at the same time, but if there are multiple latches on a bus, only one can be enabled at any given moment.

A **register** is a small, fast unit of storage within the central processing unit or other device. Figure 2-20 is the symbol for a register. Conceptually, a register is some number of latches, from one to 64 or more. Registers are described by the number of bits stored, so a register with 64 latches would be a 64-bit register. The number of outputs may be one, two, or possibly more than two. There is one WRITE input, and one ENABLE input for each output. They are connected internally to every latch in the register so that

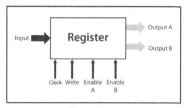

Figure 2-20

A register

all latches store data at the same time and all latches enable their outputs at the same time. A register that holds only a few bits is sometimes called a latch even though it may hold more than one bit.

2.11 Summary of Learning Objectives

*This section of the chapter tells you the things you should know about, but not **what** you should know about them. To test your knowledge, discuss the following concepts and topics with a study partner or in writing, ideally from memory.*

Boolean algebra is an algebra over finite sets of discrete values. It was developed in the 19th century by George Boole. The logical operators of the Boolean algebra important to computing are NOT, AND, OR, XOR, EQUIV, NAND, and NOR. The NAND and NOR operators are each functionally complete. Others, including C. S. Peirce and Jan Łukasiewicz, used truth tables to represent two-valued Boolean expressions. In the 20th century, Claude Shannon developed the switching algebra, a Boolean algebra in which functions and variables have only two states. Shannon showed that switching devices could compute any function that could be represented by a truth table. Switching elements are on or off. In proper arrangement, they can compute functions such as NOT, AND, OR, XOR, EQUIV, NAND, and NOR. Such devices are called digital logic gates, or just gates.

Switching devices of the early to mid 20th century were mechanical relays or vacuum tubes. Mechanical relays are slow; vacuum tubes were faster, but fragile and with a limited life. The invention of the transistor and then the integrated circuit increased both the speed and the operating lifetime of digital logic gates.

Multiple digital logic gates can be arranged to compute much more complex functions, including arithmetic operations like addition. A relatively few types of circuits are the building blocks of modern computers. Circuits that perform computation but do not have memory are called combinational circuits.

The time required for a switching device to change states is non-zero, so the time for the output of a gate to reflect a change in the input is non-zero. This time is called the gate delay. The time for an electric signal to propagate from one device to another is also non-zero. The time for a combinational circuit's output to reflect a change in the input is the sum of the gate delays and propagation delays of the longest path through the circuit, and is called the propagation delay.

Because digital logic circuits take non-zero time to complete each computation, we need a mechanism to indicate when computations are complete. A clock is a circuit that generates a regular train of pulses, the period of which is long enough for the longest computation.

Digital logic circuits incorporating feedback from output to input can be used for storage of data. The simplest of these is the S-R latch, which can store one bit of data. The clocked D-latch extends the S-R latch by providing a single data input and a mechanism to enable the storage element to be loaded from the data input. The clocked D-latch is a level-triggered device. If the value of the data input changes while the clock signal is asserted, an incorrect value can be stored. Instead, edge-triggered storage devices can be used. Sampling and storing the input takes place on the transition of the clock input, and not based on its level.

A clocked latch with one or more outputs can send its output to one or more buses. A register is conceptually one or more latches, up to 64 or more bits wide. If two or more registers are connected to the same bus, only one may be enabled for output at any given time.

2.12 References

Tanenbaum, A. S. (1990). *Structured Computer Organization* (3rd ed.). Prentice-Hall.

Tanenbaum, A. S. (1999). *Structured Computer Organization* (4th ed.). Prentice-Hall.

Chapter 3
The CPU and Memory

"It would appear that we have reached the limits of what it is possible to achieve with computer technology, although one should be careful with such statements, as they tend to sound pretty silly in 5 years."

—John von Neumann

The defining component of any computer system is the **central processing unit**, or **CPU**. The design and architecture of the CPU determine what instructions are available for programming it, how fast it will be able to run, and how data are organized and addressed. The CPU receives data and instructions from memory, performs arithmetic or logical operations on the data, and returns the data to memory. The CPU can perform billions of such operations every second. Even though each operation is relatively simple, the CPU can perform complex actions very quickly by combining those relatively simple operations.

Figure 3-1
John von Neumann
Los Alamos National Laboratory

The first commercially available CPU, that of the UNIVAC I computer delivered to the Census Bureau in 1951, was about 14 feet long, about eight feet wide, and over eight feet tall. By 1970, the progress of Moore's Law reduced the CPUs of some computers to a single circuit board. In 1971, Intel introduced the first CPU on a chip, intended for use in electronic calculators and incorporating about 2,250 transistors. Modern CPU chips have tens to hundreds of billions of transistors. In the late 20th century, chips with multiple processing units were introduced. When a chip has more than one processing unit, the processing units are called **cores**.

Also in the late 20th century, supporting circuitry like memory and bus controllers began to be added to CPU chips. These evolved to become systems on a chip (SOCs). Today, CPU chips with external supporting circuitry are used where performance is the major factor, such as in servers and workstation computers. SOCs are used where small size and low power consumption are driving forces, such as in phones and tablet computers.

3.1 The von Neumann Architecture

John von Neumann was a Hungarian-born American mathematician and mathematical physicist. He made numerous contributions to mathematics, physics, and game theory. His most important contribution was a design for a programmable electronic computer. That is why the design has come to be called the von Neumann architecture.

Von Neumann suggested the use of binary numbers in computers, but his contributions in the 1945 *First Draft of a Report on the EDVAC*[53] went much further. The *First Draft* described a binary, sequential, stored program computer with a memory that held both instructions and data. Although other computer architectures have been tried, every commercially successful computer has used this design.

Figure 3-2 shows the organization of a von Neumann architecture computer. The registers are fast memory that are a part of the CPU. Typically the registers are the same size as the word size of the computer. Word size is discussed in Section 3.5.2. The arithmetic-logic unit performs, as you might expect, arithmetic and logical operations on data. It is made of combinational logic circuits like those discussed in Section 2.7. The control unit generates the digital logic signals that cause the CPU to carry-out its operations. Not shown in the diagram, but present in the *First Draft*, is a system clock that generates a regular stream of pulses that synchronize the operation of the CPU as described in Section 2.9.

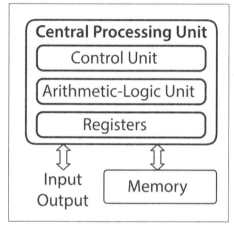

Figure 3-2
Organization of the
von Neumann architecture

The instructions that a computer can perform are stored in the computer's memory as numbers. A part of the number, called the **operation code** or op code, tells the control unit what operation is to be performed. Other parts, called **operands**, tell what data should be used in the operation. Those numbers are the machine language of a computer. At first these were written by hand. It wasn't long before a notation more easily used by humans was developed, and the translation to numbers was performed by a computer program. The idea of translation by a program led to the high-level programming languages of today.

The **program counter** is a fundamental concept in the von Neumann architecture. The program counter does not "count" anything. Since both instructions and data are held in the same memory, there must be a way to keep track of the flow of instructions. *The program counter holds the address of the next instruction.* Since the instructions are executed in sequence, often the next instruction will be the one at the next sequential memory location. The execution of an instruction can modify the program counter when it is necessary to change the flow of the program.

---

53   "Electronic Discrete Variable Automatic Computer." Although only von Neumann's name appeared on the report, several others contributed to the ideas it contained.

3.1.1 Instruction Set Architecture

You are no doubt aware of different types of CPUs. A desktop or laptop computer might have an Intel CPU while a phone or tablet might have an ARM CPU. In 2020 Apple Computer announced that they would begin using Apple-designed CPUs in Mac computers. These different types of CPU cannot run each other's programs because they use different machine languages.

Every computer design has some number of basic machine language operations it can perform. The repertoire of basic operations for a computer is called its **instruction set**. The number of instructions in an instruction set can range from about a dozen to several hundred depending on the complexity of the CPU.

In the early history of electronic computers, every new computer had a new instruction set. Buying a new computer meant rewriting software. That was tolerable when the number of computers and their collections of software were small. By 1960, government, business, and universities had amassed a large number of software applications, and the thought of rewriting all that software was daunting. Computer upgrades were postponed because of the cost of converting software.

In 1964, IBM made an extraordinary promise with the announcement of its System/360 line of computers. They promised potential buyers that, if the software were rewritten one more time, for the System/360 instruction set, it would never have to be rewritten again.[54] Although it seems obvious to us now, it was IBM's innovation that led to "families" of CPUs that are compatible at the level of binary machine instructions. The newest Intel CPU chips of the 21st century will run programs written for the Intel 80386, announced in 1985.

A family of computers has a similar instruction set, called the **instruction set architecture**, although newer members of such a family may have instructions not available in older implementations. This is called **backward compatibility**. A newer member of a family will run anything that older members of the same family will run, but the reverse is not true. Older members of a family of computers eventually become obsolescent, but the software written for them does not, or at least not as quickly.

3.1.2 Microarchitecture

Newer computers can run the same software as their older counterparts because they share the same instruction set architecture. They often provide improved performance because the underlying hardware is faster. The extra speed comes not only from faster transistors in the CPU, but from improvements in the CPU design. The design of a CPU is called its **microarchitecture**. Although the functions of a particular computer family may be con-

---

54   Not only was IBM's promise extraordinary, they did an extraordinary job of keeping that promise. IBM zEnterprise mainframes of the 21st century will run programs written for the System/360 of 1964.

strained by the instruction set architecture of that family, the chip designer is free to use the newest innovations in CPU design. Such innovations might include instruction pipelining or the inclusion of more functional units. These are discussed in Section 3.6. We will shortly examine a design for a control unit that is fast but relatively expensive because of the number of gates needed, and remark that there is a way to build a slower but less expensive device that will do the same work.

3.2 The "Little Man" Computer

The "Little Man Computer," or LMC, devised by Stuart Madnick[55] in 1965, imagines a computer as a room with mailboxes representing memory and a calculator to perform arithmetic. The calculator and mailboxes are manipulated by a hypothetical "little man" who can perform only a very few, very limited, operations. This model allows teaching the principles of a von Neumann architecture computer while abstracting away most of the details. Several people have developed LMC emulators that allow students to write and run programs in the LMC's language.

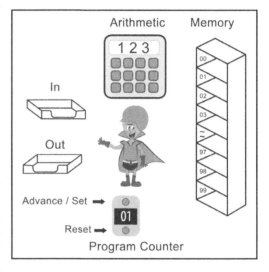

LMC has 100 mailboxes (memory locations), numbered zero to 99, each of which can hold three decimal digits, a calculator that can hold a single result, and a two-digit counter, the **program counter**, that can be advanced by one or set to an arbitrary value by the little man. The program counter can also be reset to zero from the outside the computer; this action starts or re-starts the computer. The little man of LMC performs the actions that result in computation.

Figure 3-3
The Little Man Computer

Each memory location can hold either an instruction or a three-digit decimal number. Instructions consist of a one digit operation code and a two digit operand address. No more than ten instructions are possible.

Although it was designed primarily as a tool to teach concepts, interesting programs can be written for the LMC.

3.2.1 The Instruction Cycle

A fundamental feature of the von Neumann architecture is that *the program counter holds*

---

55   Madnick is a professor at the MIT Sloan School of Management.

the address of the next instruction. The importance of that concept will be clear from what follows.

The little man in the Little Man Computer does the same things repeatedly.

1. Read the number in the program counter. (It will be zero when the LMC is first started.)
2. Read the three-digit number at the memory location given by the program counter. The little man assumes that the first digit is an operation code and the remaining two digits are a memory address.
3. Advance the program counter by one. The program counter now holds the address of the instruction which will (usually) be executed next.
4. Perform the operation indicated by the first digit of the value read in step 2. Often this will require another trip to memory to read or store a value. Reads are non-destructive, but storing a value to memory replaces whatever was there before. If the instruction is a branch, the next instruction will be read from a non-consecutive location; the little man sets the program counter to the last two digits of the value obtained in step 2.
5. Go back to step 1.

This process is called the **instruction cycle**, or the fetch, decode, execute cycle. It repeats continuously in LMC and in every von Neumann architecture computer for as long as the CPU is running.

The little man could remember the address of the memory location needed and the value to be entered into the calculator. In a real computer, **registers** are used to store such data temporarily.

3.2.2 Programming the Little Man Computer

The Little Man Computer is programmed using abbreviations for the operations the computer can perform. These abbreviations are called **instruction mnemonics**. The instruction mnemonics must be translated to their numeric equivalents before the program can be executed. The instruction mnemonics of LMC are listed in Section A.2

The program in Figure 3-4 reads two numbers using the INP instruction, stores them in memory, performs the subtraction, and outputs the result. The halt (HLT) instruction stops the program.

```
           INP
           STO   minuend
           INP
           STO   subtrahnd
           LDA   minuend
           SUB   subtrahnd
           OUT
           HLT
minuend    DAT
subtrahnd  DAT
```

Figure 3-4
LMC program to subtract two numbers

The program in Figure 3-4 is written in LMC's **assembly language**. Assembly language instructions generally have a one-to-one correspondence with machine instructions of a particular computer architecture and so are architecture-dependent. Programs written in a computer family's assembly language are translated to the target machines hardware instructions by a program called an **assembler**.

3.2.3 Problems with the Little Man computer

The essential problem with LMC is that it is a decimal computer. That obscures some fundamental relationships between binary representation and computer architecture. For example, LMC has 100 memory locations. We need seven bits to enumerate 100 locations, but with seven bits, we can actually enumerate 128 locations. Such a computer would be designed to support up to 128 memory locations. Similarly, four bits are needed to enumerate up to ten instruction operation codes, but four bits allow enumeration of 16 instruction codes, so the design need not be limited to ten.

The concept of the "little man" is problematic because there is nothing volitional about the execution of instructions in a CPU. The CPU performs the steps given in the previous page.

3.3 Let's Build a CPU – the Tiny Binary Computer

The hypothetical little man of the Little Man Computer can perform addition and subtraction using the calculator, can enter numbers into the calculator, and can copy the results. The little man is also able to increment the program counter. In this section, we'll design an arithmetic logic unit (ALU) that can perform the functions required of the LMC. We are undoing the abstraction of the LMC to see how a real, but very simple, computer might work.

A CPU consists of an **arithmetic logic unit** (ALU), some number of **registers**, which are small, fast storage within the CPU, the electrical connections, called **buses**, between them, and a **control unit**. Although all four components are essential, it is the ALU that determines what a particular CPU can do, so we look first at the ALU.

3.3.1 Architecture of the Tiny Binary Computer

Our Tiny Binary Computer , or TBC, should be able to execute the same instructions as the Little Man Computer.[56] That means the instruction operation code must be four bits to allow for nine operation codes. Seven bits are needed to address 100 storage locations, but can actually address 128 locations. The change from decimal to binary increases the number of possible instructions from ten to 16 and increases the maximum addressable memory from

---

56   Although the Tiny Binary Computer executes the instruction set of the Little Man Computer, its architecture and design were heavily influenced by Andrew Tanenbaum's MIC-1 design. (Tanenbaum, 1990)

100 locations to 128. The magnitude of the largest representable data item is also increased. That is a concrete example of the use of binary numbers increasing the expressive power of binary circuits.

Four bits of operation code and seven bits of address makes a total word size of 11 bits, distinctly odd for even a tiny, hypothetical, computer. If eight bits are used for addresses, one gets a maximum addressable memory of 256 locations. That makes a data word of twelve bits, allowing signed numbers from -2048 to $+2047$ in twos complement form. Twelve bit words are unusual, but the hugely-successful PDP-8 computer of the 1960s used twelve bit words.

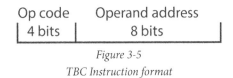

Figure 3-5
TBC Instruction format

The TBC's data registers must be twelve bits wide and address registers must be eight bits wide. The instruction format is shown in Figure 3-5, with four bits of operation code and twelve bits of operand address.

3.3.2 A One Bit ALU

We saw in Figure 2-7 that an AND gate can implement an *enable* function, either propagating an input value to the output or holding the output to zero. If one input to an AND gate is zero, the output will always be zero. If one input, which we call *Ena* or *Enable,* is one, the output will be equal to the other input. We also saw that the XOR gate can be used as a controlled inverter. When *Inv* is zero, the value of *In* appears at the output. When *Inv* is one, the value of the output is the inverse of the input and the circuit behaves like a NOT gate. Used

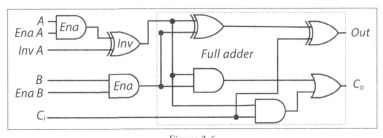

Figure 3-6
One-bit arithmetic logic unit

in this way, the XOR gate can be used to choose whether to invert a signal or not. These concepts are shown as truth tables in Figure 2-7 and Figure 2-8.

It is important to remember that these are just ordinary AND and XOR gates. The difference is that they are put to a specific use, namely using one input to control how the signal on the other input is propagated through the gate.

We can now examine the arithmetic logic unit of Figure 3-6. In the following discussion, saying that a signal is **asserted** means it is set to a logic one to cause the circuit to act.

The gates on the right side of the circuit are a full adder. The arrangement of the gates has been changed slightly to minimize line crossings, but the full adder is logically equivalent to the circuit in Figure 2-12(c).

The two AND gates labeled *Ena* perform the *enable* function for the two inputs, *A* and *B*. The XOR gate labeled *Inv* is a controlled inverter for the *A* input.

If input signals *Ena A* and *Ena B* are asserted and *Inv A* is false, the circuit functions as a full adder, adding *A*, *B*, and C_i to produce the sum at *Out* and the carry-out at C_o.

If *Ena A*, *Ena B*, and *InvA* are false, the adder computes 0+0 and emits a constant zero. This very simple ALU can perform a number of other operations. Those necessary for the TBC are listed in Figure 3-8.

3.3.3 Functions of the ALU

To see what other functions this ALU can perform, it is necessary to extend the ALU to operate on more than a single bit. That can be done in a manner similar to the ripple car-ry-adder of Figure 2-13. Such an arrangement is shown in Figure 3-7. (TBC will need twelve bits in its ALU, but that only requires adding eight more one-bit ALUs.) Carry-in to the rightmost bit (ALU 0) has been relabeled *Inc*, increment. The other con-trols, *Inv A*, *Ena A*, and *Ena B*, are connected to all of the ALU units.

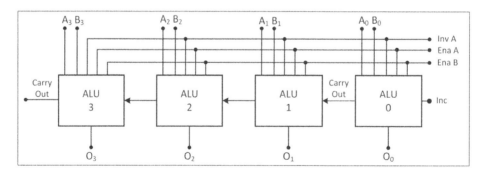

Figure 3-7
Four bit "ripple carry" ALU

There are 16 possible combinations of four control bits, but not all of them are useful. Ev-erything necessary to execute the LMC/TBC instruction set can be accomplished with four control combinations as shown in Figure 3-8. A bullet in a cell means that control signal is asserted, true, or one; a blank cell means that signal is false, or zero.

The subtract function applies the subtraction rule for two's complement numbers explained in Chapter 1, namely take the two's complement of the subtrahend and add it to the minuend. The ALU forms the two's complement of A by inverting the A bits using *Inv A* and adding one by setting *Inc*. The adder completes the operation.

Function	Inv A	Ena A	Ena B	Inc
Add (A+B)		●	●	
Subtract (B–A)	●	●	●	●
Copy A		●		
Increment A		●		●

Figure 3-8

Functions and control signals for the ALU

The copy A function actually computes A+0 by turning off *Ena B*. The increment operation enables A and asserts the *Inc* control, adding one to the A input.

Those are the operations needed to execute the LMC/TBC instruction set. This ALU can perform several more useful operations, including Copy B, Increment B, Constant zero, Constant one, and Constant minus one. Those operations aren't needed for the LMC/TBC instruction set.

3.3.4 Testing the ALU Output

We aren't quite finished. Both LMC/TBC and real computers have instructions to test the result of calculations performed by the arithmetic logic unit. For example, LMC and TBC have a BRP, branch on positive, instruction that goes to a different location in the program if the result of the last calculation was positive and a BRZ, branch on zero instruction. We need to be able to test the output for positive and zero. Because the ALU performs finite-precision arithmetic on twelve-bit operands, it is possible to compute a result that is too large to be stored. That condition is called **overflow** and is an error for which the ALU must check.

The zero condition is checked with an *n*-input NOR gate. If all inputs to that gate are zero, the gate produces a one or true; otherwise, it is zero or false.

The positive condition depends on the fact that the leftmost bit of a two's complement number is the sign bit. If the leftmost bit is a one, indicating a negative number, the NOT gate of Figure 3-9 produces a zero, or false; otherwise, it produces a one, or true indicating a positive result.

The **overflow rule** for two's complement addition is: *overflow has occurred if two numbers of the same sign are added and the result is of the opposite sign.*

The overflow condition is checked by comparing the carry-in to the leftmost bit with the carry-out from the leftmost bit. Recall that an XOR gate produces a one, or true, when the input bits are equal and a zero, or false when they're different. There are two ways that can happen.

Case 1: If the carry-in to the leftmost bit is zero, the only way the carry-out can be one is if both A and B of the leftmost bit were one, i.e. both negative. The sum of 1+1 (plus zero for the carry-in) will be zero with a carry-out. The two operands were negative, but the leftmost bit of the result will be zero making the result positive, and overflow has occurred.

Case 2: If the carry-in to the leftmost bit is one, the only way carry-out can be zero is if both A and B of the leftmost bit were zero, *i.e.* positive. The sum of 0+0+1 will be one. The two operands were positive, but the carry-out will be zero and leftmost bit of the result will be one, or negative, and overflow has occurred

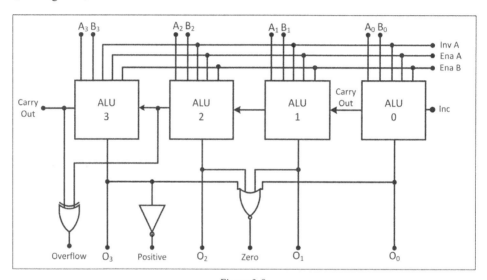

Figure 3-9
The ALU with checks for output

TBC processes only signed numbers. The mechanism above does not work for unsigned integers. In the case of unsigned integers, a carry-out from the leftmost bit indicates overflow.

Overflow is an error, and neither LMC nor TBC has an instruction like BRV, branch on overflow, to test for such an error. The error must be handled by having the TBC emulator print an error message and halt. In a real computer, overflow might be handled by a **trap**. In the event of overflow, the CPU would force a branch to the operating system's overflow handler. Traps for other errors would branch to the appropriate handlers.

The zero and positive values must be saved so they can be tested in subsequent instructions. A real computer with a less-limited instruction set might also save the overflow and carry-out bits. Conceptually, these would be stored in a four-bit **flags register** at the same time the result of the operation was stored. The flags register always holds the result of the last arithmetic operation. In TBC, the flags register holds only two values and is called is called the **P/Z latch**.

3.3.5 The Registers and Datapath

A **register** is a small, fast memory component that is a part of the CPU or similar device. Generally, registers store a single word of data. A storage device smaller than one word is often called a **latch**. The Little Man Computer has two visible registers, the calculator display and the program counter. The little man remembered the memory location to be read or written, the contents when reading from memory, and the instruction being performed. In a real computer, however simple, that remembered data is held in registers.

To do the things the Little Man Computer can do, TBC needs five registers and a latch. They are listed in Figure 3-10 .

Register	Function
Accumulator	Receives the results of ALU operations; the accumulator is represented by the calculator display in LMC.
Program Counter	Holds the address of the next instruction.
Instruction Register	Holds the operation code and operand address of the current instruction.
Memory Address Register	Holds the address to be read from or written to memory.
Memory Data Register	Holds data to be sent to memory; receives data read from memory.
P/Z Latch	Holds the positive and zero flags from the last ALU result to be stored in the accumulator.

Figure 3-10
Registers of Tiny Binary Computer and their functions.

The **datapath** of a computer is the ALU and possibly other functional units like multipliers, shifters, or incrementers, the registers, and the buses that connect them. The datapath and control unit together comprise the CPU. Figure 3-11 is a diagram of the CPU of the TBC. Units with light gray background are combinational circuits; those with white background are registers. The symbol for the ALU is a truncated V, shown at the bottom right. Using that symbol abstracts away the details of the ALU. The buses that connect the units are darker gray with arrows to show direction of data flow. Buses that cross are not connected.

Registers and Buses

The A, B, and C buses and the memory data bus are twelve bits wide; they have twelve electric conductors and can transfer twelve bits at a time. The memory address bus is eight bits wide.

The memory address register and program counter hold addresses, and so are eight bits wide. When the program counter's output is enabled, the eight bits appear on the rightmost eight bits of the A bus and the remaining four bits are zero. When the memory address register is loaded from the C bus, the rightmost eight bits are copied into the MAR.

The remaining registers are twelve bits wide. The connections from the instruction register are described below.

3.3.6 The TBC Datapath Cycle

The clock cycle of TBC is that of Figure 2-18. On the falling edge of the clock pulse the control unit sets up the necessary signals. After a delay determined by the signal propagation time through the buses and the characteristics of the register memory, the selected registers place their contents on the A and B buses. The ALU is combinational logic, so it is computing continuously but the output is not valid until some time after the data on the A and B buses is valid. The period of the clock is set so that the output of the ALU will be valid and propagated back to the registers on the C bus. on the rising edge of the clock The clock period has a small amount of additional time to allow for reliable operation.

The process of sending data from the registers through the ALU and back to the registers is called a **datapath cycle**. TBC performs one datapath cycle per clock period.

The operations necessary to execute an instruction in TBC's CPU are described using a register transfer language similar to the notation of Davidson and Fraser (1980).

This line

```
MAR ← PC; read
```

means that the contents of the program counter are copied to the memory address register and the memory read control line is asserted. The control unit accomplishes this by doing the following:

- Enable the PC register, placing its contents on the A bus.
- Send a "copy A" command to the ALU by asserting the *Ena A* control.
- Load the MAR from the C bus by asserting a write signal to the MAR; the register will be loaded on the rising edge of the clock.
- The read control line to memory is asserted, also at the rising edge of the clock cycle.

Since the program counter holds the address of the next instruction, that sequence causes the next instruction to be read from memory and delivered to the memory data register. However, the memory is slower than the CPU. The memory data register will not contain the instruction until one full clock cycle after the memory read control line is asserted. Real

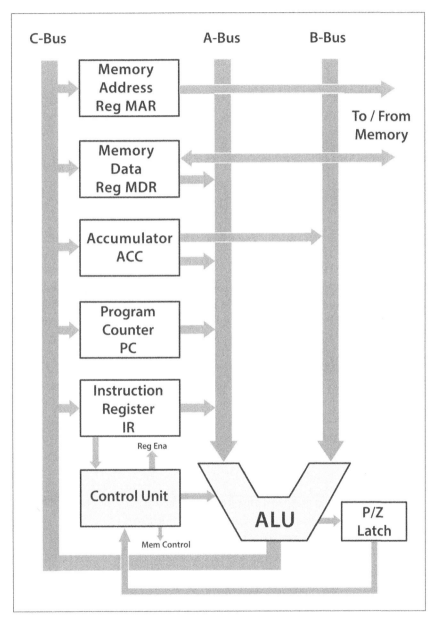

Figure 3-11
The datapath of the Tiny Binary Computer

computers take 50 or more clock cycles to read memory, although cache memory, described in Section 3.5.4, mitigates this speed mismatch somewhat.

The control unit can generate a wait operation by not asserting any of the control lines. A clock cycle goes by with nothing being stored.

The CPU performs an ADD instruction

The LMC / TBC ADD instruction fetches a value from memory at the address given in the operand field and adds that value to the accumulator. It takes six datapath cycles, and so six clock cycles, to perform an add instruction. Here is the register transfer language description of the ADD instruction.

```
MAR ← PC; read           Start a memory operation
PC ← PC + 1              Increment the program counter
IR ← MDR                 Copy the instruction to instruction register
MAR ← IR[addr]; read     Start fetch of operand value
wait                     Wait for memory to complete
ACC ← ACC + MDR          Perform the addition
```

The first three datapath cycles are the same for every instruction. The first operation fetches the instruction as described above. The second one increments the program counter so that it again points to the next instruction. During the same datapath cycle that updates the PC, memory is completing the read from step one and delivering the instruction word to the memory data register. That completes the fetch part of the fetch-decode-execute instruction cycle.

In the third datapath cycle, the instruction word is copied from the MDR to the instruction register. The control unit enables the MDR onto the A bus, sends a copy command to the ALU, and a write signal to the IR. The signal that enables the write to the IR also signifies that an operation code is available. The control unit is fast enough to determine the next steps during the high part of the clock cycle. That is the decode part of the fetch-decode-execute instruction cycle.

The last three register transfer operations are the execute part of the cycle. The address part of the instruction register is loaded into the memory address register and memory is commanded to read from that address. There is nothing to do until the memory operation completes, so the next datapath cycle is a wait cycle. The last step performs the addition. The MDR is enabled on the A bus, the accumulator is enabled on the B bus, and the ALU is sent the signals for addition. At the end of the clock cycle, the accumulator is loaded from the C bus, replacing the prior contents with the sum from the addition and setting the P/Z latch. The other instructions that are part of the TBC instruction set work similarly. There is a complete list in Appendix B.

How branch instructions work

If you have written programs in a high-level language like Java or Python, you are used to writing procedures or methods, then using them as though they were like any other feature of the language. The procedure gets executed, then the statement following the invocation of the procedure is executed. At the level of machine language, which is where things really happen, a procedure call involves saving the program counter, then branching to the first instruction in the procedure. Code in the procedure restores that saved program counter when the procedure has finished. We will discuss how a procedure completes the return in Section 3.5.5.

The mechanism for calling a procedure, performing a loop, or doing anything other than executing the next instruction in sequence is a **branch instruction**. Computer architectures implement both unconditional and conditional branch instructions. An unconditional branch always transfers control to another location within the program. A conditional branch only transfers control if some specific condition has been met. LMC and TBC implement two conditional branches, branch on positive and branch on zero. The branch is taken only if the last arithmetic operation resulted in a positive or zero value, respectively.

Branch instructions take advantage of the fact that the program counter holds the address of the next instruction. In TBC, the program counter is updated while the CPU is waiting for the instruction word to be delivered by the memory subsystem. The process is slightly more complex in computer architectures with variable-length instructions, but the program counter is always updated before the execute phase of the fetch-decode-execute instruction cycle.

To execute a branch, the datapath stores the branch target address, which is given in the branch instruction, into the program counter. Here is the register transfer language for a branch on positive.

```
MAR ← PC; read          Start a memory operation
PC ← PC + 1             Increment the program counter
IR ← MDR                Copy the instruction to instruction register
IFP; PC ← IR[addr]      Branch target address stored in PC
                        only if the P flag is set
```

The first three clock cycles are the same for every TBC instruction. In the fourth cycle, the branch target address from the instruction is copied into the program counter, but only if the P flag is set. For an unconditional branch, the IF part is removed.

The branch target address is available from the instruction register, without another memory access.

Now it should be clear why the program counter must be incremented before the execute phase of the instruction. If it were incremented after the execute step, then incrementing the program counter would incorrectly change the branch target.

The control unit

The TBC control unit generates five sets of control signals. It generates ALU control signals as shown in Figure 3-8 to perform the operation needed for the instruction. It generates signals to the registers to enable their contents onto a bus and also to load a result from the C bus. Registers can send their contents to the A bus, or, in the case of the accumulator, to either the A or B bus. Only one register can be enabled to the A bus and only one to the B bus during any datapath cycle. More than one register can be loaded simultaneously from the C bus, although that capability is not used in TBC.

When the accumulator stores data from the C bus, the P/Z latch is also signaled to store the positive and overflow bits from the ALU. That means the P/Z latch values always correspond to the value currently held in the accumulator, even though the output from the ALU may have changed.

The instruction register is twelve bits wide like the others, but is wired so that only the low-order eight bits, the operand address, will be transferred to the A bus if the instruction register is enabled. The four bits of operation code are connected directly to the instruction decoder and control unit by a dedicated bus. (The instruction format is shown in Figure 3-5.)

Finally, when a memory operation is needed, the control unit sends either a read command or a write command to memory.

Because the TBC instructions take more than one datapath cycle, the control unit needs a counter to keep up with the current step in the instruction. Such a counter is fundamentally similar to the adder we have explored in detail. It will also have a RESET input that returns the counter to zero. No TBC instruction needs more than six datapath cycles, so a three-bit counter is needed. The counter is input to a three-to-eight decoder. (See Figure 2-14 for a two to four decoder.) It's not necessary to decode values six or seven, so we can design the decoder with only six outputs for values zero to five.

In the fourth datapath cycle, the operation code is available through the connection from the instruction register to the control unit. The operation code is four bits, and so needs a four-to-16 decoder. The branch instructions need two bits from the P/Z latch. That gives a total of 24 bits, six from the counter, 16 from the instruction decoder, and two from the P/Z latch. Those 24 bits are input to a combinational logic circuit that generates the proper signals for each datapath cycle. The combinational logic circuit also generates the RESET signal to the counter after the last datapath cycle of each instruction, which causes the operations to repeat for the next instruction.

We can build a combinational logic circuit for any function for which we can write a truth table. Before decoding, we have nine bits of variable, three from the counter, four from the instruction register, and two from the P/Z latch. Such a truth table would have $2^9 = 512$ rows, but there are automated tools to help with designing such circuits. It isn't necessary to produce a complete design to see that we can build a control unit that will do what is needed. One can get a good conceptual understanding of how the CPU works without going further into the details.

A control unit that uses combinational logic and perhaps a few registers to generate the necessary control signals is called a **hardwired control unit**. The alternative is a microprogrammed control unit, in which the steps for the datapath cycles are stored in a fast read only memory. We won't go into the details here, but for the curious, a microprogrammed implementation of a control unit for TBC is described in Appendix B. Hardwired control units are generally faster, but also more complex and hence more expensive than microprogrammed control units.

It is important to recognize that TBC is a very simple computer, and so has a very simple control unit. Real computer control units are substantially more complex.

3.4 Instruction Formats and Addressing Modes

The TBC instruction format, shown in Figure 3-5 is about as simple as one could get. Even so, it is worth a more detailed look. There is a four-bit operation code, which allows up to 16 different operations. The eight bits of **operand address** allow for addressing any of the possible 256 twelve-bit words. The TBC addresses are **direct addresses**, meaning that no other information is needed to specify a memory location. Most computer operations involve two operands. In TBC, the second is an **implicit operand**. For example, the ADD instruction has an operation code and address. The second, implicit operand is the accumulator, which supplies one of the addends and receives the result of the addition. The accumulator is an implicit operand for LDA, SUB, and STO. The INP and OUT instructions are a bit different. They have the same operation code and use the address field to distinguish between input and output.

3.4.1 Instruction Formats

Most computers have more than one register that can receive the results of an arithmetic operation or participate in load and store operations. That means that, in most cases, implicit operands can't be used and both operands must be explic-

Figure 3-12
General format of an instruction

itly specified in the instruction. A general format for an instruction with two operands is shown in Figure 3-12. Some computers specify the destination operand, the operand where the result will be stored as the first operand and some specify it as the second operand. The operand that will be overwritten is called the **destination operand**.

The size of an operand field depends on how many possibilities must be enumerated. For a computer with 16 registers, four bits are enough to specify one of them. A computer with four gibibytes of memory needs 32 bits to specify a direct memory address. Both of these considerations have influenced the way CPU designers format instructions. Memory was initially very expensive and the designers of CPUs used as little as possible. An IBM mainframe instruction with two register operands is 16 bits long, eight bits for an operation code and four bits each for the register numbers. The IBM mainframe instruction set has over 20 different instruction formats and three different instruction lengths, making the instruction decoder very complex. The trade-off is that programs for those early mainframes, and for today's mainframes, used less memory than otherwise. The Intel x86 instruction set also has multiple formats and instruction lengths.

The other consideration is the number of bits needed for direct addressing of large memories. Instruction formats that must be retained for backward compatibility do not have room for large direct address fields. As a result, CPU designers provided a number of ways of generating the address actually used by the memory controller to address a word of memory.

There are instruction formats other than the two-address format shown here. Some architectures have three-address instructions. That allows two operands to participate in an operation and the result stored in a third location instead of overwriting one of the operands. Some instructions use implicit operands, particularly when referring to specialized registers.

The Intel instruction set, especially, provides for instruction modifier bytes. These modify the meaning of operation codes and further complicate the control unit design.

3.4.2 Addressing Modes

There are three general forms of addresses. A register-to-register instruction format specifies two registers as operands. The number of bits required depends on the number of registers but will generally be small.

The register-to-memory format needs one register address and one main memory address. The main memory address is necessarily larger than a register address.

Some architectures include memory-to-memory instructions, in which both operands are main memory addresses.

An **orthogonal** instruction set would allow any addressing mode for any operand. Although that was a design goal fifty years ago, modern instruction sets are not orthogonal. The Intel instruction sets can be said to be somewhat orthogonal due to design decisions made early in the design of the CPU family.

The **effective address** of an instruction operand is the address actually used to address the operand held in a register or main memory and is often the result of arithmetic performed by an address generation unit or its equivalent. An effective address in main memory is also used for the target address of some branch instructions.

Addressing modes for data and for flow of control (branching) are slightly different in many computer architectures.

Addressing modes for data

Direct addressing requires that the full memory address of data be stored in the address field of the instruction. Often the only way to do this is to make instructions more than one word long.

Displacement addressing, also called **base addressing,** forms an effective address by adding the address constant from the instruction to a **base register**. That requires fewer bits in the address field of the instruction provided the base register is wide enough to address all of memory. The size of the address field in the instruction determines the amount of memory that can be addressed with a single base register.

With **register indirect** addressing, the address of the data is held in a register and the address field of the instruction need only be large enough to enumerate the registers. **Memory indirect** addressing loads the effective address from a location in main memory. That requires both address arithmetic to locate the address in main memory and a memory access to retrieve the address before data can be accessed.

Indexed addressing adds the contents of an **index register** to the address arithmetic process. For example, a base register may hold the address of an array in main memory, and the contents of the index register selects one element of the array. A program can step through an array by manipulating only the index register.

Immediate mode addressing does not actually use a register or memory address at all. Instead, the data value is encoded directly in the instruction. It is "immediate" because no main memory access is needed to retrieve a value; the value is available in the address field of the instruction register. Andrew Tanenbaum (1978) examined over 10,000 lines of program text and found that over 81% of all the constants in a program are zero, one, or two. Even if only a few bits are available to hold immediate data, a substantial performance increase can be achieved by avoiding memory accesses for small constants.

Addressing modes for flow of control

Sequence is the natural operating mode of von Neumann architecture computers. In the absence of a specific instruction to change the flow of control, the next instruction in sequence is executed.

With **direct addressing**, a branch or call instruction has the full memory address of the branch target. As with addressing modes for data, the operand field must be large enough to address all of memory.

An **indirect branch** uses a table of effective addresses stored in main memory. Address arithmetic first selects an entry in the table, then places that address in the program counter. Indirect branching is used in interrupt handling, where an interrupt number determines which branch table entry should be used.

Relative addressing forms an address from the program counter and an address constant in the instruction. The principal advantage is that a few bits of address constant allow branching to "nearby" addresses. An eight-bit signed address constant is enough to allow jumping forward 127 bytes or backward 128 bytes. Each additional bit doubles the range. In well-modularized code, branches are likely to be to nearby addresses. Returns from a module are likely to use a stack indirect or register indirect branch. Another advantage is that such code is position-independent; it can be loaded anywhere in memory without need to adjust addresses.

In **register indirect** addressing, the branch address is taken from the register specified in the instruction's address field.

Stack indirect addressing is used for returns from procedure calls. The branch target address is taken from the memory location specified by the stack pointer register and the stack pointer is adjusted to remove that item from the stack. The use of a stack in this way is described in Section 3.5.5.

Some architectures implement a SKIP instruction. This is a conditional instruction which, if the condition is true, causes the *next* instruction to be skipped. The following instruction is often an unconditional branch. The advantage of using SKIP rather than a conditional branch is that the CPU pipeline need not be flushed when a branch is taken. Pipelined execution is discussed in Section 3.6.3.

3.5 Memory

Memory is the digital circuitry that holds programs and data immediately available to the CPU. Memory is also called RAM (random access memory), primary memory, or main memory. It is sometimes called main storage, although this book reserves the word "storage" for semi-permanent storage on devices like disks or flash drives. The term *random access memory* means that any location in the memory system can be read or written in about the same time as any other location.

The main memory system is connected to the CPU with data, address, and control buses. The control bus can signal the memory to read or write. The address bus holds the address of the memory location to be read or written, and the data bus transfers data between the CPU and memory. A memory management unit (MMU) handles the details of communication between the CPU and memory.

3.5.1 Memory Technology

Memory requires a technology capable of maintaining and distinguishing two states that will represent bit values zero or one. A device that can maintain either of two states is called **bistable**. Some of the earliest commercial memories used tiny ferrite rings called *cores*[57] that could be magnetized either clockwise or counter-clockwise. Such core memory was mostly assembled by hand and used in early commercial mainframe computers. The first core memories cost about a dollar per bit. By the 1960s, prices had come down to about one cent per bit, which would have made a gibibyte of memory cost over 86 million dollars.

Memory can be either volatile or non-volatile. **Volatile** memory depends on electrical power to maintain storage and loses its contents when power is removed. **Non-volatile** memory retains its contents even when power is removed.

Four memory technologies, used for distinctly different purposes, predominate in modern general-purpose computers.

Dynamic RAM

The main program and data storage memory of modern computers is synchronous double data rate dynamic RAM (DDR SDRAM). In dynamic RAM, each bit of storage comprises one transistor and one capacitor. A capacitor is an electronic device for temporarily holding an electrical charge. Operation of synchronous memory is controlled by a train of clock pulses, and double data rate means the memory can transfer data on both the rising edge and falling edge of a clock pulse.

Progress in the development of dynamic RAM has been in favor of higher densities, that is, more memory, and lower cost. Speed of dynamic RAM has increased as well, but it remains tens of times slower than typical CPU speeds.

Because the capacitor in each bit position can hold a charge only temporarily, dynamic RAM must be refreshed periodically. A refresh cycle reads and rewrites each bit, renewing

---

57   The ferrite cores used for memory are not the same as the multiple cores in some CPUs. The latter are complete processors.

the charge on the capacitor. Refresh times for modern memory are in the tens of milliseconds. Refreshing is handled by the memory controller, which is often in the same chip package as the CPU. The requirement to refresh memory periodically imposes a small performance penalty on dynamic RAM.

Improvements in dynamic RAM are identified by numbered generations, standardized by the JEDEC Solid State Technology Association, an independent trade and standards association. Differences in generations include chip density, operating voltage, and clock speed. DDR4 memory modules began supplanting DDR3 modules in 2017. The DDR5 specification was published in July 2020, but did not reach widespread use until early in 2023, when CPU chips with native support for DDR5 became available.

Dynamic RAM can be buffered or unbuffered. Buffered memory provides a transistor buffer between the memory module and the memory bus. This reduces the load on the bus and so allows more memory to be installed. There can be a performance penalty to using buffered memory.

Memory configurations are generally not interchangeable. For example, a computer designed for DDR4 memory will not accept DDR5 memory. A computer designed for buffered memory generally will not accept unbuffered memory. It is important to know the system specifications when adding or upgrading dynamic RAM.

Static RAM

Static RAM uses six or more transistors per bit of storage, similar to the clocked D-latch of Figure 3-9. That makes a static RAM module physically larger than a dynamic RAM module of similar capacity. There is a dramatic difference in the time / cost trade-off. Static RAM can operate at CPU speeds, but costs 100 or more times as much as the equivalent amount of dynamic RAM.

Static RAM is used for registers within the CPU and for cache memory. Cache memory is discussed in Section 3.5.4.

Mask ROM

ROM is read-only memory. It can be read, but not written or changed. The name **mask ROM** comes from the fact that both the pattern of the memory and also the contents are set when a chip is manufactured. Mask ROM is very fast; it can operate faster than the CPU clock, which makes it suitable for holding a chip's microprogram. Some controller chips are built with their start-up code in mask ROM. A disadvantage of mask ROM, and any other read-only memory, is that it cannot be changed.

NOR Flash

Nor flash memory is used to hold executable code used to start a computer system. The name comes from the fact that the storage elements are similar to, but not identical to, the NOR gates described in Chapter 2. Nor flash memory can be read a word at a time in much the same way as dynamic or static RAM. That makes it suitable for holding executable code, such as the code used to start an operating system. It is this memory that is updated when one "flashes the BIOS"[58] of a computer. Nor flash is a different technology from the NAND flash used for storage.

3.5.2 Memory Organization and Addressing

Modern general purpose computers almost universally organize memories into addressable units of eight bits, called **bytes** or **octets**. Octets are further organized into **words**, often of 64 or 32 bits, that is, eight or four octets. Other memory organizations are possible; for example, some digital signal processing chips organize memories into 16-bit units. Section 3.3.1 describes a memory organized into twelve bit words.

The amount of memory a computer can accommodate physically depends on several factors, some as simple as the number of connectors available for installing physical memory. A fundamental limitation is that the maximum physical memory is limited to 2^m addressable cells, where m is the number of physical address lines. A computer with 32 address lines cannot address more than 2^{32} memory cells. In the case of byte-addressable memory that means 2^{32} bytes or four gibibytes.

The amount of memory a program can logically address depends on the number of address bits available to the programmer, which may be different from the number of physical address bits. A program can directly address at most 2^n cells where n is the size of the logical address available to the programmer.

Computers with 32-bit addresses became common with the introduction of the Intel 80386 chip in 1985. At the time, memory was measured in mebibytes, and a computer for use by an individual might have one or two mebibytes of memory installed. Operating systems used the features of the CPU to implement virtual memory, simulating a four gibibyte address space in a few mebibytes of memory. Performance was poor for programs that required more than the available physical memory. Virtual memory is explored in Chapter 6.

The Pentium Pro, introduced in 1995, provides an interesting case study. It was a 32-bit processor capable of addressing 64 GiB of memory. Intel accomplished this by providing 36 physical address lines through a feature called physical address extension. These larg-

---

58   BIOS, pronounced "BY-ose," is "basic input output system" and is the executable code that loaded and started the operating system's loader in earlier computers. The term BIOS is obsolete. Most modern computers use the unified extensible firmware interface (UEFI) to start the operating system.

er physical addresses were managed by the operating system's virtual memory facility. User programs were still limited to four gibibytes each because the internal registers used for addressing were only 32 bits. Similar techniques, with names like bank switching or extended memory management, were used as far back as the 1980s to work around the addressing limitations of processors. Current Intel processors provide 64-bit registers, but "only" 48 address lines. "Only" is in quotes because 2^{48} is an extremely large number, equivalent to 256 tebibytes. It is unlikely that even very large computers will have that much memory in the near future.

Address decoding

Physically activating a given memory cell presents another kind of problem, namely decoding addresses. Decoding a 32-bit address in the straightforward way would require a 32 to 4,294,967,296 decoder. Four billion wires is unwieldy to the point of impossibility even with modern semiconductor technology. A 48-bit address is correspondingly worse. The solution is to think of memory not as a line, but as a plane with rows and columns. One can address a four gibibyte memory with 16 bits of row address and 16 bits of column address, quantities that are much easier to deal with. A memory with 36 bits of address would use 18 bits for row address and 18 bits for column address.

Word boundary alignment

Computer hardware generally transfers data between CPU and memory in units that are multiples of the size of the computer's word. For modern computers, that is often 64 bits, or eight bytes. Unless complex circuitry has been added to memory and the memory control unit, these transfers take place on a **word boundary**. For a computer with 64-bit words, that means an address divisible by eight. Compilers automatically insert padding as necessary to make sure that data items longer than one byte and less than or equal to one word are aligned on a word boundary.

Byte ordering

The way bytes of a word are numbered is a choice made when the architecture of a computer family is designed. The two choices are **big-endian**, in which the most significant byte of a word is stored at the lowest address, and **little-endian**, in which the least significant byte is stored at the lowest address.[59] IBM mainframes are big-endian.

The Datapoint 2200 computer of the 1970s did bit-serial arithmetic and, as a consequence, needed the low order bit at the low address to handle carries. When Intel designed the 8008 chip to Datapoint's specifications, it necessarily had a little-endian architecture for compatibility. Current x86 and x64 processors from Intel and compatible processors from AMD are little-endian.

---

59 The terms big-endian and little-endian come from Jonathan Swift's *Gulliver's Travels*, and refer to the war over which end of an egg to open. They were applied to computer byte ordering by D. Cohen (1981).

As long as a computer architecture is internally consistent, it makes no difference what byte ordering is chosen. Problems can arise when data are transferred between machines with different byte ordering and the unit of transfer is larger than one byte. That case arises with 16-bit Unicode UTF-16. Unicode defines a **byte order mark**, the hexadecimal characters FEFF. If data are transferred between systems of different-endianness, the two bytes will be swapped, and all following byte pairs must also be exchanged. The byte order mark is optional, and if not present at the beginning of a file or transmission, big-endian encoding is to be assumed.

Byte order mismatches also cause problems when transferring binary data such as binary integers and floating point numbers. For that reason, data exchanges are often based on values encoded as streams of characters.

3.5.3 Error Detection and Correction

The technology used in the memory systems of general-purpose computers is such that it's possible for one or more bits to change state erroneously, often because a cosmic ray passes through the storage element. However, current DRAM technology is very stable and errors are extremely rare. This book was written on a computer without memory error detection or correction.

The simplest error detection mechanism is **parity**. One additional bit is stored for each memory cell. When a write to the cell occurs, the additional bit is set so that the total number of one-bits is even.[60] This is quickly computed using a bitwise XOR function. When the cell is read, the one-bits are counted. If they are no longer an even number, an error has occurred and the memory subsystem can signal the error to the memory control unit and the CPU. Often the only action that an operating system can take in the case of such an error is to halt the operation of the computer system, possibly displaying an error message.

A parity system can detect only errors in an odd number of bits.[61] If two bits are changed erroneously, the parity will be correct even though the contents have been corrupted.

Error correction with Hamming codes

Error detection with parity depends on redundancy. An additional bit is added to each cell of memory to be checked. By adding more than one bit, it becomes possible to detect errors of more than a single bit, and even to correct errors.

In 1950, Richard Hamming of Bell Laboratories devised such a system, now called a **Hamming code**. The principle of the Hamming code is that every data bit is checked by more

---

60   Requiring an even number of one-bits is called even parity. Odd parity, requiring an odd number of one-bits, works equally well. The only requirement is consistency.

61   Detecting errors in an odd number of bits is often expressed as detecting only single-bit errors.

than one parity bit. Figure 3-13 shows four data bits being checked by three parity bits. If data bit *d0* were corrupted, parity bits *p0* and *p1* would both indicate errors. The only data bit checked by both *p0* and *p1* is *d0*. If we know which single bit is incorrect, it can be corrected by complementing it, *i.e.* flipping it back to the other possible value.

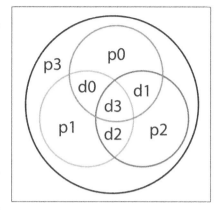

A fourth parity bit, *p3*, checks the parity of all the other parity and data bits. A Hamming code like this can correct single-bit errors and detect double-bit errors.

The example uses four parity bits to check four data bits, an overhead of 100%. However, the overhead diminishes as the number of data bits to be checked by a Hamming code increases. A 32-bit word can be checked with seven parity bits, six of which check individual data bits and one of which checks the overall parity.

Figure 3-13
Error correction using a Hamming code.

Error correction with triple module redundancy

The calculations needed to validate Hamming codes take time, even when performed in hardware. Some triple-bit errors can be incorrectly recognized as single-bit errors and wrongly "corrected."

Another approach is to use three separate memory modules. When a write to memory occurs, data are sent to all three modules. When a read occurs, the data are sent through a bit-wise majority function. For example, if a bit from each of the three memories is 111, a one is returned. If the three memories return 110 a one is still returned, on the assumption that the third memory is in error. If the three memories return 100, a zero is returned. Thus, the majority function performs "voting" among the three memories. The majority function can be computed with two gate delay times. This technique is called **triple module redundancy**.

3.5.4 Cache Memory

Cache[62] **memory** is small, fast memory that is between main memory and the CPU and physically and logically close to the CPU. Cache memory helps to compensate for the fact that main memory is so much slower than the CPU.

Cache memory is effective because the nature of the von Neumann architecture is such that both data and instructions exhibit **locality of reference.** Locality of reference means that when particular instructions or data are needed by the CPU, nearby instructions or data

---

62   Pronounced "cash."

will likely also be needed. That is especially easy to see for instructions. Sequential execution, part of the nature of the von Neumann architecture, means that the next instruction in memory is likely to be the next one executed. Similarly, data are arranged in structures so that nearby data are likely to be used soon after any data item. The probability that nearby instructions or data will be needed is **spatial locality of reference**.

Temporal locality of reference is the circumstance that when an instruction or item of data is used, it will likely be used again in the near future. This is also easily observed for instructions. A program loop involves executing the same set of instructions repeatedly. It is also true that data are frequently reused during the execution of many programs.

Locality of reference is part of the nature of the von Neumann architecture; programmers need not do anything special to take advantage of this nature. It is, however, possible to create a circumstance for which locality of reference fails. For example, if an array is stored column-wise, then accessed row-wise, successive references are likely to be far apart.

In a system with a single cache, when a word of data is needed by the CPU, the cache control unit first checks the cache memory. If the needed word is present, called a **cache hit**, it is delivered to the CPU and no access to main memory is necessary. If the needed word is not in the cache, called a **cache miss**, it and nearby data are fetched from main memory and stored in the cache. The needed word is delivered to the CPU. Cache memories are organized into blocks, and when a reference to main memory is needed, an entire block is transferred to the cache from main memory.

Modern caches are usually organized as multi-way associative caches. "Multi-way" means there are two more places in the cache where a block of data from main memory can be stored. **Tag bits** indicate the main memory address from which a particular block was loaded. "Associative" means the tag bits are checked in parallel to see whether a particular main memory address is in the cache. Associative checking is very fast, but also expensive in terms of the number of transistors needed.

Multi-level caches

The discussion above assumes one cache memory and one main memory. Modern computers implement multiple levels of cache memory. The cache physically and logically nearest the CPU is called the level 1 cache or L1 cache. The L1 cache is likely to be implemented on the same silicon chip as the CPU. L2 and sometimes L3 caches can be on the same silicon as the CPU, or in the same package.

There is a diminishing return with additional levels of cache. Intel has built systems with four levels of cache, but architectures with three levels of cache are more usual.

The L1 cache might be 32 or 64 kibibytes for a modern CPU. The L2 cache could be eight or more times larger, perhaps 256 or 512 kibibytes. The L3 cache might be four or eight mebibytes. Each succeeding level is many times larger than its predecessor, but also much slower. However, even the L3 cache is much faster than main memory. Some 21st century CPUs use embedded dynamic RAM, called eDRAM, for the L3 cache.

In multi-core chips, it is usual for each core to have its own L1 cache, and sometimes its own L2 cache.

Instructions and data exhibit different locality of reference behavior. For that reason, the L1 cache is often a **split cache**, with one cache for instructions and another for data.

Cache and memory coherence

With multiple levels of cache and separate cache memories for each of several cores, no item of data has a canonical home. The same word may

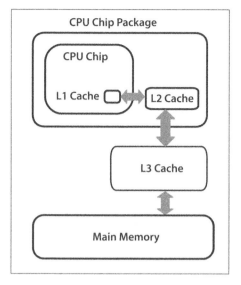

Figure 3-14
One organization for a multi-level cache

exist in main memory, in an L3 cache, and in two or more L1 or L2 caches. Since multiple cores may update the same word, it is possible for two copies of a word to differ. This is called the **cache coherence problem**. It is solved by circuitry through which the various caches communicate, so that only one copy of a particular word is considered the valid one if their values differ.[63]

Even with a cache coherence protocol mediating among the caches, if a CPU updates a word, the contents of the cache can differ from the same word in main memory. That is problematic if an output operation from main memory takes place when cache and memory do not match. That is partially addressed by the **cache write policy** of a CPU architecture. A **write through policy** updates memory every time a cache entry is modified at a cost of using extra memory bandwidth. A **write back policy** flags a cache block as changed but defers writing until the block must be replaced or the corresponding entry in main memory is accessed. That saves memory bandwidth at a cost of additional circuitry in the cache controller.

3.5.5 Stacks and Stack Pointer

Writing a method, procedure, or function in a high-level language is like adding a new instruction to the language. When a procedure is called, control passes to the first instruction in the procedure. When the procedure completes, control returns to the instruction imme-

---

63 Cache coherence protocols are beyond the scope of this book, but interesting. For further reading, look up the MOESI protocol.

diately following the procedure call. We saw in Section 3.3.6 how a branch instruction can pass control to the first instruction in a procedure by storing a new value in the program counter. Procedures have the same difficulty that Hansel and Gretel did; getting there is easy, the problem is how to get back.

That difficulty is solved easily with a data structure called a **stack**. A stack is a last-in first-out (LIFO) structure, functionally like the stack of trays in a cafeteria.

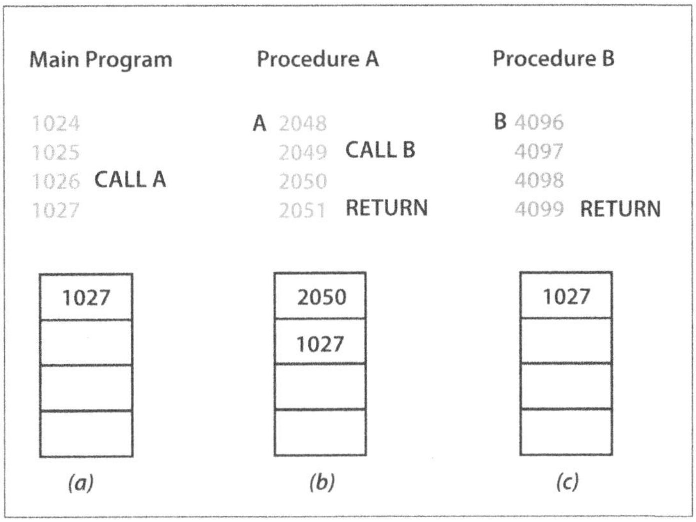

Figure 3-15
Procedure call and return using a stack

Figure 3-15 shows the use of a stack to store return addresses. Numbers in gray are example addresses. The main program has a CALL A instruction at location 1026; procedure A starts at location 2048. The CALL instruction first **pushes** the program counter at the top of the stack. Since the program counter holds the address of the next instruction, and has already been adjusted by the time the execute phase of the CALL instruction is reached, the value 1027 is stored as shown in Figure 3-15(a). Once the return address has been stored, the CALL instruction executes a branch to the procedure's address, 2048 in the example, by storing the branch address in the program counter.

The real value of the stack becomes clear in Figure 3-15(b) when procedure A calls procedure B. The CALL B instruction pushes the program counter, now 2050, onto the stack, then branches to procedure B at location 4096. Placing a value on the stack is called pushing because prior values are pushed down, like the stack of trays in the cafeteria.

Procedure B could call yet another procedure because of the flexibility of using a stack to hold return addresses; it's unnecessary for this example.

When Procedure B executes the RETURN instruction at location 4099, the address at the top of the stack, 2050, is popped off the stack and stored in the program counter. The next instruction to be executed will come from location 2050, immediately following the CALL B instruction of Procedure A. Figure 3-15(c) shows the stack *after* the return instruction has been executed. Similarly, the return instruction in Procedure A will transfer control to location 1027, in the main program and immediately after the CALL A instruction.

Many computer architectures, including the Intel x86 and x64, include a **stack pointer** register to allow manipulation of the stack address at register speeds. Architectures that support stacks generally include POP and PUSH instructions in addition to CALL and RETURN. The presence of POP and PUSH allow arbitrary data, not just return addresses, to be stored on the stack. In that way, arguments for procedure calls can be passed on the stack and results returned.

Procedures can receive data as well as the return address on the stack. The data passed to a procedure or method is called a **stack frame**, and consists of more than the return address. Operating systems prescribe a set of **calling conventions** that tell how arguments, return values, and return addresses are to be managed, and so describe the stack frame for that OS. High-level language processors are written to follow the calling conventions of the OS on which they're running.

Because the stack grows and shrinks as it is used, it is generally placed at the highest address in a program's memory space and grows downward.

3.6 Modern CPU Architecture

The von Neumann architecture of Figure 3-2 is how computers were designed and built in the middle of the 20th century. It still serves as a useful abstraction for thinking about the function of modern computers: a memory, a CPU, and sequential execution of instructions. Modern CPUs behave that way from the outside looking in, but there are a lot of moving parts in the actual implementation. We've already seen that, instead of one main memory, there is a hierarchy of main memory and multiple levels of cache with complex protocols implemented in hardware to control the flow of data. CPU architecture has acquired an even greater level of complexity over three quarters of a century.

A "better" CPU would be smaller, more powerful, faster, and consume less electric power to make batteries last longer. Each of these presents challenges to the designers of CPU chips.

Making chips smaller and more powerful means making the transistors on the chip smaller. There are two difficulties with making transistors smaller. One is the photolithography process by which chips are made. The wavelength of visible light is too great to make the tiny transistors of modern chips. Chip makers are using extreme ultraviolet light, x-radiation, and immersion lithography in the chip making process to get features smaller than 20nm.[64] The other difficulty is that, as transistors get smaller, quantum effects overwhelm classical semiconductor physics. The development of the FinFET[65] by Chenming Hu[66] and others overcomes quantum leakage and extends Moore's law for perhaps another decade. (Perry, 2020) Developments on the horizon include the Gate All Around transistor and the 3D complementary metal oxide transistor that will further extens Moore's Law. (Radosavljevic and Kavalieros, 2022)

CPU designers' challenges

Making a chip run faster poses three challenges. The first two are power consumption and heat. If the CPU clock runs faster, more power is consumed, which is counter to the desire to use less power to extend battery life. Even worse, consuming more power produces more heat. Heat sinks and fans can remove some of the heat from desktop computers and to some extent even from laptops. The process is much harder in phones and wearable devices.

The third barrier is the speed of light. Light in a vacuum can travel a little under a foot in one nanosecond.[67] Electrical signals travel somewhat more slowly in the conductors of a chip. Each digital logic gate contributes its propagation delay to the time required to transfer a signal. Complex circuits have a large number of gates chained together. The CPU's clock must run "slowly" enough to be sure that the signals within the CPU have settled into valid states before a clock pulse commands storage of a result. In a CPU with a four GHz clock, that could be as little as 0.25 nanosecond.

Figure 3-16
*A nanosecond is
this long*

Logical equivalence of hardware and software

Computing hardware and software are logically equivalent. (Tanenbaum, 1990) Specialized hardware can be built, if you have enough transistors, to perform any computation that can be performed in software. Conversely, software can be written to do anything that can be done with hardware. Software has been written to simulate entire computers. Such a software system is known as a **virtual machine**. The limitation, of course, is that there must be some actual hardware in order to run software.

---

64 A nanometer (nm) is a billionth of a meter.

65 A metal oxide semiconductor field-effect transistor with a three-dimensional "fin" that helps overcome quantum effects in very small transistors.

66 Dr. Hu and others at UC Berkeley developed the FinFET under a DARPA grant around the turn of the century. Hu received the IEEE Medal of Honor in 2020 "for a distinguished career of developing and putting into practice semiconductor models, particularly 3-D device structures, that have helped keep Moore's Law going over many decades."

67 Grace Murray Hopper used to demonstrate "nanosecond" with pieces of copper wire a bit less than a foot long.

It is the equivalence of hardware and software that allows chip designers to move functions formerly performed by software into the hardware. The CPUs of the 1970s and 1980s were microprogrammed. That meant a sequence of steps controlled by the CPU clock issued the register transfer commands that interpreted the "machine" instruction set. Microprogramming made it relatively easy to add new machine instructions. Some IBM mainframes of the 1970s had writable control stores, the storage for the microprogram; that meant new instructions could be added to existing machines already deployed to customers. CPU designers added machine instructions to each generation of CPUs to do more things that were needed by high-level languages. That meant a high-level language statement could be completed in one or a few machine instructions rather than several. The trade-off was that CPUs became increasingly complex; there is no such thing as a free lunch.

3.6.1 RISC Computers

Beginning about 1980 several researchers, among them David Patterson at the University of California, Berkeley developed the concept of reduced instruction set (RISC) computers. They observed that the most complex instructions of current computers were used by compilers infrequently if at all and reasoned that it made no difference if five machine instructions were needed to accomplish what formerly needed only one if the new machine could run ten times as fast.

RISC machines did run much faster and there were several commercially successful RISC designs, among them the MIPS architecture, the ARM architecture, the Sun SPARC, and the IBM POWER architecture.

Mainstream processors, including IBM mainframes, the Motorola 68000 line, and the Intel x86 family were trapped by the need for backward compatibility. They could not jettison the complex instructions already built into their CPUs without sacrificing backward compatibility.

The RISC principles did influence the evolution of even those systems trapped by the need to maintain compatibility. The RISC principles included:

- Simple and regular instruction formats, which made possible…
- Fast hardwired (*i.e.* digital logic) control units in place of microprogrammed control.
- Many general purpose registers, which made possible…
- Fewer memory references.
- Aggressive pipelining to allow…
- Completion of one instruction per clock cycle.

Designers of complex instruction computers (CISC) were able to incorporate many of the lessons learned from RISC designs to improve performance.

3.6.2 Hardwired Control Units

The complex instructions required for backward compatibility in some computer families were possible because of microprogrammed control units. With more transistors available because of Moore's Law, it is often possible to design hardwired control units that will execute those instructions. It is possible to profile a large sample of programs to determine which instructions are executed most frequently. If the full instruction set cannot be implemented in hardwired control, designers can implement those frequently-used instructions in hardwired control and the remainder with microprogrammed control. The instructions needed for backward compatibly will run more slowly, but they will be available, and the most frequently-used instructions can run at hardwired speeds.

3.6.3 Pipelined execution

Pipelining in a CPU is similar in concept to an automobile assembly line. Although it can take 18 hours or more to build an automobile, an assembly line can produce a finished car every one to two minutes because many cars are in different stages of assembly at the same time.

In computer architecture, pipelining means starting a new instruction before the current instruction finishes to provide instruction level parallelism. The simplest approach to pipelining, and one of the earliest to be adopted, is instruction pre-fetching. Because of the nature of the von Neumann architecture, almost always the next instruction needed will be the one following the current instruction. Even in the case of an unconditional branch, the next instruction address is known as soon as the current instruction is decoded.

Figure 3-17
Ford Model T assembly line, 1926
Ford Motor Company/ Wieck

The obvious next step is a separate decode stage, so that a three stage pipeline might have one instruction in the execute phase, the next one being decoded, and the one after that fetched. More pipeline stages tend to make each state less complex, and so potentially faster. Ten-stage pipelines are not uncommon, and one Intel chip had an astonishing 31-stage pipeline. Instructions may still take several clock cycles, but the goal is to *finish* one instruction every clock cycle, much like an automobile assembly line finishes one car every minute or two.

Pipelined computers introduce the problem of **hazards**, conditions which would cause incorrect results if the pipeline kept running. There are three general types of hazards. **Data hazards** occur when data from an earlier instruction, not yet complete, are needed, and when completing an instruction would overwrite data still needed. **Structural hazards** occur when a functional unit of the CPU is needed, but is already in use. Structural hazards are also called resource hazards. **Branch hazards** occur when incorrect instructions are brought into the pipeline as the result of a branch. Branch hazards are also called control hazards. For data and structural hazards, sometimes the only option is to **stall** the pipeline until the needed data or resource becomes available. In the case of a branch hazard, if the wrong instruction stream has been fetched, the entire pipeline must be **flushed** and restarted at the correct address.

Branch hazards occur because the next address is not known until the execute phase of the fetch-decode-execute cycle. Sometimes the instruction fetch unit will have fetched the wrong instruction, and the pipeline would have to be flushed and the correct instruction fetched. That led to attempts at **branch prediction**. A simplistic approach is to predict that a backward branch will be taken and a forward branch will not. The rationale is that a backward branch is likely to be part of a loop and a forward branch is an exception handler. Branch prediction became more sophisticated with the implementation in silicon of branch history tables.

Starting the instruction at the predicted branch target is called **speculative execution**. If the branch prediction was incorrect, then the work done in speculative execution must be undone and the pipeline flushed. If enough resources are available, the hardware could start execution of both possibilities. Once the branch target is known, the work done on that branch is kept and the work done on the other branch is discarded. Executing both branches and selecting which one to keep is called **eager execution**.

3.6.4 Many Registers

Some types of data hazards can be avoided if there are more registers for storing data. Adding more registers seems like an easy thing to do until one considers that current applications were written with a particular set of registers in mind. The Intel x86 family of computers had eight 32-bit registers, and software was written to use those registers. A change in architecture does provide an opportunity. The Intel x64 architecture added eight more registers and doubled the size of each to 64 bits. Those registers went unused until software was rewritten for the 64-bit CPU. The Intel Itanium processor had 128 64-bit registers. Because it could not run software written for the x86 processor family, it was never a commercial success, and Intel stopped taking orders for the processor in January, 2020.

However, there's a way to provide more registers, and thus reduce memory accesses without rewriting software. It is called **register renaming**. Consider the following snippet of TBC code:

```
LDA    A
ADD    B
STO    A
LDA    C
```

That code adds B to A, then stores the result back into memory location A. If TBC were pipelined, the load from location C could not start until the store instruction completed, and the pipeline would have to stall. If TBC had more than one general purpose register, a clever programmer could have used a different register for that second load, allowing it to start before the store completed. But TBC doesn't have extra registers.

In a CPU with register renaming, the hardware would detect that the LDA C instruction has no **dependence** on the previous contents of the accumulator and use a **shadow register** to start the load. When the store completed, the hardware would **rename** the shadow register as the accumulator so that subsequent instructions get the newly loaded value.

The AMD Zen processor executes the x64 instruction set, and so appears to the programmer to have 16 64-bit registers. The hardware actually has 168 64-bit integer shadow registers and 160 128-bit vector floating-point shadow registers.

3.6.5 Superscalar Architecture

Even with pipelining, branch prediction, speculative execution and shadow registers, a CPU can complete at most one instruction per clock cycle because there is only one arithmetic logic unit. Needing a computational resource that's not available results in a structural hazard, at which the pipeline must stall. A CPU with superscalar architecture might have not just a single ALU, but two integer units, a floating-point unit, and a load/store unit. Given the right instruction mix, such a CPU could complete four instructions on every clock cycle. Hardware that can check for dependencies can execute instructions **out of order** provided that no instruction depends on the results of an instruction to be executed later.

3.6.6 Multiple Cores

Clock speeds on the fastest production processors are around five GHz, with three to four GHz being more usual. Power use, heat, and propagation time make higher speeds very difficult, but Moore's Law has given designers a lot of transistors. With limits to the clock speed, CPU designers did those things discussed above to try to complete one instruction every clock cycle. With a four GHz clock, that meant four billion instructions every second.

To go even faster, designers placed more than one complete CPU in the silicon. When a processor has more than one CPU, they are called **cores**, and the entire package is called a multi-core CPU. Each core has its own L1 and perhaps L2 cache and can complete instructions at the full clock speed.

In theory, if one has four cores, each running at four GHz, one has a CPU capable of completing 16 billion instructions every second. In practice, it's not that neat. In order to get 16 billion instructions per second, the computational job must be completely partitionable, in other words, four separate jobs that can run independent of one another. Not all tasks are partitionable. In the context of software development, Frederick Books (1975) pointed out that bearing a child takes nine months no matter how many women one assigns; the task is not partitionable.

Taking advantage of the parallelism offered by multiple cores requires attention at the level of programming. The hundreds of thousands of applications written before multi-core CPUs became available did not do that because there was no need. Some, particularly multimedia applications and scientific applications, have been rewritten to take advantage of multiple cores. The average application, if there is such a thing, will not run any faster on an eight-core CPU than on a single-core CPU of the same clock rate.

3.7 Summary of Learning Objectives

*This section of the chapter tells you the things you should know about, but not **what** you should know about them. To test your knowledge, discuss the following concepts and topics with a study partner or in writing, ideally from memory.*

The von Neumann computer architecture was designed in 1945 by John von Neumann and others. It is characterized by a central processing unit consisting of an arithmetic and logic unit, a control unit, and registers. The CPU communicates with a memory and with input and output devices. Instructions are executed sequentially unless changed by a branch instruction. Modern computer architectures incorporate a great deal of internal parallelism, but the von Neumann architecture still serves as a useful abstraction of the 21st century digital computer.

There are several families of computer architecture, including CPU chips from Intel, the ARM architecture, and IBM's z/Series mainframes. Each architecture is characterized by an instruction set, which defines the programmer's view of the architecture. The microarchitecture of a CPU is the physical design.

The Little Man Computer is a hypothetical computer used as an instructional aid, particularly in understanding the instruction cycle. The fact that the Little Man Computer is a decimal computer, and all real computers are binary obscures some important points about the relationship between computers and binary numbers.

The Tiny Binary Computer (TBC) is a binary computer that can execute the same instructions as the Little Man Computer. It has a very simple arithmetic and logic unit and five registers. The arithmetic and logic unit is constructed of digital logic.

Real computers have more complex instruction formats and addressing modes beyond the direct addressing of TBC.

Modern computers use different memory technologies for different purposes. Memory speeds for the dynamic RAM used in main memory have not kept up the speed of CPUs. Multiple levels of higher-speed cache memory between main memory and the CPU attempt to compensate for the difference. Most modern general-purpose computers have byte-addressable memories with addresses supplied as row and column addresses. Some memory systems have error detection and correction technology.

The CPU of the 21st century has many registers, even though most of them may not be accessible to the programmer or compiler writer. It has hardwired control for the frequently executed instructions but may keep microprogrammed control for particularly complex or particularly infrequent instructions. It has an aggressive pipeline with branch prediction and speculative execution. It has multiple functional units, permitting multiple instructions to be executed in parallel. Perhaps most important from the user's viewpoint, it has multiple cores.

3.8 References

Brooks, F. P. (1975). *The Mythical Man-Month.* Addison-Wesley.

Cohen, D. (1981). On Holy Wars and a Plea for Peace. *Computer,* 14(10), 48–54. https://doi.org/10.1109/C-M.1981.220208

Davidson, J. W., & Fraser, C. W. (1980). The Design and Application of a Retargetable Peephole Optimizer. *ACM Transactions on Programming Languages and Systems*, 2(2), 191–202. https://doi.org/10.1145/357094.357098

Perry, T. S. (2020). The father of FinFets: Chenming Hu took transistors into the third dimension to save Moore's Law. *IEEE Spectrum*, 57(5), 46–51. https://doi.org/10.1109/MSPEC.2020.9078456

Radosavljevic, M., & Kavalieros, J. (2022). Taking Moore's Law to New Heights: When transistors can't get any smaller, the only direction is up. *IEEE Spectrum*, 59(12), 32–37. https://doi.org/10.1109/MSPEC.2022.9976473

Tanenbaum, A. S. (1978). Implications of structured programming for machine architecture. *Communications of the ACM*, 21(3), 237–246. https://doi.org/10.1145/359361.359454

Tanenbaum, A. S. (1990). *Structured Computer Organization* (3rd ed.). Prentice-Hall.

Chapter 4
Input and Output

"On two occasions I have been asked, 'Mr. Babbage, if you put into the machine wrong figures, will the right answers come out?'"

—Charles Babbage

Without a way to get data in and results out, the CPU and memory are useless. The mechanism for getting data in and results out is called input and output. It may surprise you to learn that one of the most important technologies for input and output was invented long before electronic computers. Herman Hollerith invented methods for using cards with holes punched in specific locations for recording and later tabulating information. Hollerith's machines were used in the United States census of 1890. The punched cards Hollerith invented were an important input medium for computers well into the 1970s. Hollerith's company, The Computing-Tabulating-Recording Company, became IBM.

Figure 4-1
Herman Hollerith invented punched card tabulating equipment

When a program developer needs an input or output operation, almost always the mechanism is to use a function that's a part of the programming language. Dig a little further and you will find that the programming language calls on the operating system to perform the operation.

Although application program developers rarely do input or output at the machine level, those who develop operating systems do. An understanding of the process will help the application program developer write better and more efficient programs. In short, we will study what CPU instructions make input and output happen and how they work, something that is glossed over in LMC and, to an extent, in TBC.

The input and output devices are sometimes called **peripherals** because they might be considered to form an outer circle, or periphery, around the computer and memory. The phrase "input and output" is frequently shortened to I/O.

Networks

From the viewpoint of the CPU, the operating system, and application programs, a network interface controller is like any other I/O device. However, the network interface is a gateway to communication with potentially millions of other devices. The external connection of the network interface is likely to be more demanding of attention than its nature as an I/O device. For that reason, we cover networks separately in Chapter 5.

4.1 Input and Output Concepts

The central processing unit can initiate input or output operations. Sometimes input operations happen as a direct result of an action by a program running on the CPU. Reading a block of data from a disk is an example. In other cases, a program must be able to "listen" to a device until it presents input. The CPU can't read a character from the keyboard until someone presses a key. Even in that case, there must first be a command from the CPU.

4.1.1 Architecture for Input and Output

The CPU and programs running on the CPU need to communicate with the computer's input and output devices, or more usually, with device controllers. Device controllers off-load some of the work of managing I/O devices from the CPU, leaving more CPU resources for other tasks. Four categories of information need to be exchanged between CPU and controller: device address information, commands from the CPU to a device, status information from the device to the CPU, and data, which may flow in either direction depending on whether an input or output operation is taking place.

Memory-Mapped and Port-Mapped I/O

There are two architectural approaches to exchanging information, memory-mapped I/O and port-mapped I/O. In memory-mapped I/O, some of the addresses that would otherwise be part of main memory instead refer to device registers. Often these addresses are at the highest part of the logical address space, where one might not expect actual memory to be installed in any case. It is up to the address decoder (see Section 3.5.2) to sort out which addresses are actual memory locations and which refer to device registers.

In port-mapped I/O, there is a separate address space of I/O ports. This has the advantage of allowing the full physical memory address space to be used for memory and of separating I/O devices, which are usually slower than memory, from the operation of the memory subsystem. The disadvantage is that separate instructions for input and output are needed, as with the Intel x86 IN and OUT instructions.

It is possible to combine the two approaches, as in some early small computers in which display memory was mapped into the main memory address space, but other input and output was handled separately.

Regardless of the addressing approach chosen, the actual operation of input and output is nearly the same.

Block and Character Devices

Some I/O devices transfer data a character at a time and some transfer larger blocks of data.

It is obvious that the keyboard produces data a character at a time. Someone running a word processing program presses a key and the resulting character appears on the screen. It may be less obvious that the mouse sends data for every increment that the mouse moves, but it is also a character device. The text-only displays that one might see on a gas pump or cash register are character devices.

Magnetic disks, solid-state disks, flash storage, and similar devices are block devices. Such devices have a physical block size established when the device is manufactured, or possibly when it is first initialized by the operating system. All transfers are in multiples of that physical block size. You cannot read or write a single byte on disk. To update one byte, the entire block where it is located must be read, the byte changed, and the entire block written back to disk. For disks, blocks are likely to be 512 or 4,096 bytes. Solid state drives (SSDs) present a special problem for the developer of device drivers: they can only be erased a block at a time, and the blocks are big, up to half a mebibyte. That problem is discussed in more detail in Section 4.2.3.

4.1.2 Interrupts

The CPU could command an I/O device to take some action, then repeatedly check the device status to see whether the action was complete. Such a process is called **busy waiting** because the CPU can't do anything else while it is repeatedly checking the I/O device. It is clearly better to have the I/O device send a signal when the requested operation is complete. Such a signal is called an **interrupt**. An interrupt is an electronic signal to the CPU that changes the flow of instructions. In other words, it interrupts what the CPU is doing and causes it to do something else. Although an interrupt can arrive as a signal directly connected to the CPU, in modern computers, it is more likely to arrive through an interrupt controller that offloads some of the work from the CPU, or as a message on an input/output bus.

An interrupt will cause the machine state to be saved[68] so that the interrupted program can be resumed. Then the operating system runs an interrupt handler routine to deal with the signal from the I/O device. Finally, the interrupted program is resumed.

For example, when the operating system is initialized, it may command the keyboard controller to read a character. The associated interrupt is not generated until a key is pressed. The keyboard interrupt handler will translate the code from the keyboard into a character code and pass it along to the active program. Until the key is pressed the CPU can do other work. As this example shows, the time when an interrupt will occur is unpredictable.

A **software interrupt** is a signal generated within the CPU itself that changes the flow of

---

68 Saving the machine state means saving the program counter, the contents of the registers, and possibly a small amount of other information. Since the program counter holds the address of the next instruction, restoring the machine state will cause the interrupted program to resume at its next instruction. The machine state can be saved on the stack or in an area called a process control block.

instructions. Software interrupts are caused by the execution of special instructions, such as when an application program wants to call on the operating system for some service.

A **trap**, as discussed in Chapter 3, is a third kind of interrupt and happens when an error like arithmetic overflow or division by zero occurs. A trap causes a call to the operating system, which generally handles the error, usually by producing an error message and ending the failed program.

Sometimes it is necessary to suspend handling of interrupts. This is called **disabling interrupts** or **masking interrupts**, although the interrupt signals will be held until interrupts are re-enabled. One reason is to perform an atomic operation, such as setting a semaphore[69] for inter-process communication. Interrupts should only be disabled for very short periods, a few instruction times at most.

Some interrupts indicate serious errors, such as a memory error. These **non-maskable** interrupts can occur even when interrupts are disabled.

4.1.3 I/O Completion

All input and output operations start with a command issued through the CPU, usually by the operating system. There are three ways of completing I/O operations. One is busy waiting, as described in Section 4.1.2. Busy waiting is found only in special circumstances because busy waiting means the CPU cannot do other work. Since most CPUs can execute millions of instructions in the time needed for one I/O operation, this is a serious drawback. The other two ways of completing I/O operations are interrupt-driven I/O and direct memory access I/O, or DMA.

Interrupt-Driven I/O

In interrupt driven I/O, the I/O device or device controller raises an interrupt each time a character is available on input or has been processed on output. The interrupt causes the operating system's device driver to run. On input, the device driver reads the character from the device's input data register and passes it to the appropriate application program or operating system routine. On output, the device driver places the next character in the output data register and signals the device that the next character is available or concludes the I/O operation.

Interrupt-driven I/O is used for character-oriented devices like keyboards, mice, and touch screens. While it might at first seem wasteful to interrupt a running program every time a character is typed or a mouse moves one increment, there are two important considerations. The first is that computer users expect immediate feedback when operating user interface

---

69 You will study semaphores in a course on operating systems. When one process is changing a semaphore, the operating system must ensure that no other process can read it until the change is complete. Some architectures include a hardware instruction to accomplish that. In other cases, the operating system must disable interrupts.

devices. Second, the CPU can execute millions of instructions between such interrupts.

Direct Memory Access I/O

Block devices can be attached to the computer system using a direct memory access (DMA) controller which has access to the memory bus. When the CPU initiates a DMA I/O operation, it provides the address of the device, the location of the data on the device, perhaps as a logical block number, and whether a read or write is wanted. In addition, the CPU provides a memory address. The DMA controller transfers data from device to memory on a read, or from memory to device on a write. The CPU receives an interrupt only after the entire operation is complete. Instead of hundreds or thousands of interrupts, there is only one indicating the completion of the entire operation.

The trade-off is that, while a DMA device is using the memory bus, memory access is not available to the CPU. This drawback can be mitigated through using dual-ported memory, increasing the cost of the system. In systems where each DMA-capable device has its own DMA controller, there may be multiple devices contending for memory access.

Nearly all modern memory systems include cache memory. If a copy of a memory location is stored in a cache and a DMA operation overwrites that portion of memory, the cached value no longer matches memory. Being sure cache and main memory match is called **cache coherence**. The problem of cache coherence can be mitigated by having the cache subsystem monitor the memory address lines and invalidate any cache entries that are written by direct memory access. This is called a snooping cache and increases hardware cost. Since DMA operations are initiated by the operating system, the OS is aware of memory locations that will be overwritten and can invalidate any cache entries for those locations. In that case, the penalty is time rather than money.

In addition to storage, video, sound, and network devices may employ DMA to speed up I/O operations. In some architectures, DMA can be used to move blocks of data from one memory location to another.

I/O Channels

Mainframe computers often take a different approach to input and output, the I/O channel. An I/O channel extends the concept of DMA I/O by removing even more work from the CPU. Each channel is itself a computer, programmed to handle the details of input and output and capable of controlling many devices. It is through the use of I/O channels that mainframe computers are able to handle transactions from thousands of computer terminals for an airline or bank or manage hundreds of disk drives.

4.1.4 I/O Buses

A bus is a collection of electrical conductors or optical fibers that transmits data, address information, control signals, and sometimes power over distances from millimeters or less up to a few meters at relatively high speeds. There are buses internal to chips themselves, such as the CPU and memory chips, buses on the circuit board that holds the CPU and other components, and buses that connect peripheral devices, either within the computer enclosure or external to it. The buses that connect peripheral devices are I/O buses.

Principal characteristics of I/O buses are signaling speed and whether data are transmitted one bit at a time or several bits in parallel. If multiple devices are connected to the same bus, there must be a mechanism for bus arbitration to share access to the bus among the multiple connections. Some buses transmit power as well as data and control signals. There have been numerous bus standards for various purposes since the 1980s. The computer industry is now focusing on relatively few modern standards.

Twenty-first century I/O buses transmit data serially, that is, one bit at a time. The reason is a problem called **bus skew**. Earlier buses attempted to achieve high transfer rates by using multiple data conductors and transmitting eight or more bits at a time, each on its own conductor.[70] For all the bits to arrive at the destination device at the same time, the conductors must be exactly the same length or nearly so. For relatively slow signaling speeds, that wasn't a problem. As bus speeds increased, bus skew became a problem. A bit that arrived late became a part of the following byte of data, introducing errors. If bits are transmitted serially, one after another, they necessarily arrive in the order they were sent.

There are three main types of I/O buses in current use, the universal serial bus (USB), the serial ATA bus (SATA), and the PCI express (PCIe) bus. Two other bus types, high-definition multimedia interface (HDMI) and DisplayPort are used primarily for display devices.

Universal Serial Bus

The universal serial bus (USB) is primarily an external bus. It was developed in the 1990s to address the problem that every device such as keyboard, printer, game controller, or modem connected to a computer had a different interface. To keep users from plugging a device into the wrong interface, the connectors were made different, requiring different cables. Several hardware and software companies led by Ajay Bhatt of Intel, came together in 1994 to develop a common interface for such devices. Goals of the group included ease of use, robust connectors, simplicity of interface design, and not adding manufacturing cost to computers. The interface should also supply power to devices with low power requirements like keyboards and mice. Devices should be hot-swappable, that is, it should be possible to plug and unplug devices with power on.

---

70 Such a bus is called a parallel bus.

Although Apple was not one of the original developers of USB, the fact that the iMac, released in September 1998, had only USB ports attracted attention and USB became widely accepted. The line of Apple Macs announced in late 2020 may be the first computers to incorporate USB4. The USB standard has evolved through four generations. The USB Implementers Forum currently maintains the standard and assigns USB vendor IDs. Every USB device has a 16-bit vendor ID and a 16-bit product ID assigned by the vendor (manufacturer) that in combination make a unique identifier. Together these identify a suitable device driver for the device. Every device also has an eight-bit device class, such as human interface device, printer, or mass storage device.

The original design of USB included a single host per bus, almost always a computer, and some number of peripheral devices. One computer can support more than one USB host, and so more than one bus. One physical connection can include more than one function; for example, one device with a single connection might include both a camera and a microphone. All activity on the bus is controlled by the host.

The design of USB includes hubs, which allow connecting multiple peripheral devices to one host or upstream connection. The host is called the root hub and is at the top of the connection hierarchy. Additional hubs can be connected downstream from the host, up to seven levels. Each hub can connect multiple peripheral devices, up to a total of 127 devices.

Original USB cables had a host or upstream end, called A, and a device or downstream end, called B, with incompatible connectors. This was necessary because the bus provides power, and the different connectors prevent connecting two power sources together. The two connectors were designed so that they could only be inserted face up, preserving the orientation of the electrical conductors within the cable.

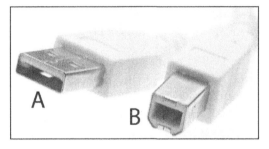

Figure 4-2
USB cable showing host connector A
and device connector B

USB 1.1 had a 1.5 megabit per second low speed mode which did not require shielded cable and was used for devices like mice which need a thin, flexible cable. The specification also had a twelve megabit per second high-speed mode for devices like printers. The high-speed mode required a thicker, shielded cable.

USB 2.0 introduced a 480 Mb/sec high-speed mode and maintained backward compatibility with older devices. The specification also included mini and micro-USB connectors for devices like smartphones and tablet computers, for which the standard connectors were too thick.

One of the most interesting features of USB 2.0 was USB On the Go, also called USB OTG or dual role mode. It is useful to have smartphones and tablets emulate mass storage for connection to desktop or laptop computers. Doing so requires them to have the role of peripheral devices. It is also useful to connect devices like keyboards and printers to smartphones and tablets which requires them to have the role of hosts. USB OTG solved that problem by allowing a device to be either a host or a peripheral device. That is accomplished by using a five-pin connector in which the fifth pin, called the ID pin, is connected to ground on the host or A end and unconnected on the B end. An addition to the USB protocol allows a role swap.

USB 3.0 introduced five additional pins in plugs and sockets that are backward compatible with USB 2.0. USB 3.0 connectors with the additional pins are marked by blue inserts. The additional pins provide two more pairs of shielded signal conductors and, as of USB 3.2 Gen 2x2, provide transfer speeds of 20 gigabits per second.

Type	USB Version	Cable Length
CC2	USB 2.0	≤ 4 m.
CC3G1	USB 3.2 Gen1 and USB4 Gen2	≤ 2 m.
CC3G2	USB 3.2 Gen2 and USB4 Gen2	≤ 1 m.
CC4G3	USB4 Gen 3	≤ 0.8 m.

Figure 4-3
USB-C Cables
Current carrying capacity is indicated by a suffix
USB 3.0 Promoter Group

The USB Power Delivery standard, USB PD, was completed in 2012. It allows a powered device and an unpowered device to negotiate the amount of power to be delivered by exchanging data between the two devices. Version 3.0 of USB PD can provide up to 100 watts of power at 20 volts and five amperes.

The USB-C connector was finalized by the USF-IF in summer, 2014. It removes the distinction between A and B cable ends. Because the pins are rotationally symmetrical, the connector has no concept of face up or face down; it can be plugged in either way. The distinction between power supplying and power consuming ends is now handled within the devices themselves rather than by requiring different connectors.

Not all cables with USB-C connectors are alike. There are four defined types of USB-C cables as shown in Table 4-1. Each type has a variant that can deliver power at three amperes and another that can deliver power at five amperes, a total of eight variations. All but the USB 2.0 three ampere version are required to include an E-Mark[71] or electronic mark circuit in the cable's connector that can be interrogated to find the capabilities of the cable. "Full featured" USB-C cables have 18 electrical conductors, including two shielded pairs for data and a power conductor that will support three or five amperes of current.

Active cables include circuitry in addition to the E-Mark circuit that amplifies and conditions the data signals to allow cable lengths longer than defined in the specification. All fiber optic USB-C cables are necessarily active cables.

---

71 This is not the same as the European Union automotive safety E-Mark.

There are cables with USB-C connectors on the market with unsafe combinations of connectors that could allow connection of two power sources, and even cables that are reported to have damaged equipment to which they were connected. Cables that allow more current than they are designed to carry could overheat and cause fires. The USB-IF has a program for certification of cables. Looking for the "USB Certified" mark is one way to avoid substandard cables.

The USB4[72] specification, announced in 2019, provides up to 40 gigabits per second; USB-C cables are required. USB4 includes Intel's thunderbolt specification, which Intel released to the USB-IF for use in USB devices. Thunderbolt compatibility is likely to be found mainly in desktop and laptop computers and less frequently in smartphones or tablets. In addition to fast data transfer, USB4 provides mechanisms for tunneling DisplayPort and PCIe signals.

Serial ATA Bus

The serial ATA (SATA) bus is used to connect mass storage devices like disk drives, optical drives, or solid-state disks to host bus adapters. It replaced the earlier ATA bus, also called the IDE bus, to allow for higher transfer rates without problems from bus skew.

Beyond replacing the ATA interface, SATA provides advanced features such as capability for being hot-pluggable. Hot-pluggable means that a SATA device can be removed from the computer and replaced while power is on. Hot pluggability requires support from the controller and operating system as well as the interface. It is implemented in part by having the ground pins on the connectors be slightly longer than the others so that they make contact first.

The SATA specification includes the Advanced Host Controller Interface (AHCI) which, if supported by controller and operating system, provides controller functions not found in ATA.

Current versions of SATA provide for transfer rates of 600 megabytes/second. There are small form-factor versions for solid-state drives and a specification, eSATA, for attachment of external drives. There is a cable specification that provides both data and power to external drives with one cable.

Because getting higher speeds from SATA interfaces would require major changes in the interface specification, SATA Express defines an interface that will accept either a SATA storage device or a PCIe storage device. SATA Express was a part of the SATA 3.2 specification, released in 2013. SATA Express provides for transfer rates of up to 16 gigabits per second.

PCIe Bus

The Peripheral Component Interconnect Express (PCIe) bus is an expansion bus designed

---

72 The official spelling does not include a space.

to connect peripherals to a computer system. PCIe is built on bidirectional serial connections. The devices attached by PCIe can use one, four, eight, or 16 lanes. More lanes mean higher transfer speeds. Each lane is a separate serial bus. Bidirectional operation is achieved by having two pair of signal conductors, transmit and receive, for each lane. Low speed devices can keep cost down by using a single lane. Higher speed devices can be designed for multiple lanes at a corresponding increase in cost and complexity. A device can operate using fewer lanes than its design maximum, but at lower speed. For example, a device designed for four lanes can operate when connected to a one lane socket, but only at about 25% of its rated speed.

The concept of multiple lanes seems very like a parallel bus, and it has many of the advantages of a parallel bus. The problem of bus skew is avoided in two ways. First, PCIe initially used an 8B/10B code. That means each eight-bit byte is encoded using ten bits. The extra bits guarantee enough transitions in the signal to allow the receiving device to recover timing from the signal itself and determine where the bit transitions occur. PCIe 3.0 (2010) changed from 8B/10B encoding to 128B/130B encoding, greatly reducing the overhead introduced by the encoding scheme. PCIe 6.0 (2019) changed to pulse amplitude modulation with four levels, allowing two bits to be transmitted with each signal event. The additional bits for timing were replaced by an error correcting code similar to the Hamming code described in Section 3.5.3.

The second method of avoiding skew is that each lane transmits one byte at a time. So, in a two-lane configuration, lane zero would transmit the first byte of a 16-bit word and lane one would transmit the second byte. The bits of each byte are transmitted serially so no skew is possible.

PCIe is really a packet-switched protocol, but the interface circuitry hides the complexity of packet switching and presents an interface similar to a parallel bus to attached devices and to the CPU.

There are PCIe specifications for small form-factor devices such as M.2 solid-state disks. The current specification is PCIe 7.0, announced in the summer of 2022.

Connection to the CPU

The original design for microcomputers involved a bus connection at the CPU package, with pins for data, address, control, and status signals. The CPU bus connected to multiple input/output controllers for different classes of I/O devices. Some designs limited the bus clock speed to that of the slowest device on the bus, and all required bus arbitration circuitry to control access to the bus and prevent multiple devices from trying to use the bus at the same time.

Moore's Law allowed designs to evolve so that fewer physical components provided greater functionality. By the beginning of the 21st century, designs for personal computer class machines used a bridge architecture, with a high-speed interconnection device called a **host bridge** connected directly to the CPU's bus pins. The connection to the CPU bus was called the **front-side bus** to distinguish it from other buses in the computer design. High-speed devices, at first main memory and graphics devices, were connected directly to the host bridge. The widespread adoption of the PCI express bus resulted in designs that included a PCIe root node as an attachment to the host bridge.

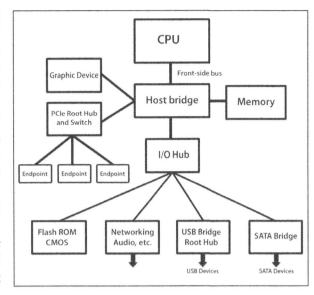

Figure 4-4
Computer organization with bridge architecture

By the second decade of the 21st century, increasing transistor density allowed the functions of the host bridge to be migrated to the CPU die[73], and so packaged with the CPU cores. Still later, some designs replaced the functions of the host bridge with a PCI Express root complex with integrated memory controller. This design presents the CPU with a bus interface but connects devices, including graphics devices, with the packet-switch PCIe interface.

4.2 Storage Devices

Storage is a primary use of computer systems. Programs to be run must be stored until needed and data to be used by the programs might be retrieved or stored. Some computer systems are used primarily for storing data.

Computer storage can be **volatile**, meaning that the contents are lost when power is removed, or non-volatile. Non-volatile storage systems like disk drives retain data even when without power. It is usual to refer to volatile storage directly accessible to the CPU as **memory**.

An important consideration for both data access and device capability is sequential or random access. For data, the use case may be **sequential access** or **random access**. In the case of sequential access, a file of data is read from beginning to end. For example, the entire

---

73 A semiconductor die is the actual piece of silicon from which a chip is fabricated. Putting the host bridge on the CPU die makes it a part of the CPU package.

word processing document or spreadsheet is read into memory, so it is retrieved from storage by reading from the beginning of the document to the end. A huge majority of files on personal-use computers are read sequentially. In some cases, it may be necessary to read a particular part of a file. For example, a database application might request the record for employee 1234. It is possible to read the entire employee file from the beginning until the record for employee 1234 is found, but it is more time-efficient to read that record directly. That is random access.

The use case for data may influence the choice of storage technology for secondary storage. Tape devices provide only for sequential access. Disk devices, whether magnetic or solid-state, can provide either sequential or random access as needed by the application.

4.2.1 Hierarchy of Storage Devices

Storage mechanisms used in computing have several characteristics in addition to being volatile or non-volatile. One obvious characteristic is cost. The **latency** of a storage mechanism refers to the time it takes to begin transferring data after a request is made, and the **transfer rate** is the amount of data that can be delivered per second. Latency is also called **access time**. Storage in a computer system can be thought of as a hierarchy, with the fastest but most expensive storage, namely the processor's registers, having relatively low capacity but being closest to the processing mechanism. The registers operate at the clock speed of the CPU and so have very low latency and very high transfer rate. The number of registers varies from 16 to perhaps a few hundred.

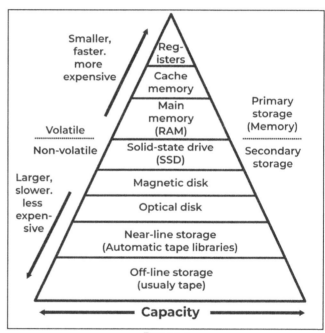

Figure 4-5

Hierarchy of computer storage.

Next in the hierarchy is cache memory. There may be two or more levels of cache memory as explained in Section 3.5.4, with the lowest level on the same chip as the CPU. Each level has greater capacity, is less expensive per bit, slower, and farther from the CPU than the levels above it.

The next level is main memory or RAM. Main memory holds the programs and data currently being used by the CPU. For all but the smallest computers, main memory sizes are measured in gibibytes.

The registers, cache memory, and main memory are all volatile and together are referred to as primary storage or memory.

The layers below main memory are called **secondary storage**. These layers hold programs and data not currently needed by the CPU. The first layer of secondary storage is **solid-state drive** or **SSD**. The SSD uses non-volatile semiconductor memory and has no moving parts. The fact that no mechanical motion is needed to access data on an SSD makes latency in the 100 microsecond range. At the end of 2022, two-terabyte SSDs cost about three times as much as magnetic disk of equivalent capacity.

The next layer is the magnetic disk. There is detail in Section 4.2.2. Details for near-line storage and magnetic tape are in Section 4.2.6.

4.2.2 Magnetic Disks

Figure 4-6
Magnetic disk with the cover removed

Alexgrec/123RF

Magnetic, or hard[74] disks were the principal storage medium for computers large and small from 1956 when IBM introduced the RAMAC 350[75] magnetic disk storage system through the first decade of the 21st century. They continue to be important, especially when cost or storage space are a primary consideration. Magnetic disks are *random access* devices. Any block of data on the disk can be read or written in about the same time as any other. A block of data can be updated by rewriting it.

A hard disk consists of one or more platters, non-magnetic metal or glass discs coated on top and bottom with a material that can be magnetized or demagnetized a small area at a time. The large silvery disc in the photograph of Figure 4-6 is a platter. You can see the edg-

---

74 "Hard" as opposed to flexible or floppy disks, a now-obsolete removable storage medium.

75 Strictly speaking the RAMAC 350 was only for large computers because only large computers existed in 1956. The RAMAC 350 was the size of two refrigerators and rented for over $3,000 per month, the equivalent of over $30,000 per month in 2022 dollars. It had a storage capacity of 5 MB.

es of three more platters below it. Each platter has a recording surface on top and bottom, so this four-platter disk has eight recording surfaces.

The object extending over the platter is a read-write arm, and at its very tip is a magnetic read-write head that can sense magnetic areas on the surface of the platter and also magnetize or demagnetize an area. The areas themselves are very small and each holds one bit of data. When the disk is in operation, the platters spin at speeds from 2,500 RPM to 10,000 RPM or more. The speed of the spinning platters creates an air bearing that allows the read-write head to fly a few nanometers above the surface of the disk. Even a fingerprint is more than a few nanometers thick, so disks are sealed to keep foreign matter out. If the read-write head touches the spinning platter, a small amount of the recording material may be scraped off. This is called head-disk interference, or more colorfully, a head crash. A physical shock can also cause a head crash. Once a head crash has occurred, the material scraped off will cause further head crashes, releasing still more material, and leading very quickly to complete failure of the disk.

Figure 4-7
Disk damaged by head crash

When power is removed, the disk's electronics move the heads to a lubricated landing zone on the disk or lift the heads completely away from the disk with unloading ramps so that head crashes do not occur during normal start-up or shutdown.

There is a disk head for each surface, and so eight heads for the disk shown in Figure 4-6. As the platters spin, a circle, called a **track**, sweeps under each head. The heads are connected, so all are in the same relative position with respect to the platters. Each head is in the same track position, but on its own platter. That "stack of tracks" is called a **cylinder**. The schematic diagram of Figure 4-8 shows cylinder, track, and head. The head stack connects all the heads so they move in unison. The head motor rotates the head stack in a shallow arc from the innermost track to the outermost track.

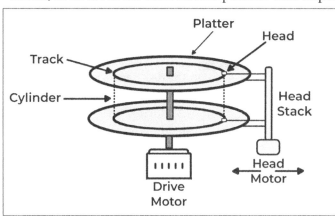

Figure 4-8
Schematic diagram of magnetic disk

Each track is divided into many **sectors**. Each sector

holds a fixed number of bytes, called a **block**. The size of a block is fixed during disk manu-facture. Blocks were originally 512 bytes; 4,096-byte blocks are more common on modern disk drives. Any block on the drive can be selected with cylinder, head, and sector number.

The circumference of the innermost track is much less than that of the outermost track. If the number of sectors were equal, bits would have to be written at a much lower density on the outer tracks than on the inner tracts. To prevent what would otherwise be a loss of re-cording capacity, modern disks use **multiple zone recording**. There are more sectors per track on the outer tracks than on the inner tracks. There are bands or zones between the inner and outer tracks with differing numbers of sectors. The aim is to hold the recording density, the number of bits per linear inch, to near the optimum value for a particular drive.

Because the number of sectors per track depends on the track number, modern disk drives use logical block addressing or LBA. The blocks on the disk are numbered beginning with zero. The device driver specifies a logical block number for read and write requests and the drive electronics convert that to the physical address of cylinder, head, and sector.

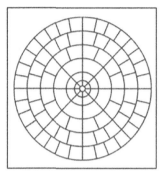

Each block of a magnetic disk contains a header that provides synchronization information to the drive electronics, a fixed size data block, a cyclic redundancy check (CRC) code and a Reed-Solomon error correcting code (ECC). The Reed-Sol-omon code is conceptually similar to the Hamming code described in Section 3.5.3. Both the CRC and the ECC are

Figure 4-9
Multiple zone recording

computed and saved on each write to the disk. The drive electronics compute a CRC on each read and compare it with the CRC read from disk. If they are equal, the assumption is that no error has occurred. If not, the drive electronics attempt to use the ECC from disk to correct the error. If that fails, the drive electronics signal a read failure to the operating system. The usual operating system action is to retry the read some number of times before signaling a fatal error.

Disk drives have a few spare blocks, perhaps a thousand. When the drive electronics recog-nize that a block is bad, the drive will remap that block so that future reads or writes for that block actually use a block in the pool of spares.

Magnetic Disk Access Time

There are three components to the access time of a block on magnetic disk. **Seek time** is the time to move the disk heads from their current position to the needed track. If the heads are already in position, the seek time is zero. Manufacturers publish an average seek time, often in the range of a few milliseconds, which is approximately the time to seek across a third of the total number of cylinders. **Rotational latency** is the time for the needed block to rotate under the disk head. On average, it is half the time for a full rotation of the disk. Together seek time and rotational latency make up the **total latency** of the disk access, the time from the request until input or output can begin. **Transfer time** is the time to complete the read or write operation once a transfer has begun. Like rotational latency, it is dependent on the rotational speed of the disk.

Disk manufacturers love to quote high transfer rates for their disks. However, *total latency is the most important throughput measure for magnetic disks*. A high-performance magnetic disk might have latency (seek time plus rotational latency) of 10 milliseconds and a transfer time for one block of 16 microseconds, a difference of three orders of magnitude. Total access time for one sector of a magnetic disk is measured in milliseconds and cycle time for a CPU is measured in nanoseconds, six orders of magnitude different. To put it another way, a CPU is about a million times faster than a magnetic disk. *This* is what makes solid-state secondary storage so attractive.

Shingled Magnetic Recording

Shingled magnetic recording is a technique developed about 2013 that packs more data onto a disk of given size without a need to increase the linear recording density. SMR takes advantage of the fact that, while a relatively wide write head is needed to change the recording layer on a disk, a much narrower area can be used for reading. Conventional magnetic disks have a small space between tracks. In SMR disks, the tracks are overlapped like the shingles from which the technique takes its name.

That means that any track can be read randomly, but random writes require rewriting all adjacent tracks that contain valid data. Random reads work as expected, but random writes require rewriting an entire zone on the drive with a large impact on performance. The trade-off for increased capacity is poor random write performance. SMR drives are good for write few, read many archival applications, but very poor for the usual case which is a mix of random reads and random writes.

Drive-managed SMR drives handle the necessary updates from non-sequential writes with electronics that are part of the drive. Host-aware SMR drives use internal electronics to handle updates, but the host operating system is aware of the SMR nature of the drive and so can optimize sequences of writes. Host-managed SMR drives expect the host operating system to handle the complexity of random writes.

Error Control

Magnetic disk drives may suffer permanent or temporary failure, including catastrophic failure. Such things as aging electronic components, loose cables, or variation in supply power can cause variations in the magnetic field when recording that may make particular blocks unreadable. Every block contains an error-correcting code that can detect multi-bit errors and correct single-bit and some multi-bit errors. Often re-reading a block will correct an error.

Failures in the CPU, bus, or connection to the disk drive result in incorrect data being recorded. In that case, the error correcting code will be computed using incorrect data and cannot indicate the error when the block is read. This is **silent data corruption**. It is rare, but problem of concern to those who work with large disk arrays. Silent data corruption can occur with solid-state drives or main memory as well because the cause is incorrect data delivered to the storage device or memory.

4.2.3 Solid-State Secondary Storage

Solid-state secondary storage, also called a **solid-state drive** or SSD, is non-volatile semi-conductor storage, which means it operates at electronic speeds, not mechanical speeds. Modern solid-state drives typically use NAND flash storage. This storage technology is named for the similarity to the NAND gate discussed in Section 2.4, although the actual storage cells are not NAND gates.

Internally, the NAND storage cells are grouped into pages, typically 2K, 4K, 8K, or 16K bytes. Pages are organized into blocks, usually 128 or 256 pages. Reading is done at the page level, that is, the operating system can ask for a single page, similar to reading one block from a magnetic disk. Writing can also be done at the page

Figure 4-10
2TB M.2 format NVMe device

level with an important restriction: *pages cannot be overwritten*. A page can only be written into a space that has been erased, and erasures can happen only at the block level. Writing a page means finding a block with an empty page, writing to that empty page, and remapping the page address. The **flash translation layer** (FTL), a controller within the solid-state device handles the mapping of logical block addresses given by the operating system to physical block and page addresses in NAND storage.

The flash translation layer handles two other important functions, wear leveling and garbage collection. As a reminder that pages cannot be overwritten, writing a page is called *programming* the page. Each page of NAND flash cells has a limited number of program/erase (P/E) cycles before it fails. The limit is large, often into the hundreds of thousands of P/E cycles, but it is finite. The wear-leveling function of the FTL tries to keep the number of writes to each block approximately equal so that no area fails before the predicted lifetime of the device.

When a block no longer has any active pages, the block can be erased so that it is ready to be reused. The garbage collection function keeps track of blocks with no active pages, erases them, and adds them to a list of free blocks.

As with magnetic disks, there can be errors in reading and writing solid-state storage, and solid-state storage uses error detecting and correcting codes in much the same way as magnetic disks. Solid-state storage is susceptible to silent data corruption, but as with magnetic disks, it is rare.

Solid-state storage is available in consumer and enterprise grades. As with magnetic disks, the trade-offs in design and manufacture are different between the two.

Interfaces and Form Factors

When the technology to replace magnetic disks with solid-state devices was first available, the NAND flash memory was packaged in an enclosure the same size and shape as the 2.5-inch disk drives used in laptop computers and equipped with a SATA interface. That allowed direct replacement of a magnetic disk with an SSD.

Even large-capacity SSDs didn't need as much physical space as a 2.5-inch magnetic disk, and the SATA interface was a bottleneck. While SSDs with the 2.5-inch form factor and SATA interface are still available, devices with much smaller form factors and PCIe interfaces became available shortly before 2010.

NVMe (non-volatile memory express) devices were available in 2013. The current revision of the NVMe standard (2.0c) was published in October 2022. An NVMe module is shown in Figure 4-10. The connector is at the right end of the image. The notch in the connector, called a key, prevents the device from being plugged into an incompatible socket. The device in the figure is 3.15 inches long, 0.87 inches wide, and 0.09 inches thick, about the size of a stick of chewing gum. The PCIe four lane interface gives write speeds of 2,100 MB/second and read speeds of 3,500 MB/second according to the manufacturer's specification. Price for the 2 TB version at the beginning of 2023 was about $160. By comparison, a 2 TB magnetic disk cost about $50.

M.2 form-factor NVMe devices with SATA interfaces are also available. These have two key notches on the connector. Because transfer speeds are limited by the SATA interface, lower-cost designs can be used for the storage and FTL, making these devices less than half the price of the PCIe-connected device.

In addition to the obvious speed advantages, the fact that solid-state secondary storage devices have no moving parts makes them resistant to mechanical shock, unlike magnetic disk drives. That shock resistance is a huge advantage in mobile and portable devices. Lower power consumption makes them appropriate in devices that must be battery powered.

4.2.4 Redundancy: RAID

Data storage systems fail. Magnetic disk systems suffer disk crashes and wear-related problems, and solid-state storage systems wear out after some number of program/erase operations. Other kinds of problems can cause particular areas of storage media to fail. For reasons described below, the RAID arrays that provided protection against such failures are less effective when used with today's large disks. However, the same techniques used by RAID can be used by advanced file systems to guard against failures, so it is worthwhile to understand how RAID works.

In 1987, David Patterson, Garth A. Gibson, and Randy Katz[76] at the University of California Berkeley were looking for a way to get large for the time amounts of disk storage without buying what they termed SLEDs, single, large, expensive disks. At the time, mainframe disks were very expensive, but smaller, inexpensive[77] disks were beginning to be available for personal computers. They wrote and published a paper titled "A Case for Redundant Arrays of Inexpensive Disks (RAID)." Most of the technology they described was already in use; their paper brought it all together in one place.

RAID can be implemented in hardware in the disk controller or in software as drivers that are part of an operating system. Some levels of RAID, such as RAID 5 described below, require computation for each disk block read or written. For those levels of RAID, best performance comes from hardware RAID because otherwise the CPU would have to perform the necessary computations. RAID provides logical disks, not a file system, so a Windows Server system using RAID would have an NTFS or ReFS file system housed in the RAID array. RAID arrays can be made from magnetic disks or solid-state drives.

There are several "levels" of RAID, a few of which are described here; the others are infrequently used in practice.

RAID 0 instantiates one large logical volume from two or more physical disks. Data are striped across the physical disks, so parts of a large data file will be stored on each of the physical disks of a RAID 0 array. That can improve performance when reading large files. There is no redundancy with RAID 0; if a physical disk fails, all data are likely lost.

RAID 1 consists of mirrored disks. All data are written to two disks and can be read from either one. This obviously imposes a penalty when writing because two physical write operations are necessary. On the other hand, it provides a chance for substantial improvement in reading because data can be read from either disk and the operating system can select the less busy one. A failure of a single disk in a RAID 1 array causes no loss of data, but the array

---

76   You are likely to encounter one of Dr. Patterson's books if you take a computer architecture course in a computer science department, and one of Dr. Katz's if you take a digital logic course in an electrical engineering department.

77   People who do marketing hate the word "inexpensive," so you will see other words like "independent" and "individual" in some definitions of RAID. The original description said *inexpensive*.

is no longer redundant. The failed disk must be replaced, and all the data copied to regain redundancy.

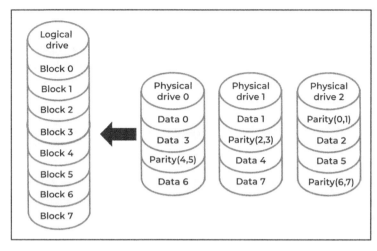

Figure 4-11

A single large logical drive is mapped on to three smaller physical drives. This configuration can tolerate the loss of one physical drive without loss of data

For reasons to be explained shortly, RAID 5 is no longer recommended for arrays of large disks, but the easiest way to understand RAID with parity is to understand RAID 5. Refer to Figure 4-11, a RAID 5 array that presents a single logical volume from three physical drives. This array has the property that the complete failure of any one drive will not cause loss of data provided no other failures occur.

To understand that, we need a review of parity, which was introduced in Section 2.5.2 and used for error-checking in Section 3.5.3. The XOR function computes even parity. The parity block is the result of an XOR of all bits in the two disk blocks it is checking. Here is an example with six bits:

$$\begin{aligned}
&\text{Disk A} \quad 101101 \\
&\text{Disk B} \quad 101011 \\
&\text{Parity} \quad 000110
\end{aligned}$$

Each parity bit is the XOR of the corresponding bits from Disk A and Disk B. The XOR function computes even parity, and you can see that the total number of bits in each column above is even. The value of parity in this case is that, given any of the two rows above, the value of the third can be calculated. Continuing with the example, suppose Disk A has failed but the data for Disk B and the parity information are available.

```
Disk B  101011
Parity  000110
 XOR    101101
```

The columnwise XOR of the Disk B bits and the parity bits recovers the data from Disk A.

Refer again to Figure 4-11 and assume that physical drive zero has failed. It held data blocks 0, 3, and 6 and the (4,5) parity block. Data block 0 can be recomputed using data block 1 which is on drive 1 and the parity (0,1) block on drive 2. Similarly, every other block on physical drive zero can be recomputed using data and parity blocks available from other drives. If the other two drives remain in operation, the RAID array can respond to read requests for physical drive zero by computing the needed data as shown above. It can even respond to write requests to physical drive zero by recomputing the appropriate parity block to reflect the change. However, inability to read either of the two remaining drives is likely to mean total loss of data.

A RAID 5 array like the one described would be made using hot-pluggable disks, that is, disks that can be replaced while power is on. It would probably have a "hot spare" disk. A hot spare disk is mounted in the RAID enclosure and powered on, but not used for storing data. If a hot spare were available, the RAID controller would immediately begin rebuilding the contents of the failed drive and writing the contents onto the hot spare. When that operation completed, the array would again be redundant. If no hot spare were available, rebuilding would begin as soon as the failed drive was replaced.

RAID 5 is not recommended for large capacity disk drives. Operating a RAID 5 array in a degraded state puts stress on the remaining drives. Rebuilding the failed drive adds to that stress. For RAID 5 to be effective, the other drives must perform perfectly until the rebuild operation completes. An uncorrectable read error on another drive before a failed drive is rebuilt causes complete failure of the array because the redundant data to correct that error does not exist. As drive capacities increase and rebuild times stretch from hours to days, the chances increase that an uncorrectable read error on another drive will occur during a drive rebuild. Manufacturers' reliability claims are optimistic. One study revealed that "the probability of seeing two drives in the cluster fail within one hour is four times larger under the real data" (Schroder & Gibson, 2007).

RAID 6, which provides for two parity blocks and can tolerate up to two simultaneous failures provided a solution for a time, but as disk capacities grow, RAID 6 also appears fragile.

Various solutions like triple-mirroring, where there are three copies of data instead of two, attempt to address the problem in very high-capacity drives. More robust solutions are likely to come from adoption of file systems specifically focused on preserving data integrity such as Microsoft's ReFS and the open-source ZFS. ZFS uses the techniques of RAID. ReFS and ZFS are discussed in Chapter 6. **Fountain codes**, not discussed here, may be more suitable than parity or mirroring when large storage devices are involved.

It is also important to remember that *RAID is not backup*. Redundant configurations of RAID protect only against storage failures. RAID provides no protection against accidental or malicious corruption of data, accidental or malicious erasure, or disasters like data center fire or flooding.

4.2.5 Optical Drives

The principles of optical recording and reading are similar across CD, DVD, and Blu-ray drives. We will examine CD recording in detail and the other two technologies in less detail.

The first optical recording devices started with the compact disc (CD), a project of Philips NV and Sony in 1982. CDs were intended for music as a replacement for vinyl phonograph records. The technical details were established as an international standard, known as the red book, which allowed music companies to make CDs and electronics companies to make CD players with confidence that they would be compatible. Because the CD was developed for music, it has one continuous spiral track rather than the concentric tracks of magnetic disks.[78] The spiral is over 22,000 revolutions long, and if unwound would be almost 3½ miles long (Tanenbaum, 1999).

To keep the flow of music bits constant, players rotated the disk at about 530 RPM when reading near the center down to 200 RPM near the outer edge, maintaining *constant linear velocity*.

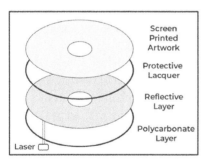

Figure 4-12

A CD has four layers

CDs are recorded by using a laser to burn holes into a master disk which is then used to make a mold. The mold is used to mass-produce CDs. The holes are called pits; the spaces between pits are lands.

A mass-produced CD has four layers. The polycarbonate layer at the bottom accounts for the thickness of the CD and has the molded-in pits. A very thin reflective layer of aluminum or other metal is deposited on top of the polycarbonate layer. It is protected by a coating of lacquer. The CD artwork is printed over the lacquer. The polycarbonate layer is arranged with the pits on top, so they are bumps when viewed from below by the laser. That construction makes the top surface of the disc more sensitive to damage than the bottom surface. Errors due to damage are likely to affect a run of bits and are called burst errors.

An audio CD is played by positioning a laser light source and photo-detector under the

---

78   If CDs had concentric tracks like magnetic disks, there would be a break in the flow of music data each time the playback head had to move to the next track.

polycarbonate layer and spinning the disk. The head follows the spiral track from the center outward. Light from the laser is reflected from the lands but weakened by an interference pattern when it strikes the pits so the photo-detector can distinguish pits and lands. Bits are encoded as transitions. A transition indicates a 1-bit; no transition indicates a 0-bit. This is called non-return-to-zero inverted (NRZI) encoding. To assure that there are enough transitions to maintain timing, each eight bits of data are encoded as 14 bits, a technique called **eight-to-fourteen modulation**. Three additional bits separate each 14-bit encoded value, so each eight bits of information occupies 17 bits on the disc. Each 512-byte data frame has an additional 76 bits of error correcting code information appended prior to the eight-to-fourteen modulation (Roberts et al, 1996). The error correcting codes are designed to detect and correct both random and burst errors.[79]

In 1986 Phillips and Sony published a specification, the yellow book, for recording computer data on CD with a file system compatible with the major operating systems of the time. These CD-ROM discs were widely used to distribute software.

For data CDs, frames are grouped into sectors of four frames. Depending on the recording mode, a sector may hold 2,048 or 2,336 bytes of data. In either mode, a three-byte address field permits logical sector addressing. Mode 1 recording, with 2,048 byte sectors, includes error checking bits in addition to those in each frame.

Since CDs have a continuous spiral groove, there is no concept of a track as with magnetic disks.

A recordable CD, or CD-R has a physical spiral groove, called the pregroove, molded into the polycarbonate layer. The pregroove is used for tracking. It has regular sinusoidal variations called the "**wobble frequency**" that can be read by the laser to generate timing information. The polycarbonate layer is covered with a layer of dye, then the thin, reflective metal layer and protective coating. A laser operating at high power can heat the dye layer causing a physical change that can be detected by a low-power laser when the disc is read. Recordable CDs are very sensitive to environmental and storage conditions and may become unreadable over a very short time in unfavorable conditions.

Instead of a dye layer, rewritable CDs have a thin layer of silver alloy that can be made to change phase to an amorphous state using a laser at high power. The alloy can be returned to the crystalline state using an intermediate power. The amorphous state is less reflective than the crystalline state. The difference can be detected by a low-power laser to read the disk. The allow can later be returned to the amorphous state with a high-power laser for rewriting.

---

79 Details of the error correction mechanism are beyond the scope of this book. The principle is similar to the Hamming code discussed in Section 3.5.3. For those who would like to investigate further, the mechanism is called cross-interleaved Reed–Solomon coding.

Digital Versatile Discs

The DVD was originally developed for distributing motion pictures and originally called the digital video disk. At first there were competing, incompatible formats. The companies developing the successor to the CD reached agreement on a single standard in 1996. Most DVDs are the same 12 cm size as a CD and, in the single-layer format, use the same construction. The standard also allows for smaller 8 cm discs. Pits and lands are smaller, requiring the use of a red laser in place of the near-infrared laser of CDs.

The original standard included dual-layer discs. In a dual-layer disc, the metalized coating of the bottom layer is made semi-transparent. By changing focus, the laser can read either layer. The standard also included double-sided discs and dual-layer double-sided discs. The manufacture of the latter two formats was complex and expensive.

Recordable DVD-R[80] discs with a single layer hold 4.7 GB of data. Rewritable DVD-RW discs are also available. DVD-R and DVD-RW devices use information called land prepits, marked on the grooves when the DVD blank is manufactured, to position the laser when recording.

A competing format, DVD+R, uses a wobble frequency for laser positioning. DVD-R and DVD+R are compatible for reading. Most modern DVD recorders will write discs designed for either format. DVD+RW devices can rewrite data.

DVD+R DL is a recording mechanism for storing 8.5 GB on one DVD through double-layer recording. There are no rewritable double-layer discs.

DVD-RAM was a recordable DVD technology that recorded data on concentric tracks, like a magnetic disk, on a rewritable medium. The last manufacturer of DVD-RAM discs stopped making them in 1999.

Blu-Ray

Blu-ray discs are the same 12 cm size as CDs but in single-layer format, store 25 GB of data using a violet laser with much shorter wavelength than the red laser used for DVDs. Sony demonstrated a prototype in 2000; Blu-ray players were generally available in 2006.

BD-R discs are write-once recordable discs. BD-RE are recordable and erasable discs that can be rewritten. Both types are available with capacities of 25, 50, and 100 GB. A 128 GB BD-R format is also available. Prices at the end of 2022 for 25 GB BD-R discs were about $2.00 each; 100 GB BD-R disks were about $22.00.

---

80   Pronounced "dash R."

4.2.6 Magnetic Tape and Near-Line Storage

Magnetic tape is a thin strip of Mylar or other polymer coated with material that allows writing and reading of data by magnetizing the material. The strips are hundreds to thousands of feet long, often about ½ inch wide, wound on spools. The spools are enclosed in a case that allows the spool to be self-loaded in a computer tape drive. Current magnetic tapes follow the Linear Tape Open (LTO) standard. LTO 9 cartridges provide 18 TB capacity in a single cartridge.

Magnetic tapes are sequential access devices. Reading any block of data on a tape requires passing over all prior blocks. Although data can be appended at the end of a file on tape, there is no reliable way to rewrite a block of data in the middle of a tape file.

Tape drives can have cartridges loaded manually or with a robotic loader as described below. Once a tape is loaded, the drive opens an access gate and winds a portion of the tape around a spool internal to the drive. The tape can then be passed between the spool within the cartridge and the internal spool. Many such cartridges contain a semiconductor memory chip that can describe the cartridge's contents and so provide for automatic indexing.

Near-line storage is storage that is accessible to the operating system and application programs without human intervention, but which may have latency times of many seconds. Near-line storage is implemented as automated libraries of magnetic tape with robot loaders. When data from a particular tape cartridge is needed, the robot loader mechanism locates the tape cartridge and loads it into a tape drive. When the load operation is complete, the tape contents are available to the operating system and application programs. Near-line storage devices are available with capacities ranging from a dozen tape cartridges and one drive to thousands of cartridges and dozens to hundreds of drives.

The current generation of tape cartridges provide 18 TB of storage uncompressed or up to 45 TB of storage with compression. A modest near-line device with one drive and sixteen tape cartridges provides a near-line capacity of up to 720 TB. A device with a single drive and multiple cartridges, any one of which can be loaded automatically, is sometimes called an *autoloader*. Larger devices are called **tape libraries**.

Near-line devices are used for automated backup and for hierarchical storage systems which automatically migrate infrequently used files to tape and automatically copy them back to disk when needed. Tape cartridges with write-once, read-many (WORM) capability can be used to maintain archives for legal or other reasons.

A completely different type of near-line storage is the **MAID**, or massive array of idle disks. Large numbers of magnetic disks are configured to "spin down" after a period of no access. When access to such a disk is needed, a read or write command from the CPU will cause it to spin up, then process the command. The premise is that most drives will be idle most of the time and that will increase drive longevity, decrease power consumption, and decrease heat generation. Capacities of MAID arrays are likely to be lower than tape-based solutions because of cost. At the end of 2022, cost per TB for tape storage was about half that for magnetic disk storage and the useful life is about 30 years. Six or more disk replacements would be required in that time.

4.3 Other Input and Output Devices

There are many input and output devices. We will consider in detail displays, including touch screens, printers, keyboards, and mice.

4.3.1 Displays

There are special-purpose displays for applications like calculators, cash registers, and gasoline pumps, and for applications requiring very large displays like signage applications and event venue displays. Probably most computer displays are intended for use by one person at desktop viewing distances or are a part of a mobile device.

The most visible characteristic of displays is **size**. Size is measured diagonally. There are displays as small as a few inches and as large as 40 inches or more. A comfortable size for most desktop displays is about 24 inches. Related to size is the **aspect ratio**, the ratio of width to height. Current desktop, laptop, and tablet displays are nearly universally 16:9, the aspect ratio of high-definition motion pictures. The other important physical characteristics are **pixel density** and **resolution**. The pixel density of a display is the number of pixels per inch. For ordinary display devices that is likely to be 90 to 144 pixels per inch. Apple's trademarked retina displays are designed to have a pixel density of 300 PPI or higher. The concept is that one cannot discern individual pixels at normal viewing distances. The resolution is the height and width of a screen measured in pixels.

The **refresh rate** is the number of times each second the image on a display is updated, measured in Hertz. A common refresh rate is 60 Hz but high-performance refresh rates are available, up to about 240 Hz. Whether a higher refresh rate will improve application performance depends on the application. Motion pictures present frames at 24 per second, so high refresh rates cannot improve performance of motion pictures.

Response time is the time it takes for a pixel to change states. Response times for liquid crystal (LCD) displays are a few milliseconds and less than a millisecond for organic LED (OLED) displays. Both types of displays are described below.

Connectivity is the other important consideration for stand-alone displays. The connectivity of the display must match the device to which it will be connected. Common connectivity options are DisplayPort, HDMI, and USB-C. It is not unusual for a display device to have two or more connectivity options.

Finally, there will be a choice of display technologies and possibly touchscreen technologies. Modern general purpose and mobile displays are generally either liquid crystal displays or organic LED displays.

Liquid Crystal Displays

Liquid crystal displays depend on the ability of a class of material called liquid crystals to change the polarity of light when stimulated electrically. The basic operating principle is that light from an LED backlight is sent through a polarizing filter, then through a thin layer of liquid crystal material that can selectively change the direction of polarization when an electric field is applied to the liquid crystal material. The light then passes through color filters to produce red, green, and blue sub-pixels, and a second polarizing filter with the same axis of transmission as the first filter. The liquid crystals polarize the light with an axis of transmission 90 degrees from the two filters except in those areas where an electric field applied to the liquid crystals allows light to pass through. The electric field is applied by a thin film transistor (TFT) matrix with a transistor in every red, green, or blue sub-pixel position.

The description just given is of an active-matrix in-plane switching LCD display, the prevalent technology for mobile, desktop, and larger displays. It provides a wider viewing angle than earlier technologies, and does not show shadowing when touched, an important consideration for touchscreen displays. Because there are no phosphors, LCD displays are very resistant to burn-in, the presence of a static image on a screen caused by displaying the same content for long periods of time.

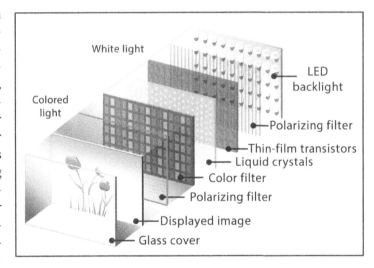

Figure 4-13
Structure of an LCD display

Pattarawit/stock.adobe.com

The change in the liquid crystals that allows or blocks light is a physical change that takes time measured in milliseconds.

Quantum dot monitors are beginning to be available at the end of 2022, but at high prices. Quantum dots are nano-scale particles that, when excited by light from a blue LED, can emit light. The color of the emitted light depends on the size and composition of the quantum dot.

There are many other designs for LCD displays including displays without backlight that depend on reflected light and displays that can show only pre-designed images like the seven-segment images used to display numbers. The other designs are important for specialized applications such as calculators, but seldom used in general-purpose displays.

Organic LED (OLED) Displays

OLED displays depend on organic compounds that exhibit electroluminescence; that is, they emit light when stimulated electrically. Because OLEDs emit light, no backlight is needed. Instead, a pattern of red, green, and blue OLEDs make up each sub-pixel.

Because there is no mechanical change as there is in liquid crystal displays, response time for OLED displays can be a millisecond or less.

OLED displays can be made transparent and flexible. The transparency property allows

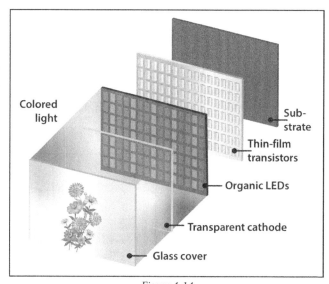

Figure 4-14
Active matrix OLED display

Pradeep Sharma

things like optical fingerprint readers to be placed under the display screen. The flexibility property allows folding screens, although smart phones with folding screens only began to be practical in 2023.

Touchscreens

Modern touchscreens allow for a wide range of responses to touch depending on the pressure and duration of the touch. Touchscreens for mobile and general-purpose display applications usually rely on resistive or capacitive technology. Both resistive and capacitive touchscreens are built as a part of the display. While mice transmit information about motion, touchscreens transmit X-Y coordinates. Multi-touch screens can transmit two or more sets of coordinates, and motion on the screen transmits sets of coordinates in rapid sequence.

Resistive touchscreens are constructed of two conductive, transparent layers separated by a small distance. When the screen is touched, the outer layer deforms to contact the inner layer. Measurement of resistance determines the X-coordinate of the touch, then voltage is quickly switched to measure the Y-coordinate. A major advantage of resistive touchscreens is that the object that touches the screen need not be electrically conductive, so a person wearing a glove or using a plastic stylus can operate one. The requirement for physical motion makes resistive touchscreens more susceptible to damage than other technologies.

Capacitive touch screens are the most common type of touch screen on mobile devices. Capacitive touchscreens depend on the fact that the human body is a conductor of electricity. There are several approaches to implementing a capacitive touch screen, but all depend on an electrostatic charge on a transparent surface. Contact with finger, thumb, or palm disturbs the electrostatic field in a way that can be measured and translated into an X-Y coordinate. A drawback is that contact with skin is required. Manufacturers of capacitive touch screens are continually improving sensitivity so that for some modern displays, a gloved finger will work. There are also conductive styluses and gloves with conductive thread woven into the fabric to allow for working with capacitive touchscreens.

4.3.2 Printers

The first consideration in selecting a printer is the use to which the printer will be put. Machinery for printing a few pages a month at home, hundreds of guest checks a day at a restaurant, and thousands of bills a day at a utility company will be very different.

The use case includes consideration of the nature of the material to be printed, including whether color printing is required, volume in pages per month, and speed requirements in pages per minute. Color printers often have different pages per minute specifications for monochrome and color printing. The use case should include a budget.

Cost of consumables should be part of the budget. It will be more important with thousands of pages a day than with dozens of pages a month. Consumables for color printing are more expensive than for monochrome printing.

Next, consider paper and paper handling. Paper can be continuous or sheet-fed, narrow format like a receipt printer, standard pages, or wide format such as for printing posters or blueprints. Paper handling considerations include whether automatic duplexing[81] is required, how many paper trays are required for sheet-fed printers, and tray capacity. Paper handling also includes finish options like collating, punching, and stapling.

That information will drive selection of a printing technology. There are three major general purpose printer technologies in use in the 21st century: laser printers, ink jet printers, and thermal printers.

The physical space available may drive some selection decisions. Connectivity options are also important. An office or data center printer might require Ethernet connectivity. A

81   In printing terms, duplexing means printing on both sides of a sheet.

printer for a small or home office might need wireless or Bluetooth connectivity to connect to mobile devices.

Finally, for small or home offices, an all-in-one device that includes copying, scanning, and facsimile might be more space-efficient and cost-effective than several stand-alone devices.

Laser Printers

Laser printers use laser light to selectively remove the charge from a negatively charged drum. A rotating mirror and other optics allow the laser beam to scan the surface of the drum and remove the charge from those areas that represent pixels to be printed. The drum is then exposed to very fine toner particles which have also been negatively charged. Toner particles adhere to the areas that were exposed to the laser beam but are repelled by those areas of the drum that still have a negative charge. The image is transferred to paper which moves under the rotating drum. The paper then passes between heated fuser rollers that melt the toner, causing it to adhere to the paper. Monochrome laser printers use black toner. Toner cartridges include a supply of toner and a waste receptacle in which toner left after printing is stored. Toner cartridges often include the drum component as well as the toner. Printers with separate toner and drum cartridges are likely to have lower consumable cost because the life-time of the drum is likely to be greater than the supply of toner in the combined cartridges.

Printing is a continuous process in which the drum is charged, exposed to toner to develop an image, the image transferred to paper, the drum is cleaned of remaining toner, then charged again. Because it is a continuous process, the printer must have a buffer big enough to hold the entire page image. The page image is composed using a page description language such as PostScript or another language proprietary to the printer manufacturer.

The most common laser printers are sheet-fed; that is, they process one sheet of paper at a time. There are continuous-form laser printers that print on fanfold computer paper at speeds up to 100 pages per minute or more.

Special toner is available to print checks with magnetic ink character recognition (MICR) characters. Although there is now widespread use of optical character recognition by banks, MICR encoding of checks is still legally required.

LED printers work like laser printers but use a line of LEDs to generate the necessary light. The moving mirror is eliminated, making construction simpler.

Color laser printers use four colors of toner, cyan, magenta, yellow, and black. The CMYK color model is discussed in Section 1.7.2. The printing process is essentially the same as for monochrome laser printers except that four colors are applied. This usually means multiple laser and optical assemblies. Color laser printers do generally well at reproducing line art, charts, and corporate logos. Ink jet printers do a better job with photographs and complex artwork.

Many, perhaps most, color laser printers and color copiers print an identifying pattern, often a pattern of tiny yellow dots called a machine identification code, on each page. The machine identification code, or "secret dots," includes the date and time a document was printed and the serial number of the printer. The dots are visible, but very hard to see. With that information, it may be possible to determine who printed a document.

Ink Jet Printers

Ink jet printers work by propelling tiny droplets of ink onto paper or another surface to be printed. Home and office inkjet printers are likely to be droplet-on-demand printers that propel droplets of ink only when needed. There are two major technologies for doing that, thermal expansion and piezoelectric systems.

Thermal expansion ink jet printers use resistive heating to heat the ink in the print head enough to cause formation of a gas bubble. The pressure from the bubble forces a droplet of ink through a nozzle and onto the surface to be printed. A thermal expansion ink jet printer can produce thousands of very tiny drops per second.

Piezoelectric materials are crystalline or ceramic materials that generate an electric charge when stressed. The reverse is also true; a voltage applied to piezoelectric material will cause it to deform, returning to its original shape when the voltage is removed. This effect can be used to propel ink droplets onto a surface to be printed. Piezoelectric nozzles can generate more force than is available with thermal expansion. There is more latitude in ink formulation that is available with thermal ink jet printers because the ink need not change phase between liquid and gas quickly.

Ink jet printers generally go through a cleaning cycle when turned off so that there is no ink residue on the print heads while the printer is idle. Interrupting printer power instead of allowing the printer to go through its power-down cycle can cause degraded printing quality.

Ink jet cartridges often include both print head and ink reservoir. Printers with separate print heads and ink supplies are likely to have lower consumable cost.

Color ink jet printers use the CMYK color model described in Section 1.7.2. To get a wide color gamut and vivid colors, it is common to use more than four colors.

Thermal Printers

Thermal printers use heat to darken areas of treated paper. These are sometimes called receipt printers and are generally narrow-format devices, printing on forms up to about four inches wide and fed from rolls of treated paper. Some facsimile machines use thermal printing technology. The printing mechanism consists of many tiny resistive heaters, from about 200 elements per inch to over 1,000 per inch. Paper is pulled past the printing element by a roller and the resistive elements quickly heated and cooled to make a pattern of dots that form printed characters.

The only moving parts are the roller that pulls paper past the printing element and possibly a cutter that cuts the paper after printing. A sawtooth tear bar might be used as an alternative to the cutter.

Thermal printers have few moving parts and no ink supply. The only routine attention needed is replacement of the paper. Some printers can generate a signal when paper is low or out.

4.3.3 Keyboards and Mice

Keyboards in the 21st century are typically attached using a USB or a wireless connection like Bluetooth. Each key on the keyboard generates a unique **scan code** when the key is depressed and a different scan code when the key is released. That allows for keys to repeat if held down, and for key-chords like shift or control and another key. It is up to the operating system to map the scan codes to the encoding scheme of the operating system, often UTF-8. The operating system also controls the repeat rate when a key is held down.

In operating systems with a windowing interface, the operating system determines which window has focus when keyboard input is received and sends the keyboard input to the application that owns that window. In command-line systems, the keyboard may be dedicated to a particular application while that application runs, then released to the operating system when the application program terminates.

 Mice and other pointing devices translate motion in two dimensions into position of a cursor on a screen. The original mouse, invented by Douglas Engelbart in 1964, had two wheels at right angles to each other and a single button on top. It was connected by cable to the computer system. Because the two wheels were at right angles to each other, the mouse had to be tilted or rocked to keep from dragging one of the wheels. Later mice had a rolling ball that could turn two internal shafts at tight angles to one another. If moved in a straight line, it would turn one shaft and slip on the other. If moved at an angle, the ball could turn the two shafts proportionately. Modern mice use LED or laser light and an optical sensor to measure motion and have no internal moving parts. Modern mice also have two (usually) or more switches and a scroll wheel which may also be attached to a switch. Modern mice can be connected to the computer system with a cord or wirelessly using Bluetooth or other short-range radio technology.

Figure 4-15
Douglas Engelbart's Mouse (1964)

Unlike touch screens, mice send units of motion rather than position to the computer. The number of signals sent to the computer system per inch of motion varies with design of the

138

mouse. For that reason, the units are called **"mickeys"** rather than units implying pulses per inch. Rates from 100 Hz to 1,000 Hz are supported by most operating systems using the USB human interface device class. Mice do not generate interrupts when there is no motion.

The operating system will present a configuration control to allow the user to match the user's desired cursor speed to the number of mickeys per second generated by a particular mouse.

The operating system's handling of mouse actions in a windowing environment is a bit more complicated than that for the keyboard. The mouse cursor is allowed to range over all the windows available. A click, usually left, in a window that does not have focus transfers focus to that window. Actions in a window that has focus are passed to the application owning the window.

4.3.4 Other Devices

There are many other input and output devices, too numerous to mention here. These include speakers, microphones, scanners, cameras, and many other classes of devices. There are also types of devices in the categories above that are not covered. For example, dot matrix printers were not covered because they are obsolete.

4.4 Summary of Learning Objectives

*This section of the chapter tells you the things you should know about, but not **what** you should know about them. To test your knowledge, discuss the following concepts and topics with a study partner or in writing, ideally from memory.*

There are four categories of information that must be exchanged between the CPU and a device controller during an I/O operation. There are two very different architectural approaches to handling input and output. There are also two basic classes of I/O devices depending on how much data is transferred in one operation.

Signals called interrupts are critical to efficient I/O operation. Some I/O device controllers can access memory directly. Access to I/O devices is accomplished with I/O buses.

There is a hierarchy of storage that relates capacity, speed, and cost. The hierarchy distinguishes between volatile and non-volatile storage and also between primary and secondary storage. Primary storage is often called memory.

Bulk online storage is provided by two different technologies, one with mechanical parts and one that is all-electronic. The two technologies have very different access times. The all-electronic storage technology has a few different form factors and a few different interface options.

RAID technology can introduce redundancy in storage, but is no longer recommended for very large storage devices. It is important not to conflate RAID technology with the need for backing up data.

Optical drives have evolved through at least three different formats and a number of different recording schemes. Most optical storage media have a structure fundamentally different from magnetic disks. The capacity of online bulk storage has increased at a different rate from the capacity of optical storage.

Near-line storage makes data available online in times varying from seconds to tens of seconds. Offline storage has much longer latency times but effectively unlimited capacity.

There are two major display technologies and also two major printing technologies. Use-case is particularly important when selecting printing equipment.

Mice and touchscreens are both pointing devices but have very different construction and send information to the CPU in very different ways.

4.5 References

Patterson, D. A., Gibson, G., & Katz, R. H. (1988). A case for redundant arrays of inexpensive disks (RAID). *ACM SIGMOD Record,* 17(3), 109–116. https://doi.org/10.1145/971701.50214

Roberts, J. D., Ryley, A., Jones, D. M., & Burke, D. (1996). Analysis of error-correction constraints in an optical disk. *Applied Optics,* 35(20), 3915–3924. https://doi.org/10.1364/AO.35.003915

Schroeder, B., & Gibson, G. A. (2007, February). Disk failures in the real world: What does an MTTF of 1,000,000 hours mean to you? 5th *USENIX Conference on File and Storage Technologies (FAST 07).*

Tanenbaum, A. S. (1999). *Structured Computer Organization* (4th ed.). Prentice-Hall.

Chapter 5
Networks and Data Communications

"...the value of a network to a user is proportional to the number of people one can contact."
—Bob Metcalfe

The 21st century is typified by devices that are always connected, often wirelessly, to each other and the global Internet. It is common to see the global Internet, and even smaller networks, represented clouds. A better representation might be a duck. On top of the water, the duck floats along nice and easy, but a lot of paddling happens underneath. Similarly, modern networks have a lot of interconnections and moving parts. Information technology professionals are expected to keep that duck floating serenely along, providing efficient, effective, and secure communications. Network problem solving requires a clear mental model of the interconnections and moving parts.

Figure 5-1
Bob Metcalfe, inventor
of Ethernet and formulator of
Metcalfe's Law

The Internet is so named because it is an **internetwork**, an interconnection of many networks. This chapter explores network technology, the mechanism by which networks operate, and the techniques for interconnecting disparate networks.

We expect our gear to communicate seamlessly and, for the most part, it does. This is because of the development of standards, the importance of which was covered in Chapter 0. A study of data communications and networks is largely a study of the relevant standards.

The Covid-19 pandemic that began in 2020 in the United States appears to have fundamentally changed the attitude of employers toward remote workers. That brings new challenges in the application and security of data communications. The security aspects of data communications are covered briefly in Section 7.7.

5.1 Messages, Protocols, Channels, and Links

At the simplest level, data communications consists of messages, protocols, and channels. Messages are exchanged between or among hosts, and nodes, which are computers equipped with the necessary hardware and software for communication. More specifically, a **node** is any device attached to a network while a **host** is a computer, such as a PC or Mac, a laptop, or even a smartphone or Raspberry Pi. A **message** might be an operating system update, a streaming video, a music download, or digital voice on its way to a grandmother's landline.

Protocols are rules. In data communications, they are rules for communication. The same word is used in diplomacy. Two hosts that share the same protocols and have suitable network interface control (NIC) hardware can communicate with each other. Figure 5-2 shows the protocol for party line telephone service.[82] Protocols are established by standard-setting organizations, among them the Institute of Electrical and Electronic Engineers (IEEE), the Internet Engineering Task Force (IETF), the International Organization for Standardization (ISO), and the International Electrotechnical Commission (IEC.) Protocols apply to the hosts at the ends of a data connection and to the data connection itself. They also govern **intermediate nodes**, which are specialized computing devices for routing signals.

Figure 5-2
Protocol for party line telephones

A **channel** is a communication facility capable of carrying messages. In network diagrams, a channel is often represented as a lightning bolt or a pipe. The physical connection between two nodes is called a **link**. The mechanism might be radio, fiber optic cable, or copper cable. A link may carry more than one channel. It is likely that more than one communication link is involved with a connection to a remote resource. A mobile device's connection to an Internet web site will involve cellular radio and probably both copper and fiber optic connections. The **bandwidth** of a link is the theoretical amount of information the link can carry per second, measured in Hertz. A channel may carry more than one link. The **speed** of a link is the transmission rate, measured in bits per second. Modern networks operate at speeds measured in megabits, millions of bits per second, or gigabits, billions of bits per second. **Latency** is the delay in transmission as signals pass through the network from source to destination.

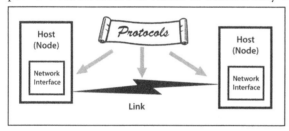

Figure 5-3
Abstract diagram of the communication process

Figure 5-3 is a high-level diagram of a data connection, showing two nodes, their network interface hardware, and the connection between them. Protocols and standards govern all parts of the process, from the signaling mechanism and shapes of the connectors to the format of the messages exchanged.

Circuit switching and packet switching

To place a telephone call in 1925, one lifted the receiver of a landline telephone instrument.

---

82 Up to the middle of the 20th century, it was not uncommon for two or more families to share a single telephone line, especially in rural areas. One had to listen to be sure the line was not in use before attempting to place a call. That is remarkably similar to how Ethernet works in a non-switched environment.

That caused an electric current to flow and alerted a telephone operator, who said "Number, please?" You spoke the number you wanted. If the destination telephone wasn't already in use, the operator physically connected the wires from your phone to those of the person you were calling using plugs and sockets. The connection remained in place until you hung up the telephone instrument. Because of the need for an end-to-end connection, long distance calls were complex and expensive. A ten-minute call from New York to San Francisco in 1925 cost $27.75. (Waldon & Lande, 1997) That's nearly $475 in 2023 dollars.

Figure 5-4
A telephone switchboard
Seattle Municipal Archives

Now consider mailing a letter from New York to San Francisco. In 1925, that cost two cents for a letter of up to one ounce, the equivalent of about thirty cents today. You had an expectation that the letter would be delivered but little or no idea of the path it would take. A little thought would convince you that many other letters traveled along with yours on various parts of that journey, and that a second letter mailed to the same person might take a somewhat different path.

The telephone call example illustrates a **circuit switched** network.[83] When a call is placed, a connection is established between caller and called party. It remains active for the duration of the call. Circuit switching is **connection-oriented** and reserves the full bandwidth of the link even when it is not carrying information, and so introduces inefficiency. While the connection is established, no other connection can be made. If computer connections were circuit-switched, one person streaming a video would lock out everyone else in the household until the video ended.

The letter example illustrates **packet switching**. Packet switching divides messages into packets of perhaps several hundred bytes. Each packet is transmitted independently. This allows use of the available bandwidth to be maximized. It also allows packets from different messages to be interleaved on the same link. One person might be streaming a video while another is browsing a news site with neither aware of the other's activity. Packet switching is **connectionless**; that is, packets can be sent from one node to another without prior arrangement. Modern data communications systems employ packet switching. Although the communication hardware is no longer circuit switched, we will see the concept of persistent connections at a higher level of abstraction as we explore communication protocols, particularly the transmission control protocol, TCP.

---

83   In 21st century landline calls all that remains of the circuit-switched network is the connection between the telephone instrument and the telephone office or multiplexing point. Until the middle of the 20th century, landline calls were circuit-switched end-to-end.

"Reliable" and "unreliable" protocols

The words "reliable" and "unreliable" are used in a way that's different from their common meanings when describing data communications protocols. An analogy with the postal service may help. If you place a properly addressed letter in the mail, it is nearly certain to be delivered, but the postal service doesn't confirm the delivery. That is an unreliable mechanism. If you pay extra for certified mail with a return receipt, you are nearly certain to get a green post card in the mail confirming that your mail piece was delivered. Note that your original mail piece can still be lost, or the return receipt card can be lost. If, after a few days, you don't get that green post card, you know that something is wrong. You don't know what, but you know there's a problem. That is a reliable mechanism.

We can now provide a definition. A **reliable protocol** acknowledges receipt of messages and an **unreliable protocol** does not. In a reliable protocol, absence of an acknowledgment is an error which is handled by having the sending node retransmit the unacknowledged message(s). The receiving node must identify and discard duplicate messages. A duplicate message results when it is the acknowledgment and not the original message that is lost.

Local and wide area networks

At the beginning of the 1970s, when researchers began to get serious about data networks, there was a clear distinction between local area networks, called LANs, and wide area networks, called WANs. In **local area networks**, the operators of the networks owned the wires that connected the hosts on the network together. So, LANs connected devices in one department, or a single building, or maybe a college or corporate campus. To connect to a location across town, one needed the help of a telephone company. Telephone service was mostly a monopoly then, dominated by AT&T. Connections were expensive and speeds were very limited. Those who operated networks soon realized that it was far more effective to connect two networks than two devices when telephone company lines were involved. So, "**wide area network**" even then was a misnomer; people were building internetworks, in the same fashion as the global Internet but on smaller scales.

Things are a little less clear today. There are still local area networks where the network owners also own the wires and wireless access points. There are still private internetworks operated by entities like banks and governments, but many organizations use the Internet as a mechanism to connect local area networks.

Your cell phone isn't a local area network, but it isn't an internetwork, either. Today we talk about local area networks, Internet service providers, and "**endpoints**," which can include a cell phone, a wired desktop computer, or a laptop with wireless access to a local wireless access point.

5.2 Protocol Stacks and the OSI Model

The concept of a **protocol stack** is an abstraction of the modularized hardware and software functions necessary for data communication. Not only is modularization good programming practice, in the case of data communications systems, it means that one part of the process can be replaced without disrupting everything else. For example, the transmission medium could be changed from copper wire to cellular radio without changing the way application programs deal with the network. A protocol stack isolates the parts of a network exchange. At the application level, for example, an email program exchanges header information, then message data, with the email server. The two applications are exchanging lines of text, and need not be concerned about how those lines are organized as frames at the data link layer, nor about how the bits are transmitted at the physical layer.

There are two protocol stacks of interest to the student of information technology, the Open Systems Interconnection (OSI) model and the Internet Protocol Suite model. The Internet Protocol Suite model is often called the TCP/IP model because the transmission control protocol (TCP) and the Internet Protocol (IP) are the fundamental protocols of the model.

5.2.1 The OSI Model

The **OSI model** is a reference model, that is, an abstract model describing interaction with a network. It does not describe any physical or programming interfaces. For that reason, the OSI model is primarily of theoretical interest. It provides arguably the cleanest separation of the various required functions of a protocol suite. More importantly, it includes the physical layer, which is subsumed in the link layer of the TCP/IP protocol suite. The seven-layer OSI model is shown in Figure 5-5.[84]

The bottom-most layer, the **physical layer**, is concerned with the physical connectors, the transmission medium, and the signaling protocol. Its job is to move bits from one network node to another.

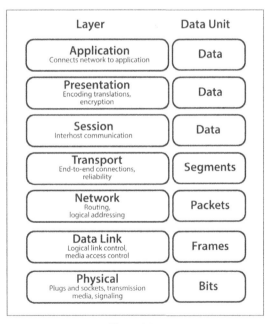

Figure 5-5

The OSI protocol stack

---

84 The names of the layers are something to look up, not to memorize. If you should ever have to memorize the layer names, the mnemonic, from bottom to top, is, "People Do Not Throw Sausage Pizza Away."

The **data link layer** organizes bits into frames, the logical unit of transmission. The data link layer is responsible for logical link control and media access control. The media access control sublayer performs media arbitration, which is deciding which nodes may transmit, and frame synchronization, which is dividing the bit stream from the physical layer into frames. The logical link control sublayer is responsible for addressing and may provide flow control and error control.

The **network layer** provides for logical addressing, for example, using IP addresses. It also provides routing between networks. The network layer is connectionless in the sense that its job is transporting individual packets.

The **transport layer** is responsible for segmenting messages, for example, cutting a large video download into smaller segments for transmission, then reassembling them at the other end. It is responsible for error control and flow control. **Flow control** means signaling a sending node to pause if data are being sent faster than they can be accepted.

The **session layer** controls exchanges of related messages between two network endpoints. The session layer establishes a connection, facilitates exchange of messages, and closes the connection at the end of the session.

The job of the **presentation layer** is data independence. For example, one end of a network connection may use double-byte UCS-2 characters while the other uses UTF-8. The presentation layer performs the necessary translation. Compressing and decompressing data and encrypting and decrypting also happen in the presentation layer.

The **application layer** provides the interface between the network and the application. The application could be a web browser or chat program, or it could be an internal application at a bank to move data between branches. The application program communicates with the application layer of the network protocol stack using an application program interface (API) to send and receive data. The application program does not need to be aware of any of the other parts of the network protocol stack. In fact, insulating applications from the details of networking is the reason for the concept of a protocol stack. From the viewpoint of the application developer, the application programs at the two ends of the network connection are communicating directly with one another using those API calls.

5.3 Ethernet, Local Networks, and the Data Link Layer

A general-purpose local area network of the 21st century is nearly always an Ethernet network, often running at gigabit speeds.[85] A local area network serves a home, a department, a building, or perhaps a campus, and connects to other networks such as the global Internet through the use of routers.

---

85 Specialized networks using technologies other than Ethernet are found in automotive, aviation, and manufacturing settings, among others.

Bob Metcalfe invented Ethernet in 1973 at Xerox Corporation's Palo Alto Research Center (PARC). Xerox filed a patent application for Ethernet in 1975. In 1976, Metcalfe and David Boggs published a paper describing Ethernet in *Communications of the ACM* (Metcalfe & Boggs, 1976). Xerox Corporation, together with Digital Equipment Corporation and Intel developed Ethernet into an open standard in 1980, and it was adopted as an Institute of Electrical and Electronics Engineers (IEEE) standard in 1985. Ethernet is named for *luminiferous ether*.[86] Metcalfe won the 2022 Turing Award for the invention of Ethernet.

The original design for Ethernet was based on a shared transmission medium, with all nodes connected to a single, long and thick coaxial data cable. A transmission by any node on the network was received by all other nodes, but was ignored by all but the node to which it was addressed. The icon still used to mark wired Ethernet connections depicts three computers connected to a common cable.

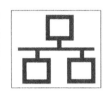

Figure 5-6

The Ethernet icon

The thick coaxial cable was cumbersome, difficult to install, and difficult to maintain. A fault anywhere on the cable could bring down the whole network. Development quickly progressed to the use of twisted-pair cable connected with devices called hubs, and by 1994, to the use of fiber optic cable.

Today, Ethernet can run at speeds of up to 400 gigabits per second. Gigabit Ethernet over twisted pair cable is common and inexpensive. Wireless Ethernet, called Wi-Fi, is also common.

5.3.1 The Ethernet Data Link Layer

Every Ethernet **network interface controller** (NIC) has a 48-bit address assigned when the device is manufactured and called the **media access control (MAC) address**. The first three bytes are assigned to the device manufacturer by the IEEE and are called organizationally unique addresses. Two bits of the first byte are reserved and are always zero in the prefixes assigned to manufacturers, leaving 22 bits, enough to assign four million organizationally unique addresses. Large manufacturers have more than one organizationally unique address. The remaining three bytes are assigned during manufacture such that the resulting address is globally unique.

MAC addresses are written as six hexadecimal pairs, separated by colons. An example is 00:11:25:d3:12:77.

An Ethernet NIC will receive all traffic on its part of the network, but ignore data not addressed to it. Exceptions are the broadcast address, 48 bits of all ones, which is acted upon

---

86 Luminiferous ether was the hypothetical substance supposed to transmit light in the way that air transmits sound. In 1905, Einstein's special theory of relativity showed that it was not necessary to assume the existence of luminiferous ether to explain the propagation of electromagnetic waves.

by every NIC, and a possibly configurable list of **multicast addresses** that allow a single message to be processed by more than one NIC. A NIC can also be placed in **promiscuous mode**, which allows it to accept and process all traffic it receives. This is useful for network monitoring applications.

Preamble 7 bytes	SFD 1 byte	Destination address 6 bytes	Source address 6 bytes	Ether type 16 bits	Payload 46 to 1,500 bytes	FCS 4 bytes

Figure 5-7

An Ethernet frame

The unit of transmission in Ethernet is the frame. Figure 5-7 shows an Ethernet **frame**. The preamble is 56 bits of alternating one and zero. This allows the sending and receiving NICs to synchronize bit timing. The one-byte start of frame delimiter (SFD) provides for byte synchronization and marks the start of the meaningful data in the frame. It is followed by the destination and source addresses, the Ether type field, the payload data being transmitted, and a frame check sequence (FCS) value. The FCS is a cyclic redundancy check. It is computed by the sending NIC and verified by the receiver. A mismatch indicates that a transmission error has occurred. In that case, the receiving NIC discards the frame. It is up to a higher-layer protocol to recognize that a frame is missing and request retransmission.

An alternate IEEE standard allows the field labeled Ether type in Figure 5-7 to contain the payload length. To allow the two uses of the field to be distinguished, the Ether type field must be greater than 1,535.

Non-standard jumbo frames can carry payloads larger than 1,500 bytes. This has the advantage of reducing the frame overhead caused by the preamble, SFD, and header information. The trade-off is that larger frames may have an adverse impact on latency.

5.3.2 Collisions and Switching

In the original design of Ethernet, all nodes are connected either to a single data cable or to each other through a hub. That arrangement is called **multiple access**. The multiple access protocol requires that each node check that the cable is idle, *i.e.* that no other node is transmitting, before beginning a transmission. Checking whether another node is transmitting is called **carrier sense**. If another node is transmitting, a node with a frame to send has to wait until the cable is idle. With this arrangement, it is still possible for two nodes to transmit at once if both detect that the cable is idle simultaneously. That circumstance is called a **collision**, and Ethernet NICs are designed to be able to detect collisions. When two transmitting nodes detect a collision, both stop, wait a random time, then listen for the cable to be idle. Since it is very unlikely that the two random times will be equal, one node will "win" and begin to transmit. The other node must wait until the cable again becomes idle. The collection of nodes for which mutual collisions is possible is called a **collision domain**.

The combination of carrier sense, multiple access, and collision detection is abbreviated **CSMA/CD**.

The CSMA/CD design works well for small networks and low traffic volumes. As network nodes and traffic increase, the number of collisions increases. At some point more time is spent recovering from collisions than transmitting data and network throughput degrades badly.

Switched Ethernet

The solution to the problem of collisions degrading network throughput is to decrease the size of collision domains or remove them completely using **Ethernet switches**. In a wired or optical Ethernet, each node is connected to a port on the switch. Both the node and the switch can transmit and receive simultaneously, an arrangement called **full duplex**. In such an arrangement, no collisions are possible because there is no longer a shared medium; communication is between a single host or node and a port on the switch.

Switching applies only to wired and optical Ethernet. Collisions remain possible in wireless Ethernet when more than one wireless device is using one wireless access point. Wi-Fi uses a technique called **collision avoidance** to minimize the number of collisions.

In normal operation, an Ethernet switch receives a frame on one port and transmits it again on a different port based on the destination address in the frame. When an Ethernet switch is first started, it has no information about which port connects each node. When the port is unknown, the switch sends the frame on all ports except the one on which it came in. As frames are received, firmware or software in the switch records which MAC addresses are on what ports, something like "00:11:25:d3:12:77 is on port 16." Within a very short time, the switch is able to direct most frames to a single destination port rather than all ports. Broadcasting is still necessary from time to time as nodes join or leave the network.

A major drawback of a switched Ethernet network is the potential for a switching loop. If two ports on a switch are connected to each other, or there are two connections between switches, such a loop exists. If a frame for which there is no entry is received, it will be broadcast to every port except the one on which it arrived. If two ports are connected together, each will receive and rebroadcast the frame continuously. That is called a **broadcast storm**, and it will render the network useless until it is stopped, possibly by resetting the switch. However, another packet with no routing entry will cause another broadcast storm.

The spanning tree protocol and shortest path bridging protocol

Loops that can cause broadcast storms can be introduced accidentally or even deliberately as a way to provide redundancy. The invention of the **spanning tree algorithm** by Radia Perlman in 1985 allowed software or firmware in switches to find those paths through the network sufficient to reach every node, that is, to span the network. Switch ports unnecessary to the spanning tree are disabled and loops cannot exist. A change in the topology of the network, such as by a connection failing, causes the spanning tree to be recomputed. That makes redundant connections possible, but only one connection of a redundant set can be used at a time. Perlman's description of the spanning tree algorithm is in Figure 5-8 (Perlman, 1985).

Another approach to preventing broadcast storms caused by loops is the **shortest path bridging protocol,** which was developed by the IEEE 802 working group beginning in 2006 and finalized in 2012. The spanning tree protocol disables redundant links; the shortest path bridging protocol allows traffic on redundant links, thereby maximizing network throughput while preventing or mitigating loops. Shortest path bridging is currently found only in enterprise and service provider grade equipment.

Algorhyme

*I think that I shall never see
A graph more lovely than a tree.*

*A tree whose crucial property
Is loop-free connectivity.*

*A tree which must be sure to span
So packets can reach every LAN.*

*First the root must be selected.
By ID it is elected.*

*Least cost paths from root are traced.
In the tree these paths are placed.*

*A mesh is made by folks like me
Then bridges find a spanning tree.*

*Figure 5-8
Algorhyme by Radia Perlman
Copyright 1985 by the Association for Computing Machinery*

5.3.3 The Ethernet Physical Layer

Standardization at the physical layer as well as the data link layer means you can buy a computer from one manufacturer, an Ethernet switch from another, and cable from a third and expect them to work together seamlessly provided they are for the same physical specification.

The physical specification for Ethernet is a three- to five-part description consisting of speed, modulation technique, physical medium, encoding method, and either number of lanes for local connections or maximum distance for wide-area connections. For example, gigabit Ethernet has a physical specification of 1000BASE-T. The 1000 is the speed in millions of bits per second, BASE indicates baseband, *i.e.* no other signals on the cable, and the -T says the transmission medium is category five twisted pair cable.

The Ethernet physical layer for ten and 100 megabit speeds describes a medium-dependent interface (MDI) which connects the transmitter of one device to the receiver of the other, and vice-versa. End devices like computers are generally MDI devices and central devices like switch are generally MDI/X devices with transmission and reception lines "crossed over." Modern 10/100 megabit devices and all gigabit and higher devices negotiate the "crossover" automatically when the cable is connected.

Modern consumer-grade and small-office Ethernet switches automatically negotiate to the highest speed common to the two devices for 100 megabit and gigabit speeds, and sometimes for 10/100/1000 speeds. IEEE Ethernet standards as of 2018 specify speeds up to 400 gigabits per second.

Wireless Ethernet

Devices participating in a wireless Ethernet are called **stations**. Wireless Ethernet uses radio signals to transfer information. For that reason, it must still operate in the carrier sense multiple access (CSMA) mode because there is no concept of a private connection to a switching device. Wireless Ethernet, or Wi-Fi, attempts to avoid collisions using the same listen-before-sending mechanism as the original wired Ethernet. In addition, a station may optionally send a request to send (RTS) control frame. The access point or controlling station will reply with a clear to send (CTS) control frame, reserving the radio link for the original station to transmit a data frame.

Wireless Ethernet is standardized by the IEEE as a set of standards numbered 802.11 and suffixed by letters. The Wi-Fi Alliance has published a set of version numbers, Wi-Fi 1 to Wi-Fi 6, which they believe to be more consumer friendly. In the United States, most wireless Ethernet equipment operates in the 2.4 gigahertz (GHz) or 5 GHz frequency bands. In 2020, the U.S. Federal Communications Commission approved a frequency allocation in the 6 GHz band for wireless Ethernet. There are also frequency allocations in the 60 GHz band, intended for wireless audio-visual applications. Although higher frequencies allow for higher data rates, they are more easily blocked by walls and other obstructions.

Particularly for wireless networking, security from eavesdropping is a concern. When a signal is transmitted by radio, not only Wi-Fi, but also Bluetooth or cellular signals, any suitable receiver within range can pick up the signal. To prevent eavesdropping, such signals are nearly always encrypted. The wireless Ethernet standards include a provision for encryption and for authentication with an access point. Encryption is discussed further in Chapter 7.

5.4 The Internet Protocol Suite – TCP/IP

The TCP/IP protocol suite is the protocol suite of the global Internet. It was specifically designed to be independent of the physical connection. A joke at the time was that it could run over two tin cans and a string. The TCP/IP model is a four-layer model, with the underlying physical and data link layers assumed, but not a part of the model. The Internet Protocol Suite model is shown in Figure 5-9.

The lowest level is the **link layer**. The link layer includes the address resolution protocol (ARP), which translates Internet Protocol addresses to the addresses used by the data link layer of the OSI model. Everything else is assumed to exist and is not explicitly specified in the protocol. The scope of the link layer is all hosts directly accessible on the local network. The data units are those of the local network, often Ethernet frames.

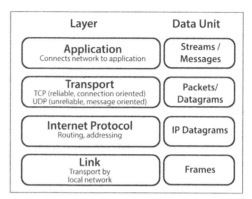

Figure 5-9
The Internet suite protocol stack

The **address resolution protocol** (ARP) solves the problem of communication on a local area network when a logical address such as an Internet Protocol address is known but the link layer address, *e.g.,* a MAC, address is not. A node or host wanting to communicate with a node or host with unknown link layer address sends a broadcast message containing the Internet Protocol address for which the link layer is wanted. The node with that address replies, and the link layer frame contains that node's link layer address. The correspondence of logical address and link layer address is stored in an **ARP table** for future communications with that host.

The **Internet Protocol layer** is responsible for addressing and routing IP datagrams. Each datagram is an independent message to be transmitted from source to destination. So, a large video download will be divided into many datagrams, each handled separately by the Internet Protocol layer. The Internet Protocol layer does not distinguish among the several protocols of the transport layer.

There are two incompatible addressing schemes at the Internet Protocol layer. IPv4 was the original addressing scheme of the Internet, numbers one to three having been used for experimental protocols. IPv4 is based on 32-bit addresses, which are discussed in Section 5.4.2. IPv6 was accepted as a standard in 1996; significant use of IPv6 addresses began in the early 21st century. The 64-bit IPv6 addressing mechanism is discussed in Section 5.4.3. IPv5 was a proposed streaming standard that was never officially adopted.

The Internet Control Message Protocol (ICMP) has as its primary purpose exchanging messages among network devices. It is visible to users in the PING and TRACEROUTE applications.

Routers are switching devices that operate at layer 3, the network layer of the OSI model, which is equivalent to the Internet Protocol layer of the TCP/IP model. The simplest routers for home or small office networks have two interfaces, a LAN interface that operates at the Ethernet data link and physical level, and a WAN interface. The WAN interface might be a cable or DSL modem or an optical interface for connection to an Internet service provider. Its principal purpose isn't really routing, it is to translate from the Ethernet physical and data link layer to the physical and data link protocol needed by the connection to the service provider. Such a device may include an Ethernet switch in the same physical package and have more than a single Ethernet port, and even a wireless access point.

Enterprise and carrier-grade routers have multiple ports and, like switches, choose a port on which to forward each datagram. The major difference is that routers use logical addresses and make routing decisions based on the network portion of the address as discussed below. The routing information protocol (RIP) and open shortest path first protocol (OSPF) are "interior" routing protocols, suitable for use within a single enterprise. The border gateway protocol (BGP) is an "exterior" protocol suitable for routing among peer systems. A thorough discussion of routing protocols is suitable for a networks course.

There are three major transport layer protocols, the transmission control protocol (TCP), the user datagram protocol (UDP), and stream control transmission protocol (SCTP). In addition, a protocol developed by Google, QUIC (a name, not an acronym), was adopted as a standard by the IETF in May, 2021. Strictly speaking, transport layer security (TLS) is implemented on top of the transport layer protocol, and is not itself a transport layer protocol. For the purposes of this book, it will be covered here, along with the transport layer protocols. There are several other Internet suite protocols not discussed here.

Transmission Control Protocol

The transmission control protocol (TCP) is a connection-oriented and reliable protocol. At the application layer, each application appears to be talking directly to the corresponding application at the other host. Communication is through an application program interface, or API. Often the API is a **socket**, an interface specification developed by Berkeley Systems Division and standardized as a part of POSIX, the IEEE portable operating system interface.

A connection is established through a TCP handshake process in which the two communicating hosts exchange sequence numbers. The sequence numbers are assigned randomly to help thwart session hijacking. The sequence numbers are used to re-order packets that may arrive out of order. Each station also acknowledges receipt of the other's packets. The TCP header includes an acknowledgment field so that a separate message is not needed for acknowledgments. Unacknowledged packets are retransmitted. If the problem that caused a retransmission was with the acknowledgment and not the original packet, the sequence number allows the duplicate packet to be identified and discarded. The TCP header contains a checksum that is verified on reception. Packets for which checksum verification fails are discarded and will be retransmitted because they aren't acknowledged.

Flag bits and other fields in the TCP header provide for flow control and optionally for explicit congestion control. One of the flag bits is used for gracefully closing the connection.

In addition to IP addresses for the endpoints, a TCP connection requires port numbers for each endpoint. Port numbers do not refer to any type of physical connection. Instead, they are 16-bit numbers that are used by the operating system to send data to the correct application. A TCP connection is completely characterized by the protocol number, the two IP addresses, and the two port numbers. A program such as a web browser wanting to make a connection to a server asks the operating system to assign a random port number for the outgoing part of the connection. The 65,536 possible port numbers are divided into well-known port numbers, registered port numbers, and dynamic port numbers. The application will usually use a **well-known port** for connection to the destination host. For example, by default an HTTP connection will be made by default to port 80 of the destination, an HTTPS connection to port 443. The Internet Assigned Numbers Authority (IANA) is responsible for assigning well-known ports, and most of the port numbers below 1024 have been assigned. Many higher-numbered ports are also used, registered to particular applications by the IANA. The destination server must be configured to listen on a particular port.

Port numbers 49,152 to 65,535 are available for operating systems to assign dynamically.

User Datagram Protocol

The user datagram protocol (UDP) is connectionless and unreliable. It provides for individual messages, called datagrams, which are not acknowledged at the protocol level. Since each datagram is handled separately, it is possible for datagrams to arrive out of order.

Because there is no handshake at the beginning of communication and no need for acknowledgments, UDP is considerably faster for short messages than TCP. It is particularly well-suited for query/response applications such as domain name system queries, discussed in Section 5.4.1. UDP is also used for streaming applications such as voice over IP, where the occasional loss of a packet is not critically important.

UDP also uses port numbers to direct messages to particular applications. Since UDP is a different protocol from TCP, the port numbers are disjoint. That is, a host may use a port number for TCP and the same number for UDP without conflict.

The theoretical maximum size of a UDP datagram is 65,536 bytes minus the length of the header, so usually 65,507 bytes for IPv4. However, large datagrams are likely to be fragmented at the IP layer. Since there is no error handling, the loss of one fragment is effectively the loss of the entire datagram. For that reason, many applications using UDP limit datagram size to around 512 bytes. That is small enough to avoid fragmentation at the IP level except in very unusual circumstances because the minimum allowed transmission unit for the Internet is 576 bytes.

Stream Control Transmission Protocol

The stream control transmission protocol, SCTP, is a connectionless protocol. Like UDP it transmits messages (datagrams) rather than providing a connection between the endpoints. Unlike UDP, SCTP provides a reliable connection. It includes other features for reliability, such as multi-homing. Multi-homing means one or both endpoints may have multiple IP addresses allowing transparent fail-over in case of a link failure.

Transport Layer Security

Transport layer security (TLS) is not an Internet Protocol transport layer; it operates on top of the transport layer and below the application layer. However, it is important in the context of securing communication between networks and so should be included in this chapter. TLS provides privacy of communications by encrypting the data traveling between endpoints. TLS uses message authentication codes to protect the integrity of communications. Digital certificates provide a measure of assurance of the identity of the server endpoint. Client certificates are optional. Modern implementations provide forward secrecy, making it impossible to decrypt future communications or past communications that may have been stored by an adversary even if the server's private key is compromised. Forward secrecy is discussed further in Section 7.7 and Section 7.8.2.

Many web site operators call their web sites "secure" when transmission between browser and web server is encrypted with TLS. However, TLS only secures *transmission* between browser and web server. It is still possible for the server itself to be carelessly managed or inadequately secured.

The QUIC Protocol

The QUIC[87] protocol was adopted by the IETF as a standard in May, 2021. Like TLS, QUIC is intermediate between the transport layer and the application layer. It uses UDP for transport. Error recovery, lost datagram recovery, and datagram reordering are performed at the QUIC level. QUIC was devised by Jim Roskind and others at Google to speed up web services by taking advantage of the characteristics of interactions between web servers and web browsers, such as establishing a TLS connection during the initial setup instead of requiring separate TCP and TLS handshake operations. It is supported by servers operated by Google, on the LiteSpeed and Ngnix server packages and by at least one commercial content distribution network. QUIC is supported by the major web browsers.

As of June, 2022, the Internet draft specification for HTTP/3 included QUIC as a transport protocol in preference to TCP. Although not yet a standard, HTTP/3 is implemented in the major browsers.

---

87   It's a name, not an acronym, pronounced "*quick.*"

TCP/IP Names and Addresses

IP-based networks use one of two formats of logical addresses. Users of such networks nearly always refer to hosts and network resources by name. They nearly always expect the machines they use to "just work," that is to be configured automatically or to be self-configuring.

Those who design, install, maintain, and troubleshoot IP-based networks must have a thorough understanding of the relationships between names and addresses and of the mechanisms used to configure hosts on the network.

5.4.1 The Domain Name System (DNS)

The job of the domain name system is to translate human-friendly domain names into logical IP addresses. The domain name system is a hierarchical, distributed database that maps domain names to IP addresses, provides inverse mapping, and provides resource records and several other functions. Its principal use is mapping domain names to IP addresses. Name servers receive requests specifying a name and return an IPv4 or IPv6 Internet Protocol address. DNS operates at the application layer of the Internet Protocol suite.

Figure 5-10 shows a portion of the structure of the domain name system. The root node does not have a name;[88] when necessary to represent it explicitly, it is represented with a dot. Below the root are several hundred top level domains or TLDs. There are several types of top level domains. The generic TLDs originally described the kind of organization to which a domain name was assigned, such as .com, .org, or .edu. There are about 200 country-code TLDs, such as .us for the United States and .ca for Canada. There is a growing list of TLDs sponsored by organizations, such as .aero for the aviation industry and .museum for museums. There is a small set of reserved names, including .arpa, .local, and .test. The second level domain names, shown as 2LD in Figure 5-10, are registered to organizations or individuals which pay an annual fee to commercial domain registrars. The commercial registrars are, in turn, accredited by ICANN, the Internet Corporation for Assigned Names and Numbers. It is possible to have three or more levels of domain names. Subdomains, if any, are named and managed by the holders of the second level domain names. At the lowest level are names of host computers or network nodes. It is the responsibility of the holders of second level domain names to maintain authoritative name servers. These name servers resolve subdomain and host names within the second level domain. Often the name servers are provided by the domain name registrar, but that isn't required.

Domain names are written with the lowest level on the left, so Kennesaw State University's web server name is www.kennesaw.edu. That is a fully-qualified domain name (FQDN) for host *www* in second-level domain *kennesaw* and top-level domain *edu*. It is possible to

---

88 The root node does not have a name, but the root name servers do. They are a.rootservers.net to m.rootservers.net.

configure a DNS search suffix list that fills in the domain name, so a client computer in the Kennesaw State network might be able to reach the web server by typing only www.

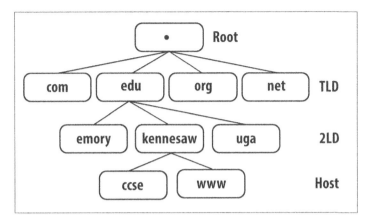

Figure 5-10
The domain name system (DNS) database is organized as a tree structure

The domain name system has some built-in assumptions that the character set is ASCII. Domain names in non-Latin alphabets, such as Cyrillic or Greek are called internationalized domain names. They are implemented by encoding Unicode characters as pure ASCII for internal handling using a scheme called *punycode*.

A client computer, such as a laptop, tablet, or phone, uses very simple software called a stub resolver to query a DNS server on the client's network. If the stub resolver has looked up the name recently, it can return an answer from its cache. If not, it will pass the query to a recursive resolver on its home network. That resolver might also be able to answer from cache. If not, it will pass the query to the next higher level continuing until an answer is received or a root name server is reached. The query then travels down the hierarchy until the authoritative name server for the domain is reached. The authoritative server provides the IP address. Once the client has received an IP address, it is cached to prevent repeated calls to DNS servers.

When a name server is asked for an address for a given name, it can provide an A (address) record with an IPv4 address, an AAAA[89] record with an IPv6 address, or both.

It is possible that a query is sent for a name that does not exist in the domain name system. The proper response from the domain name system is a "no such domain" DNS response. Various ISPs and others have engaged in the unsavory practice of presenting advertising instead of the prescribed response that the domain name does not exist.

Although there are only 13 root server names with 13 IP addresses, a technique called

---

89   Because there are four times as many bits in an IPv6 address as an IPv4 address.

anycast routing permits a geographically distributed group of over 600 root name servers. Anycast will attempt to send a query to the root server with the fastest connectivity path. The IP addresses of the root name servers change very infrequently, and are included in operating system and DNS software releases. If a DNS resolver can reach any root name server, it can find the addresses of all the others.

DNS as originally designed has some serious security shortcomings. DNS Security Extensions (DNSSEC) is an extension to DNS that is beginning to be widely adopted in the third decade of the 21st century. DNSSEC uses cryptographic signatures to allow a DNS resolver to verify that the data it received came from the authoritative name server for that domain. It provides integrity protection to allow modification in transit to be detected, and includes a mechanism to guarantee that a "no such domain" response is valid. Adoption has been slow because DNSSEC requires cryptographic signatures from the next higher level in the DNS hierarchy, and those are still typically handled manually.

5.4.2 IPv4 Addresses and Routing

The 32-bit Internet Protocol address format, called IPv4, was described in an IETF document in the fall of 1981, the same year the original IBM PC was introduced. The choice of a 32-bit address space was made earlier, in 1978 (Huitema, 1996). IPv4 addresses have been in use since 1982 and probably still carry the bulk of Internet traffic.

A 32-bit address space allows for 2^{32} or about 4.29 billion addresses. There are about 600,000 reserved addresses, leaving about 3.7 billion available for assignment. At the time, that was believed to be sufficient for the foreseeable future.

IPv4 addresses are written in dotted-quad form, four numbers separated by periods, for example, 192.168.137.97. Each of the numbers represents eight bits, and so will be in the range zero to 255.

IP addresses consist of two parts, a network part and a host part. The network part identifies a network reachable by routing and the host part identifies one host address within that network. Originally the first eight bits were the network number, allowing for 254 networks. By 1981 the standard was revised so that the first one to four bits of the first octet specified the **network class** that defined the separation between the network part and the host part. You may still hear people talk about class A, B, or C networks. By 1993, the IETF realized that three sizes[90] did not fit all, and introduced **classless interdomain routing** (CIDR).

CIDR includes the concept of a **netmask**, a bit string 32 bits long with ones marking the network part and zeros marking the host part. The netmask concept allows division of network part and host part at any bit boundary. Since the netmask is 32 bits, it can be written as a single number indicating the length of the network part of the netmask. The example

---

90   There were actually five classes, with class D being a multicast class, and class E reserved.

address above could be written 192.168.137.97/25 with the 25 indicating that the first 25 bits of the address is the network part. In some cases, the netmask is required to be specified in the older dotted quad format. A /25 netmask would be 255.255.255.128 if written as dotted-quad. That's 25 bits of ones and seven bits of zeros. The division need not be on a byte boundary, as was required with class-based addresses. The introduction of CIDR did not change the form of the address; it only changed how the address bits are interpreted.

The /25 network would have $32 - 25 = 7$ bits of host part, so 2^7 or 128 host addresses. The first address, with a host part of all zeros, is the address of the network itself. The last address, with a host part of all ones, is the network's broadcast address. That leaves 126 addresses available for network hosts or nodes. The number of host bits, h, is $32 - n$ where n is the number of onebits in the netmask, *i.e.*, the number following the slash. The number of available host addresses is

192	168	137	97	Dotted quad
11000000	10101000	10001001	01100001	Binary
11111111	11111111	11111111	10000000	Netmask

Figure 5-11
IPv4 address in dotted-quad and binary, showing a /25 netmask in binary

$2^h - 2$ to account for the first and last addresses, the network address and broadcast address, respectively.

IPv4 reserves a number of addresses for special uses. The **loopback address**, 127.0.0.1, is used for a node to send messages to itself. **Link-local addresses** are in the block 169.254.0.0/16 and are assigned by an operating system when neither manual nor automatic IP configuration is available. Link-local addresses were originally intended for automatic configuration. In a managed network, the presence of a link-local address on a machine now suggests connectivity failure or configuration failure.

In addition to the link-local addresses, the IANA has reserved three ranges of IP addresses for private networks: 10.0.0.0–10.255.255.255, 172.16.0.0–172.31.255.255, and 192.168.0.0–192.168.255.255. These private addresses are sometimes called reserved addresses, or RFC 1918 addresses after the number of the standards document that set them aside. They are also sometimes, incorrectly, called non-routable addresses. Since these addresses are reserved for private networks, many different networks can use addresses in the same ranges without conflict. Router/gateway devices for home or small business networks usually assign addresses from one of these ranges automatically by including a dynamic host configuration protocol server as part of the device. When a network using private addresses must be connected to the Internet, network address translation is required.

Network address translation (NAT) allows a network to use private or link-local addresses internally and provide a connection to the Internet using a single registered address. Registered IP addresses are generally assigned in large blocks to Internet service providers (ISPs)

who, in turn, assign them to customers as needed.[91] For home use, most addresses assigned by ISPs are dynamic, meaning they can change from time to time. Blocks of one or more fixed addresses are available, usually at extra cost, for organizations and sophisticated home users.

Network address translation takes advantage of the fact that TCP connections and UDP datagrams are characterized by protocol number, the two endpoint IP addresses, and the two endpoint port numbers. A NAT device will have two network interfaces, one for the outside, registered address, and one for the inside, private address. For outgoing packets, the NAT substitutes its registered address for the internal source address and a port number of its own, selected from the dynamic port numbers, for the source port number. The NAT device maintains a mapping of the port numbers it used with internal addresses and port numbers. For incoming packets, the NAT device uses the destination port number to look up the internal IP address and port number, rewrites the destination address and port number, and forwards the packet on its internal interface.

The entries in the NAT device table are made when a host on a private network initiates an outgoing contact. In the absence of special configuration of the NAT device, a host on a private network cannot receive unsolicited network packets. This is sometimes held out as a security advantage.

Port forwarding is necessary to operate a host that can receive unsolicited network packets while within a NAT network. Port forwarding is accomplished by making a semi-permanent entry into the NAT device's translation table. For example, to operate a web server on the machine with address 192.168.137.97 inside a NAT network, the NAT device would be configured to forward all incoming traffic directed to port 80, the HTTP port, to port 80 on the host at address 192.168.137.97. The advertised address of the web server must be that of the NAT device's registered address.

IPv4 Configuration and the Dynamic Host Configuration Protocol

An IPv4 host must, at a minimum, be configured with an IP address, a netmask, and the addresses of one or more DNS servers. If communication off the local network is needed, it must be configured with the IP address of at least one router, the **default gateway**. The default gateway receives packets for which no other route is configured. For small and medium sized networks, often it is the only router configured. If the host is to be a server and accessible by name, it must have its name and IP address configured in the local DNS servers. The existence of link-local addresses provides one way of configuring the IP address automatically, but netmask, DNS servers, routers, and possible DNS mapping must still be configured. A configuration error can result in an inoperable network host. Some errors, such as duplication of IP addresses, can result in unstable network operation.

---

91   In the United States, blocks of IP addresses are assigned directly to very large organizations, to the military, and to some educational institutions.

Manually configuring the devices for even a small network can take significant effort, especially if the network is to support portable devices that join and leave the network on an *ad hoc* basis.

The solution is to automate all or nearly all configuration tasks with a **dynamic host configuration protocol (DHCP)** server. Like DNS, DHCP operates at the application layer of the Internet Protocol suite. A DHCP server listens for broadcasts from hosts wanting to join the network. The broadcast for a DHCP server is sent on the local link network, usually Ethernet, so an IP address is not needed to send the broadcast nor receive the response. When a DHCP broadcast is received, the server will supply configuration information to the host client, which will use the configuration information to complete the configuration.

DHCP servers can configure all of the required parameters and many others, including things like the address of a network time protocol (NTP) server, which the client can then use to obtain the correct time. Some DHCP servers integrate with DNS to provide the necessary DNS records when an IP address is assigned.

Most routers designed for home or small office use incorporate a DHCP server so that client computers are configured automatically.

DHCP servers assign IPv4 addresses from a pool of addresses specified when the DHCP server is configured. Since home and small office routers generally also include NAT, common practice is to configure a pool of addresses from the RFC 1918 allocations, often 192.168.0.0/24 or 10.0.0.0/8.

IPv4 Address Exhaustion

By 1992, people planning what was then called IPng[92] projected that the 32-bit address space would be exhausted between 2005 and 2015 (Huitema, 1996). The regional Internet address registries did run out of IP addresses near the end of the predicted time. IP addresses are assigned to regional registries by the Internet Assigned Number Authority, which ran out of addresses in 2011. The regional registries still had addresses to allocate. The American Registry for Internet Numbers exhausted its supply of addresses in 2017, and the registry for Europe, Middle East and Central Asia exhausted its supply in 2019. ISPs still have pools of IPv4 addresses to allocate to customers in 2020. A major crisis was avoided through using CIDR to allocate addresses in blocks smaller than 256 and using NAT to provide internal addresses for many networks. The regional registries can also reclaim addresses not in use.

The long-term solution is an Internet protocol with larger addresses, now called IPv6. The mechanism that was adopted includes 128-bit addresses, offering the potential of 2^{128} IPv6 addresses. To put that in perspective, the mass of Earth is about 2^{92} grams. There are enough IPv6 addresses to assign one to every gram of Earth's mass with 2^{36} extra. (As a practical

---

92   IP next generation.

matter, not all 2^{128} addresses are available for assignment because some are reserved, but there are more than enough.)

5.4.3 IPv6 Addresses and Routing

IPv6 addresses are written as eight groups of four hexadecimal digits separated by colons like this: fe80:0000:0000:0000:e2b7:00ff:0000:ada0. That's a lot to write, but many IPv6 addresses can be shortened. Leading zeros in any group are not significant and can be omitted. So, 00ff above could be written as ff only. Two or more consecutive blocks of all zero can be shortened to two consecutive colons, but only once. If there are several such blocks, only one, preferably the longest one, can be shortened because the length of the shortened block is computed from the length of the block as written. Shortened, the address above is written as fe80::e2b7:ff:0:ada0.

IPv6 addresses have prefixes that serve the purpose of the netmask in IPv4 addresses, namely, to mark the portion of the address used for routing packets. The notation is the same as the CIDR notation, a slash and number following the address. For IPv6, the number must be from zero to 128. The default prefix is /64. That is, the leftmost 64 bits are used for routing.

Each IPv6 address also has a **reachability scope**. The **node-local** address is ::1/128, or all zeros followed by a single one; it has a reachability scope of the local node. The node-local address is equivalent to the IPv4 loopback address, and is used when a host wants to send a message to itself. Messages sent to the node-local address are never sent to a network interface controller.

Addresses with **link-local** reachability are used for sending datagrams to hosts on the same local network. Unlike IPv4 link-local addresses, which are a kind of last resort, every IPv6 node has a link-local address that is configured automatically. Link-local addresses have the form fe80::/10. The example address at the beginning of this section is a link-local address. The link-local reachability scope also includes a link-local multicast address and the unspecified address. The unspecified address is all zero and is used before a host or node has received an IPv6 address. The default route is also all zero, but with a different prefix: ::/0.

Addresses with **global** reachability are called aggregatable global unicast addresses and are equivalent to public IPv4 addresses. Such addresses are called aggregatable because, with proper assignment, it is possible to arrange IPv6 addresses in a hierarchy, where the next router is "up" the address hierarchy until a datagram reaches the point when it must leave that portion of the network. It is also possible to route IPv6 packets in much the same way as IPv4 packets.

Multicast addresses also have global reachability and are intended for one-to-many communication. They have the form ff00::/8.

IPv6 is designed for full **stateless autoconfiguration**. When a device joins an IPv6 network, it generates a link-local address. The first 64 bits start with fe80. The last 64 bits are formed from the device's MAC address. Once a device has a link-local address, it sends a router solicitation (RS) request to the default multicast address. A router will respond with a router advertisement (RA) response which includes the router's address and also the addresses of DNS servers (Dooley, 2015).

Once a device has a router address, it can generate a unique global address from the first 64 bits of the router address and the last 64 bits from the device's link-local address.

Devices also need to be able to find the MAC addresses of other hosts on the local network. With IPv4, that was done with ARP. The equivalent for IPv6 is the neighbor solicitation protocol. The device sends a neighbor solicitation packet, and the host with the address in the NS packet responds with a neighbor advertisement packet, which includes the MAC address. (Dooley, 2015)

Network hosts or nodes may need information not provided through autoconfiguration. That can be provided with dynamic host configuration protocol version 6 (DHCPv6). Routers can also be configured through DHCPv6.

IPv6 Transition

Although IPv6 solves the address exhaustion problem, IPv6 and IPv4 addresses are not interoperable. There have been a number of approaches to the problem of making the transition to IPv6 that also accommodate both clients and servers that still use IPv4. The accepted solution at the end of 2022 is dual-stack IP on clients and network infrastructure such as routers.

Both IPv4 and IPv6 can coexist "on the wire." The unit of transmission on a typical local area network is the Ethernet frame, and the IP datagram is payload, never used as other than data by the underlying network. The problem is to allow clients to process both IPv4 and IPv6 packets. The dual stack environment, is shown schematically in Figure 5-12. The dual stack environment is supported by current versions of all major operating systems.

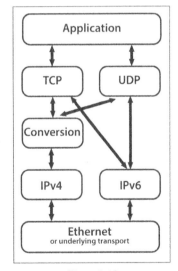

Figure 5-12
Dual stack IPv4 / IPv6
environment

The distinction between IPv4 and IPv6 is the version number in the datagram header. Dual-stack software uses the version number to select the appropriate datagram handling code. Once Internet Protocol layer processing is complete, the packet or datagram can be passed to the transport layer.

Microsoft's implementation, beginning with Windows Vista, is typical. Dual stack applications should expect to process only IPv6 packets or datagrams. If an IPv4 packet is received, it is converted to IPv6 format by using the IPv4 address as the low-order 32 bits of an IPv6 address and the constant 0:0:0:0:0:ffff as the high-order 96 bits.[93] When the application is sending, lower protocol layers recognize the prefix and select the IPv4 branch of the dual stack.

5.5 Physical Transmission

Up to this point, the chapter has focused on the logical interpretation of bits and given little attention to the mechanism by which bits are transported from one network node to another. Physical transmission is important because the choices made affect the distance over which signals can be transmitted and the maximum speed of transmission.

5.5.1 Network Topologies

The **topology** of a network describes how network signals travel, and is easiest to think about in terms of wired networks although wireless networks also have topology. The physical topology of a network is the layout of the wires or other media that carry the signals. The logical topology describes the flow of the signals themselves. Logical and physical topologies are often the same, but do not have to be.

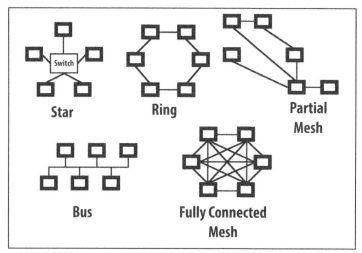

Figure 5-13
Some physical network topologies

Figure 5-13 shows five physical topologies. Modern wired networks are most often physical and logical star networks. As discussed in Section 5.3.2, modern Ethernet networks connect

---

93   The use of 0:0:0:0:0:ffff is an IETF standard, described in RFC 4291, and not a Microsoft extension.

each host or node to a central switch that is responsible for forwarding incoming Ethernet frames to the proper destination. Connections between the network nodes and the switch are **point-to-point connections**.

The original Ethernet design was a bus topology. Every node on the bus received every transmission and network interface controllers were responsible for processing broadcast messages and those with the controller's own address and ignoring others. A physical bus as shown in Figure 5-13 is a **multipoint connection**. A physical bus is difficult to install and maintain, especially when adding new network nodes. Ethernet hubs, which just connected all ports together, made a physical star and logical bus network.

IBM's token ring network was at first wired as a physical ring. Every node received messages and passed on those not addressed to it. Like a physical bus, a physical ring is difficult to install and maintain. IBM's introduction of the medium access unit allowed a logical bus network to operate in a physical star configuration, as shown in Figure 5-14.

Figure 5-14
Physical star, logical ring

A partial mesh network requires more complex software than network architectures where each node is responsible only for processing its own and broadcast messages. In a partial mesh, some nodes must be able to forward messages for other nodes. A sparse network is one in which the number of links is much less than the maximum possible number.

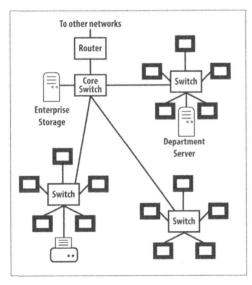

Figure 5-15
A hierarchical network

A fully-connected mesh provides the greatest redundancy, but its complexity, approximately $n^2/2$ where n is the number of nodes, increases very rapidly.

Particularly in larger organizations, networks may be arranged in a hierarchical structure. Figure 5-15 shows such an arrangement. The diagram shows three star networks, possibly for organizational units, each potentially with their own servers. More or fewer connected networks are possible. Each star network switch is connected to a core switch that provides connectivity to common resources such as enterprise storage and a router to external networks.

An arrangement like that of Figure 5-15 can simplify wiring, especially if the nodes in each of the star networks are physically close together. However, connecting several networks increases the size of the broadcast domain.[94] Broadcast messages will be sent to every node on the network. When a new device enters the network, messages to it are flooded to every port other than that on which the message entered the switch until the switches learn the location of the device. That is described in Section 5.3.2. While not strictly broadcast messages, flooding has a similar effect on network bandwidth.

One solution to limiting the broadcast domain is the **virtual local area network**, or VLAN. The VLAN standard in widest use is IEEE 802.1Q which identifies virtual LANs with a 12-bit tag field included in the Ethernet frame. The first and last values are reserved, making the number of possible VLANs on a single physical network 4,094. Other IEEE 802.1 standards offer up to 16 million VLANs on one network. Prior to adoption of IEEE 802.1Q, several manufacturers of communication equipment implemented VLANs using proprietary techniques.

In addition to minimizing broadcast domains, properly configured VLANs can improve network security. If the departmental server in Figure 5-15 held confidential information, the traditional approach to protecting it would be using passwords, perhaps with two-factor authentication.[95] A properly configured VLAN can limit which workstations are able to access the server, thereby reducing the attack surface and supplementing the password authentication.

Software defined networks expand on the idea of VLANs and include the ability to automate and optimize network configurations. Software defined networks are most suitable for large enterprises.

5.5.2   Data Transmission

Information is transmitted from sources to intended recipients by way of signals. A **signal** is a way to transfer information. Some examples are electrical voltage, sound, or even puffs of smoke. Information is transferred through meaningful changes in the signal as a function of time. The signal is conveyed from sender to recipient by a **transmission medium**, such as electric wires for voltage, air for sound, and visible light for the puffs of smoke. In data communications, a communication **link** is the transmission medium connecting two nodes and the communication controller hardware at each node. The sending node converts digital data to signals suitable for the transmission medium. The signals are then transmitted along the link, the receiving node receives the signals and converts them back to digital data. Data communication between two endpoints usually passes through multiple links and multiple intermediate nodes.

A communication link is characterized by:

---

94   Do not confuse broadcast domain with collision domain. They are different. See Section 5.3.2.

95   Two-factor authentication is discussed in Chapter 7.

- The medium used
- The signal transmission method
- Direction(s) in which a signal can flow
- Susceptibility to attenuation, noise, and distortion
- Bandwidth
- Time delay and jitter.

There are two classes of transmission media, guided and unguided. In **guided media**, also called bounded media, signals are guided along a path. Copper wire and fiber-optic cable are examples of guided media. **Unguided** or unbounded media use electromagnetic waves to transmit data. Examples are radio, microwave, and, for short distances, infrared light.

Signal transmission can be analog, that is, continuously varying within a range of values, or discrete. In discrete transmission, the signal takes on a countable set of values.

A transmission medium that can carry signals in both directions simultaneously is called **full duplex**. A medium that can carry signals in either direction, but only one at a time is called **half duplex**. A medium that carries signals in one direction only is called **simplex**.

Attenuation is the loss of signal strength, primarily due to distance, but other causes are also possible. For example, a wall will attenuate a Wi-Fi signal. Signal wires can act as antennas and pick up unrelated electromagnetic radiation, called **noise**. Noise from external sources is called interference. Noise is measured at the end of a link distant from the transmitter as the ratio of the power of the signal to the power of the noise component. That ratio is called the **signal to noise ratio**. If signal and noise are expressed on a logarithmic scale, the resulting ratio is in decibels. **Distortion** changes the shape of the waveform, particularly when signals are transmitted over long distances.

The **bandwidth** of a transmission medium is the range of frequencies it can carry without excessive attenuation. Because the bandwidth of a transmission medium limits the number of bits per second the medium can carry, the word "bandwidth" is often used to express the data-carrying capacity of a medium in bits per second.

Latency is the time from transmission of a signal to its receipt and is unavoidable. Although electrical and electromagnetic signals travel at a large fraction of the speed of light, distance and processing at intermediate nodes can cause perceptible delay. Grace Murray Hopper used to tell the story of the Navy admiral who asked her why communication via satellite took so long. Dr. Hopper answered, "Because there is a very large number of nanoseconds between here and the satellite."[96] **Jitter** is variation in latency, and can be more troublesome than delay, particularly for applications like voice and video. Figure 5-16 compares an ideal communication link, represented as a pipe, with a model representing a real communication

---

96   See the illustration of "nanosecond" in Figure 3-16.

link using copper wiring. In an ideal communication link, a signal would go in one end and come out the other unchanged after an invariant delay proportional to the length of the link.

In a real link, the signal is changed by attenuation, noise, and distortion of the wave form. Capacitance (parallel line symbols) changes the waveform and can admit noise from external sources. Resistance (saw tooth symbol) attenuates the signal. The striped triangle is a ground symbol, showing that some of the signal strength can be drained away during transmission. Inductance (coil symbol) distorts the signal and can admit external noise. A real link does not actually contain the capacitors, resistors, or inductors in the diagram. Instead, the electrical wires themselves exhibit these characteristics, which increase with the length of the link.

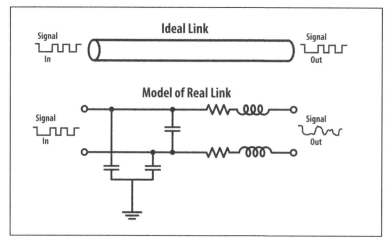

Figure 5-16
Ideal and real communication links

Information is transmitted through changes in the signal as a function of time. These changes are expressed in units of **baud**,[97] equivalent to one signal event per second. The term "baud rate" has been misused to mean bits per second; the two are not equivalent. Depending on the signaling techniques used, more than one bit may be encoded in one signal event, or baud. Other signaling techniques require more than one baud for each bit. A transmission medium must have a bandwidth at least equal to the baud rate of the signal.

In digital transmission, a signal such as the one shown at the output of the model real channel can be recovered exactly provided it has not been too degraded by attenuation, noise, or distortion. This is possible because it is a discrete signal. The expected number of levels of the signal is small, from two in a pure binary signal, up to about five levels with other kinds of discrete encoding.

---

97 Named after Émile Baudot, 19th century French telegraph engineer, who invented a telegraph code and a mechanism for time division multiplexing of telegraph messages.

Baseband and Broadband Circuits

The term "broadband" has been misused to mean "fast." In discussions of communication technology, more precision is needed. A baseband circuit is one in which the signal covers the entire frequency spectrum from zero Hz up to the maximum frequency the channel can carry with acceptably low attenuation. A gigabit Ethernet circuit, often held out as the goal to achieve in home Internet connections, is a baseband circuit. In fact, "base" in 1000BASE-T means baseband.

A broadband circuit is one in which two or more frequency bands carry two or more independent signals. A digital subscriber line (DSL) Internet connection is a broadband connection. The frequency band from 300 Hz to 3,400 Hz carries voice traffic. Two or more bands are allocated beginning at 4,000 Hz. At least one band carries data from the customer's equipment to the carrier, and at least one band carries data from the carrier to the customer. If the distance to the carrier's equipment is short and the wire line is in good condition, more bands can be used, increasing the speed of the DSL connection.

Television and radio are broadband technologies, with each television channel or radio station occupying a frequency band within some allocated spectrum, for example 88.8 MHz to 108.0 MHz for FM radio in the United States. The technique of carrying two or more signals within some frequency band is called **frequency-division multiplexing**.[98]

Baseband Signaling Mechanisms

The stream of bits that comprises a digital signal looks like the diagram labeled "Signal In" in Figure 5-16. Such a signal is called non-return to zero because there is no space or rest between each bit. Recall from Section 5.2.1 that the preamble of an Ethernet frame is 56 bytes of alternating zero and one bits, followed by a start of frame delimiter. The preamble allows the receiver to synchronize timing with the transmitter so that both agree on where the bit boundaries are. The receiver then samples the incoming signal in the middle of each bit-time. The preamble establishes bit boundaries. The start of frame delimiter establishes where each byte of the incoming signal begins.

Although the receiver is synchronized with the transmitter at the beginning of each frame, a long string of either ones or zeros would cause no changes in the signal during that time. It is possible for the receiver's timing to drift slightly during a period of no transitions. Especially at high speeds, that can mean either a missed bit or an erroneous bit inserted into the signal stream. Everything after such an error will be incorrect.

To prevent such errors, baseband transmissions are encoded in such a way that there are regular transitions in the signal even when long strings of ones or zeros are transmitted. Ten-megabit Ethernet uses Manchester encoding. According to the IEEE 802.3 standard, a

---

98 Packet switching, in which packets from multiple sources are sent one after another on a transmission medium, is one form of **time-division multiplexing**.

zero bit is represented by a high-to-low transition in the middle of the bit period, and a one bit is represented by a low to high transition.[99] That means there will always be a transition in the middle of each bit time, and often there will be two, one at the beginning and one in the middle. For example, if two ones are sent in sequence, there must be a high to low transition at the end of the first bit period so that there can be a low to high transition to represent that second one. With at least one transition per bit time guaranteed, the transmitter and receiver clocks can be kept in synchronization. However, since there will frequently be two transitions per bit time, the bandwidth of the medium must be at least twice the data rate. In fact, Manchester encoding requires that the transmitter have a clock that operates at twice the bit rate of transmission as shown in Figure 5-17. A close look at the figure will show you that the Manchester encoded signal is the XOR of the clock and data signals.

The requirement that the transmission medium have a bandwidth of twice the data rate makes Manchester encoding unsuitable for higher data rates. Hundred megabit Ethernet encodes each four bits into a five-bit group in such a way that there will be at least one transition for each five-bit group. That is called a 4B5B code. The five-bit groups are then transmitted using a three-level code called MLT-3 for wired connections. It's still a discrete signal, but the values are a positive voltage, zero, and a negative voltage. For fiber optic transmission, the 4B5B code is encoded using a method called non-return to zero inverted, or NRZI in which one and zero bits are sent as transition or no transition, rather than as levels. The 4B5B encoding means there will always be at least one transition per group to keep transmitting and receiving clocks synchronized.

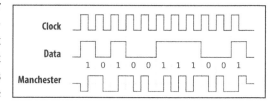

Figure 5-17
Manchester encoding (IEEE 802.3)

Successively higher speeds use different encoding mechanisms to be sure signal transitions occur frequently enough to allow the receiver's clock to remain synchronized, and to limit the bandwidth required from the transmission medium.

Broadband Signaling Mechanisms

A broadband connection is one in which the same medium carries two or more independent signals. That means there must be two or more carrier signals of different frequencies. Information is transmitted on the carrier signals by modulating, that is changing, the carrier signal in a way that represents the transmitted data stream. The received data stream is recovered by demodulating the carrier signal. This is performed by a device called a modulator/demodulator, or **modem**.

---

99   In the original Manchester encoding, invented by G. E. Thomas at the University of Manchester about 1949, the transitions are the other way around.

The fundamental waveform used in broadband signaling is a sine wave. Sine waves have the properties of frequency, amplitude, and phase. One or more of these properties can be modulated, *i.e.* changed with respect to time, to transmit data. Frequency is the number of repetitions of the sine wave per second. Amplitude is the power of the wave. Power measurements for electromagnetic waves are complex. What is important in signaling is that the received power be sufficient to have a signal to noise ratio greater than one at the lowest amplitude used.

For radio waves, frequency is measured in Hertz. For light waves, frequency is measured in nanometers (nm) between peaks of the waveform. A typical wavelength for multimode glass fiber is 850 nm, which is 352,697 GHz.

The phase of an electromagnetic wave is expressed in degrees from some reference. The upward zero-crossing of a sine wave is zero degrees, the peak is 90 degrees, and the downward zero-crossing is 180 degrees. Often phase angle is measured with respect to the carrier wave before a phase change so that it isn't necessary for the receiver to maintain a reference waveform.

Figure 5-18 illustrates modulation of the three properties. Figure 5-18(a) shows the transition of a digital signal from low to high. Figure 5-18(b) shows amplitude modulation of a sine wave for such a transition. Figure 5-18(c) shows frequency modulation, and Figure 5-18(d) shows phase modulation.

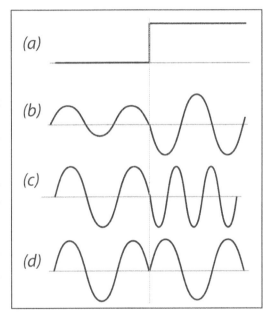

Figure 5-18

Modulation technique: (a) digital signal; (b) amplitude modulation; (c) frequency modulation (d) phase modulation

The baud rate of broadband signals is one signal event, *i.e.* one change in the carrier signal, per second. Modulation can encode more than one information bit in one signal event. For example, quadrature amplitude modulation (QAM) as used in Wi-Fi and some fiber optic systems modulates both phase and amplitude. With QAM, four or more bits are transmitted with each change in the carrier.

Demodulating a broadband signal produces a stream of bits. As with baseband signals, there must be a way to maintain synchronization of receiver to transmitter. So, data transmitted on broadband systems are encoded using Manchester coding, 4B5B, or a similar mechanism to be sure bit transitions occur frequently enough to maintain synchronization.

Transmission Media

Guided transmission media, copper wire or fiber optic cable, are used in permanent or semi-permanent installations. Unguided media, radio waves and sometimes infrared, are used for portable devices or where installation of guided media is not practical, such as in an apartment building. Focused unguided media are also used for long distance communication, such as with satellites.

The principal types of copper transmission media are coaxial cable and twisted pair cable. Both coaxial cable and twisted pair cable can have either solid conductors or stranded conductors. Solid conductors are used for permanent installation. Stranded conductors, which withstand flexing better, are used for applications like patch cables.

Coaxial cable has an insulated inner conductor covered by a conductive braid. The braid is covered by an insulating jacket. Conductor, insulator, braid, and jacket have a common center or axis, hence the name coaxial. Coaxial cable is used in broadband circuits with multiple channels, such as television or other audiovisual systems because of its high bandwidth capacity.

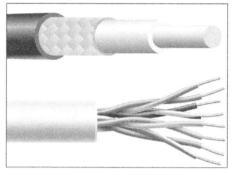

Figure 5-19
Coaxial cable (top)
twisted pair (bottom)
nitroxlmares/vinap/123RF

Twisted pair cable is used for baseband transmission at speeds up to 10 GHz. Twisting the pairs means that interference affects both wires in a pair approximately equally. Twisted pair cables for Ethernet have four pairs of wires, eight wires total. The pairs are color-coded for matching at the ends of the cable. Different pairs in a cable have different numbers of twists per meter, called pitch, to minimize interference from within the cable, known as **crosstalk**. Cable intended for higher speeds will have more twists per meter. It may have an overall foil shield, or each pair may be separately shielded. There may be a bare drain wire that is in electrical contact with the shield material and that is intended to be grounded. The drain wire, if present, should be grounded only at one end of a cable run.

Specifications for twisted pair cable are established by the Telecommunications Industry Association (TIA)[100] and the ISO / IEC. Specification for twisted pair cable are given as categories, with Category 5e being used for Ethernet up to one gigabit per second. Categories 6 and 6A are compatible with category 5e, but with higher bandwidth specifications. Categories 7, 7A, and 8 are defined for specialized uses.

---

100 TIA was formerly part of the Electronics Industries Alliance, which ceased operations in 2011. You may still see "EIA" specifications for networking equipment and media.

Fiber optic cables transmit light waves rather than electrical signals. The high frequency of light waves make optical fiber transmission suitable for very high bandwidth applications. Optical fiber transmission is not affected by external electromagnetic noise. Construction of a fiber optic cable is shown in Figure 5-20. The core is a glass fiber roughly the thickness of a human hair. The core is surrounded by glass or plastic cladding with a refractive index less than that of the core. Light hitting the boundary between core and cladding is reflected back into the core rather than being allowed to escape. The process of total internal reflection means light travels along the core. The cladding is surrounded by a protective coating, then a strength member, often aramid fibers,[101] then a protective jacket. It is common to include a number of fibers with cladding and coating within one strength member and jacket.

Near infrared light is injected into fiber optic cables with lasers or LEDs and detected at the receiver with a photodetector device. The light signal is made to carry data by modulating the light signal. Wave length division multiplexing, also called lambda division multiplexing, allows signals of two or more different wavelengths of light to be carried in the same fiber.

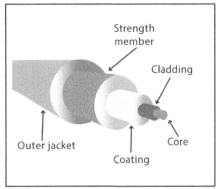

Figure 5-20
Structure of fiber optic cable
Jaouad/stock.adobe.com

Fibers for fiber optic transmission are either multi-mode or single mode. Multi-mode fibers have a larger core, typically 50μm[102] or 62.5μm, which makes connected equipment less expensive. However, the larger fiber size reduces the bandwidth and also the distance over which signals can be transmitted. Single mode fiber is much narrower, about 9 μm, requiring more precise connectors and electronics. It is suitable for longer distances, and the cable itself is less expensive. It is important that the type of fiber match the equipment to which it will be connected.

Unguided communications use radio waves, or for very short distances, infrared light. In the United States, frequency allocations in the radio and microwave spectrum are controlled by the Federal Communications Commission (FCC). Operation of transmitting devices over most of the radio and microwave spectrum requires a license from the FCC. However, the FCC has set aside some frequency bands for unlicensed operation, and allows unlicensed operation in some other frequency bands at very low power. In the United States, unlicensed does not mean unregulated. The FCC has stringent requirements for power and frequency even for unlicensed uses.

Unlike fiber optic transmission and some wired transmission, radio frequency bands are

101 One brand of aramid fiber is Kevlar, used for making bullet-resistant vests.

102 The Greek letter μ (mu) is an abbreviation for micro, so μm is micrometer, a millionth of a meter.

divided into channels, and it is the bandwidth of the channel that is available for modulation. For example, some Wi-Fi devices operate in the 2.4 GHz band, which is divided into eleven overlapping channels of 22 MHz each. It is the 22 MHz bandwidth of a channel that is available for modulation. Wi-Fi and Bluetooth use a technology called spread-spectrum transmission, which spreads a radio signal over the assigned frequency band to minimize interference.

In the United States, wireless local area networking (**Wi-Fi**) operates mainly in the 2.4 GHz and 5.0 to 5.9 GHz bands. Although the higher frequencies allow potentially higher throughput, they are also more susceptible to blocking by walls and other obstructions. In 2020, the FCC allocated space in the 6 GHz band for wireless local area networks. The Wi-Fi Alliance has defined "generations" of Wi-Fi, with the most current being Wi-Fi 6, which is equivalent to the IEEE 802.11ax standard. Six GHz equipment became available in 2021 and is branded Wi-Fi 6E.

Wi-Fi is generally operated in infrastructure mode, with one or more access points providing connectivity to portable and mobile devices. It is also possible to operate Wi-Fi devices as peer-to-peer networks without access points. With specialized antennas, Wi-Fi can be used for point-to-point transmission over line-of-sight distances of hundreds of meters.

The design of Wi-Fi attempts to secure it from unauthorized access or interception. The first attempt, wired equivalent privacy (WEP), had a major flaw in the encryption algorithm. WEP was replaced by Wi-Fi Protected Access (WPA), which also had flaws. The current version is WPA3, which supersedes WPA2.

Bluetooth was originally intended as a replacement for cables that connect devices to personal computers. It is usually lower-powered and shorter range than Wi-Fi, although a maximum range is not specified. Bluetooth also operates in the 2.4 GHz band. It is now mostly used for connecting devices to mobile equipment, such as a headset to a cellular telephone, although keyboards and mice with Bluetooth connections are common. Bluetooth 3.0 can provide speeds up to three Mb/second at a cost of increased power consumption. Bluetooth Low Energy minimizes power consumption through reduced speed and a much-simplified protocol stack.

There are other wireless networking technologies, for example ZigBee for low power and low speed personal area networks and LoRa for low power longer range networks.

Cellular communication is provided by a number of competing cellular carriers that hold the necessary FCC licenses and operate the infrastructure. Subscribers' cellular devices are covered by the carrier's FCC license. Until about 2020, there were two technologies, code division multiple access (CDMA) and the Global System for Mobile Communications (GSM), used by different carriers. The GSM standard is maintained by the European Telecommunications Standards Institute (ETSI) and legally mandated in the European Union.

ETSI establishes "generations" of mobile communication standards. United States carriers are completing a transition to 4G LTE,[103] a step in the direction of full 4G compliance. When the transition is complete, early in the 2020s, there will be no public CDMA networks in the United States.

Cellular devices are increasingly used to transfer data rather than making voice calls. Many cellular devices can function as Wi-Fi "hotspots," allowing Wi-Fi (802.11) equipment to make a data connection over the cellular network.

Cellular data speeds are increasing. At the time this is written, carriers are implementing the 5G (fifth generation) cellular standard, which will provide gigabit speeds. Doing so requires higher-frequency signals that do not penetrate obstacles well. That means slow adoption of 5G or greatly expanded infrastructure, or both.

5.6 Summary of Learning Objectives

*This section of the chapter tells you the things you should know about, but not **what** you should know about them. To test your knowledge, discuss the following concepts and topics with a study partner or in writing, ideally from memory.*

Devices that are always connected to each other and the global Internet typify the 21st century. Networks have many parts that must work together smoothly. Modern networking involves the connection of many local area networks.

Networking consists of messages, protocols, and channels. Modern networks are packet switched, and at the lowest levels, connectionless. Protocols may be reliable or unreliable.

The OSI model is an abstract model of a protocol stack. The Internet Protocol model is an implementation of a protocol stack.

The predominant local area networking technology is Ethernet, which may be wired or wireless. Ethernet network interface controllers have physical addresses distinct from the device's logical address. The unit of transmission is the frame. Ethernet was originally a bus topology, which allowed for collisions and required a mechanism for recovering from them. Switched Ethernet can eliminate collisions but introduces the possibility of broadcast storms. Broadcast storms can be addressed by algorithms implemented in the switching system.

The Internet Protocol is the principal protocol for internetworking. It implements protocols for both reliable and unreliable communication. Other parts of the protocol specification address security and access specifically to web pages.

There are two incompatible formats for Internet Protocol addresses with very different siz-

---

103 Long Term Evolution.

es, structures, and facilities. One way to handle the incompatibility is dual-stack software. The domain name system is used to map structured domain names to logical addresses. The initial standard address format, IPv4, is running out of available addresses. Network address translation allows blocks of reserved addresses to be reused among many private networks.

An Internet Protocol host or node needs several configuration options. IPv4 hosts can be configured manually or using the dynamic host configuration protocol. The IPv6 protocol was designed for fully automatic host configuration. An IPv6 host will have several addresses with different reachability scopes, including node-local, link-local, and global unicast addresses.

The physical transmission medium provides the mechanism for moving bits from one host or node to another. Physical media can be guided or unguided. Several network topologies are available, including star and hierarchical topologies. Physical and logical topologies can be different.

Signaling involves changing the state of the transmission medium over time. The signal can be analog or digital. Transmission can be in one or both directions. Transmission is subject to latency, jitter, attenuation, noise, and distortion. The signal to noise ratio is an important measure of the quality of transmission.

The bandwidth of a transmission medium limits the maximum rate at which information can be transmitted. Transmission circuits are categorized as baseband or broadband, depending on the number of independent signals the channel can carry. Signaling mechanisms differ between baseband and broadband media. In either case, there must be a way to synchronize the transmitter and receiver clocks.

Physical transmission media are principally copper wire or fiber optic cable. There are two major types of copper wire with different characteristics and uses. There are also two major types of fiber optic cable.

Unguided transmission over more than very short distances uses radio waves. In the United States, most local area wireless networking uses frequency bands that do not require licenses for transmitters. Unguided communication of voice and data over longer distances is provided by commercial cellular operators who hold licenses for the frequencies they use. Cellular communication standards are named with generation numbers. The most recent, not yet widely implemented, is 5G.

5.7 References

Dooley, K. (2015, May 12). *What Every Network Admin Should Know About IPv6.* Retrieved from Auvik: https://www.auvik.com/franklyit/blog/ipv6-network-design/ on September 6, 2020

Huitema, C. (1996). *IPv6: The new Internet protocol.* Prentice-Hall.

Metcalfe, R. M., & Boggs, D. R. (1976). Ethernet: Distributed packet switching for local computer networks. *Communications of the ACM*, 19(7), 395–404. https://doi.org/10.1145/360248.360253

Chapter 6
Software and Programming

"Software makes hardware happen."

—*Computerworld* advertising button

Modern computers are *general purpose* machines, adapted to specific purposes by the software they run. That software is usually changeable. A laptop computer can be a word processing machine, a web browsing machine, and a calculator at different times, or possibly all at once. Even the microcontroller computers used to run things like microwave ovens are general purpose machines that get their personalities as oven controllers through software. If the software is built-in using read-only memory rather than loaded on demand as in a laptop computer, it is called **firmware**. Often there will be a way to update or replace the firmware.

Figure 6-1
Grace Murray Hopper
about 1946
U.S. Navy Bureau of Ordnance

An important property of computers is that *software and hardware are logically equivalent* (Tanenbaum, 1990). Hardware can be built to perform any function that can be performed with software. Microwave ovens used to be built with mechanical timers and switches instead of computer microcontrollers. The reverse is also true; we can write software to perform any function that can be performed in hardware. In that case, there must be *some* hardware at the lowest level to run the software, and if the software is to control external devices like that microwave oven, the hardware must include the necessary actuators. In Chapter Three you learned that the control unit of a computer itself could be implemented as hardware or software, and that the hardware implementation would be faster but probably more expensive. That is true in general: an implementation in hardware will generally be faster and more expensive.

Except in the very simplest microcontroller application, there will likely be two or more layers of software running on a computer. The **application software** fulfills the purpose of the application, whether it be word-processing, routing network packets, controlling an appliance like an oven, or playing a game. **System software**, specifically the operating system, is an interface between the application software and the hardware. It is also an interface between the user and the application software because the operating system controls the input and output devices.

6.1 Undecidable and Intractable Problems

One of the most important things that practitioners of information technology must learn is that not all problems can be solved with computers. Some problems, like "solve world hunger," are clearly outside the realm of computational solution, although we can surely use computers to do things like increase crop yields. There are other problems that "look computational" but cannot be solved. Such problems are called **undecidable**. A famous example is the halting problem. Alan Turing proved that it is impossible to write a program that, given another arbitrary program and its input, can determine whether that program will loop forever or eventually halt.[104]

Another class of problems, called **intractable** by mathematicians, have the property that their run time increases exponentially or faster as the number of cases increases. In Chapter Seven you will learn that finding the prime factors of very large numbers is intractable for von Neumann architecture computers. We know exactly how to do it, but actually doing it would take decades on the fastest computers now available.

Another intractable problem is the traveling salesman problem. Given a list of cities and their distances, find the shortest route that visits each city exactly once and returns to the origin city. This problem is applicable to things as diverse as package delivery, microchip design, and DNA sequencing. A brute force solution to this problem involves checking each possible route. The run time of such a solution is proportional to the factorial of the number of cities. For seven cities, that's $(7-1)!/2$,[105] or 360 routes to check. Increase the number to eight and there are 20,160 possible routes. With only 15 cities, there are 43,589,145,600 possible routes. A program that could check 100 routes per second would require almost 14 years to run! The good news is that for many such intractable problems, there are **heuristic algorithms**[106] that will find nearly optimal solutions in much less time.

Time complexity of algorithms is represented in **big-O notation**, where O is the order of worst-case run time for n where n is the number of input cases. Many algorithms have time complexity of $O(n)$; a linear search through an unordered list is an example. If the number of items in the list doubles, the worst-case time to search the list also doubles. If the list is sorted, we can do a binary search in time $O(\log_2 n)$, much faster since we don't have to visit every element in the list. The intractable problems are those where n is an exponent, so the runtime increases exponentially as the number of cases increases, for example, $O(2^n)$. It's even worse if a problem has factorial complexity like the traveling salesman problem mentioned for which the naïve approach has complexity $O(n!)$. Exponential and factorial problems are not solvable computationally in practical lengths of time except when there are very few cases. If faced with such a problem, look for heuristic solutions.

---

104 For an amusing proof that the halting problem is undecidable, see Geoffrey K. Pullum's poem "Scooping the Loop Snooper" which you can find here https://www.cs.columbia.edu/~tal/3261/sp12/Pullum.htm and at many other locations on the World Wide Web.

105 The exclamation mark is mathematical notation for the factorial operation. Since $7-1$ is 6, $(7-1)!$ is $6\times5\times4\times3\times2\times1 = 720$. Factorials get big very quickly.

106 A heuristic algorithm trades possible completeness for time. For example, a heuristic approach to the traveling salesman problem will find the best of a subset of possible solutions, which may not the best of all possible solutions.

Algorithms also have space complexity; how much memory is required to solve the problem. A time-space trade-off is frequently possible; a faster algorithm can be used only if more memory is available. There is no free lunch.

6.2 Application Software and Software Development

The information technology professional of the 21st century will most often use software developed by others and licensed to the professional's organization. Even so, some software development will likely be necessary to prepare data for input to others' applications or to connect applications. For that reason, it is important to understand the processes and pitfalls of software development.

6.2.1 Software Engineering

Software is hard. More specifically, building large, correctly functioning software systems on schedule and within budget is more difficult than people at first imagined. Frederick Brooks (1987) wrote that he observed "the hard part of building software to be the specification, design, and testing of this conceptual construct" of data items, algorithms, and invocation of functions. The fact that it is hard has led to a culture of "design as we build" in software construction. Possibly this is because, as Brooks (1987) says, "Software entities are more complex for their size than perhaps any other human construct because no two parts are alike… In this respect, software systems differ profoundly from computers, buildings, or automobiles, where repeated elements abound." It could also come from a desire to "get started;" a belief that the process of specifying and planning is not the "real work" of software development. It is!

The fact that software is hard was a surprise to early users of computers. These were scientists and engineers solving numerical problems with known formulas, which we'd now call algorithms. The programmer's job was to translate from the mathematical notation of the formula to the language of the machine. The important thing about that is that *the job to be done by the computer was already rigorously specified by the formula*. The difficulties called out by Brooks did not arise.

As you have seen, early electronic computers in the United States and the United Kingdom were mainly funded and used by the military. Once computing moved out of the rigorously specified area of mathematical formulas, there were some spectacular failures. Some failures were spectacular in terms of money wasted or time lost. In July of 1962 a Mariner spacecraft veered off course less than five minutes after launch. The range safety officer destroyed the craft to prevent a crash into shipping lanes or inhabited areas. The cause was reported to be a single missing hyphen in a guidance program. The cost? Over 18 million dollars.

Alarmed, the leaders of NATO, a military alliance, sponsored conferences on software engineering in 1968 and 1969 with the intention of defining best practices and principles of engineering for the development of complex software systems.

There have been incremental improvements, but about the time of Brooks' essay, a programming error in the Therac-25 radiation therapy machine caused at least four deaths. In 1992, F-22 Raptor aircraft experienced computer crashes when they crossed the International Date Line. Another error in spacecraft software caused the destruction of an Ariane 5 rocket in 1996 at a loss of $370 million. The ship USS Yorktown was dead in the water for three hours in 1997 because of a divide-by-zero error.

The Institute of Electrical and Electronics Engineers (IEEE, 1990) defines software engineering as "the application of a systematic, disciplined, quantifiable approach to the development, operation, and maintenance of software; that is, the application of engineering to software; the study of approaches to the application of engineering to software."

However, the classical engineering disciplines have their foundations in the physical laws of physics and chemistry, and ultimately in mathematics. Software engineering lacks such a foundation, and so software engineering is necessarily based on a set of best practices. A study of those best practices is beyond the scope of this book but learning them is essential for anyone who will do software development.

6.2.2 Programming Languages

The earliest computers that were programmable in the modern sense were programmed in the language of the machine, that is, using numbers to represent instructions and addresses. That was both tedious and error prone. The people building and using computers developed programs that would translate abbreviations like ADD, called instruction mnemonics, into the correct numeric codes. Such programs were soon expanded to do such things as assigning addresses for data and doing the necessary address arithmetic. These programs assembled an instruction mnemonic, one or more addresses, and other data into a machine instruction, and so were called **assemblers**. An assembler in general produces one machine instruction per line of code and is specific to one hardware architecture. That meant that a company buying a new computer with a different architecture had to rewrite all their programs. In its basic form an assembler is a very simple program. It makes two passes through the source code. In the first pass the assembler determines the amount of memory needed for each instruction. It also collects all the symbols, labels for branch targets and data, into a symbol table. Because the amount of memory each line of code will occupy has been determined, the assembler can add to the symbol table the address relative to zero that each symbol represents. On the second pass it can actually generate the code, substituting addresses from the symbol table for the symbols themselves.

A desire to avoid rewriting programs each time an organization bought a new computer was one of the drivers to adoption of **high-level languages**. Programs written in high-level languages look more like the language of the programmer and less like the language of the machine. A single high-level language statement usually produces several machine instructions, which improved programmer productivity. Brooks (1987) has estimated that it improved productivity by a factor of five or more.

Early high-level languages included Fortran[107] (*Formula Trans*lation) and COBOL (COmmon Business-Oriented Language). Grace Murray Hopper, whose picture introduces this chapter, was a proponent of high-level languages, especially COBOL. She induced the Navy and much of the Federal government to require high-level languages to be available when buying computer hardware. The COBOL and Fortran languages were developed with little theoretical information about the requirements of high-level languages. More modern languages like Java and Python were designed specifically to prevent certain kinds of programming errors. That is discussed in Section 6.2.4.

A high-level language requires a translator program to read in a program in the high-level language, called the **source code** or source program, and produce a program in machine language, called the object code or **object program**. The program that does the translation is called a **compiler**. Once the source code has been compiled, the resulting object program can be run as many times as necessary without repeating the compilation step. However, the compilation step must be repeated any time there is a change to the source program.

With the availability of much faster processors, another approach to high-level languages has emerged, namely interpretation. The language translator program, called an **interpreter**, reads the high-level language source code statements, and immediately executes the machine instructions needed to perform the operation described in the high-level language statement. There is no intermediate step of generating machine code and that work is avoided. On the other hand, the work done by the compiler in compiled languages must be done each time a program in an interpreted language is run. This is especially bad in programs with loops that run thousands or millions of times; in that case, language translation might have to be performed thousands or millions of times for a single run of the program.

Modern interpreters process the source code into an intermediate form called **bytecode**, then interpret the bytecode to execute the program. That allows the resource-intensive part of translation to be done only once even when code is repeated, as in loops.

In the Java language, the production of the bytecode class file is explicit and visible to those using the program. Translation to bytecode need only happen one time unless the source program is changed. However, the class file is not machine code, it is Java bytecode, and the Java interpreter, also called the Java Virtual Machine or JVM, is needed to run the class file.

---

107 Originally written as all capitals as FORTRAN.

Python and JavaScript are also interpreted languages. Their interpreters produce and execute the bytecode in a seamless process so that the bytecode and its production are not visible to those running the programs.

In fourth generation languages like SQL, the programmer describes what is to be done, rather than how to do it. There is more about SQL in Section 6.5.1.

6.2.3 Algorithms and Data Structures

The structure, operation, and efficiency of every non-trivial program is influenced heavily by the algorithms and data structures they use. Moreover, the algorithms used will influence the data structures needed and the data structures available will influence the algorithms that can be used. The relationship between algorithms and data structures is so important that one of the foundational books of computer science is *Algorithms + Data Structures = Programs* (Wirth,[108] 1976)

An **algorithm** is the set of steps a computer program takes to accomplish the desired function. Unlike a set of directions written for a human, there are formal requirements that make a sequence of steps an algorithm. According to Schneider and Gersting (2013) an algorithm must have these properties:

- Well-ordered
- Unambiguous
- Effectively computable
- Produce a result
- Halt in finite time.

As we saw in Chapter 3, von Neumann architecture computers operate sequentially, one step at a time. While humans can often deal with an implied order of steps, computers cannot. The instructions in an algorithm must be well-ordered. The steps must be unambiguous; there can be no doubt as to the meaning of each one. They must be something the computer can actually do, that is, be effectively computable.

An algorithm necessarily produces a result. Without a result, nothing has been accomplished. Finally, to meet the formal definition of algorithm, it must complete in finite time. While not part of the formal definition, we'd like algorithms to complete in a *reasonable* time, too. There are algorithms that address the kind of intractable problems described in section 6.1, but they have little practical use.

There are a great many well-developed algorithms for a very wide variety of problems. Donald Knuth took three books to document some of them, *Fundamental Algorithms*, *Seminumerical Algorithms*, and *Sorting and Searching*. The goal of the computing practi-

---

108 Dr. Wirth says his name is pronounced "Neeklaus Veert."

tioner should be not to learn about every algorithm, but to learn about the major classes of algorithms, know that they exist, and to be able to find the right one when needed.

Data types describe how information is represented in a computing system. The selection of a data type should be driven by how the data will be used.

Wirth (1976) pointed out that, for addition of small numbers, tally marks are preferable to decimal numbers. It is intuitively clear that 卌 || + ||| = 卌 卌. Decimal numbers, which require learning several rules, are better suited to large numbers, and to operations like multiplication and division.

Floating-point numbers express very large and very small numbers easily but are subject to rounding errors and the other problems mentioned in Chapter 1. Integers do not have rounding problems but have limited range and don't represent fractions easily.

Wirth (1976) says the fundamental data types are integer, floating-point, Boolean, character and set. Integers, floating-point, and characters were described in Chapter 1. A Boolean variable can have only two values; it can only be true/false or 1/0. There is more information in Chapter 3. Set variables tell whether or not a particular item is a member of the set and are often implemented as bitmaps.

Data structures describe how individual data items are aggregated. Simple examples include arrays, which are collections of items of the same data type, like an array of integers. A list is a sequence of values; an array is a type of list. A record is an aggregation of possibly different data types that are related. For example, an employee record might include name, address, and salary. There are many other kinds of data structures, enough to occupy a semester course.

6.2.4 Structured and Object-Oriented Programming

The original high-level languages were **procedural languages**, in which the programmer described the steps to accomplishing the program's purpose. The control structures of the early high-level languages were modeled after the instructions available in the hardware. Unless a programmer was extremely careful, that resulted in "spaghetti code," pieces of code intertwined with branches and nearly impossible to follow.

In 1966, two Italian computer scientists, Corrado Böhm and Giuseppe Jacopini, proved the **structured programming theorem**, which states that the only control structures needed in programming are sequence, selection, and iteration. Sequence is the execution of statements in order, and is the natural operation of von Neumann architecture computers. Selection is conditional branching, and iteration is repetition or looping. In 1968, Edsger Dijkstra wrote a now-famous letter, "Go To Statement Considered Harmful," published in *Communications of the ACM*. The Böhm-Jacopini proof and Dijkstra's letter fueled the structured programming movement with the goal of writing clearer programs with fewer errors.

Of course, with GO TO still present in the high-level languages, people could still write spaghetti code, and did. Modern languages like Java and Python make spaghetti code much less likely by eliminating the GO TO instruction.[109] One area where GO TO was particularly useful was exception handling. Modern languages implement some version of TRY … CATCH blocks for exception handling, removing the need for GO TO for that purpose.

Another important innovation in programming language design was object-oriented programming. The concept is that programs are implemented as collections of objects, each of which has specified attributes, or data, and behaviors, or executable code. For example, a DATE object might hold a single calendar date and be able to return it in one of several forms. It might include operations like incrementing itself to find a date 30 days in the future.

The three identifying properties of object-oriented programming languages are encapsulation, inheritance, and polymorphism. Encapsulation hides the internal data and algorithms of an object from anything outside the object itself. So, a more efficient algorithm could be substituted so long as it did not affect those parts of the object explicitly declared as public. Inheritance allows creating a new object with the attributes and behaviors of an existing object and adding new attributes and behaviors. An example might be a class PERSON with attributes such as date of birth. The class STUDENT might inherit from PERSON and gain attributes like student number and grade point average. The usefulness of this approach becomes clearer when we consider another class, FACULTY, that also inherits from PERSON and gains attributes like department and academic rank. In general, an object should be something that either cannot be further decomposed, or for which it doesn't make sense to do so. Returning to the DATE example, a calendar date can obviously be decomposed to year, month, and day, but when considering operations on dates, it doesn't make sense to do so. Objects designed this way will have relatively small amounts of executable code.

Polymorphism literally means "many shapes" or "many forms." The form of an operation or result can depend on the number or type of the parameters, or on the object on which a method is called. A very simple example of the first type is the multiplication operator. In most languages, the same operator, often *, can be used to multiply integers, floating point numbers, or a mixture. An example of the second type might be a method to return an ID number. If used in reference to a STUDENT object, one gets a student ID number, but if used in reference to EMPLOYEE, one gets a payroll ID number. It is important not to misuse polymorphism by making catch-all objects. In the multiplication example, procedures for multiplying integers and floating-point numbers are very different, but the result is the same.

---

109 The word GOTO is included in the Java set of reserved words but is not implemented in the language. Python has functions that can simulate the GOTO, including one that was written as an April Fools' Day joke.

6.2.5 Development Environments and Version Control

It is possible to do software development using only a text editor and the programs necessary to compile or interpret the language being used. However, for most languages, an **integrated development environment**, or *IDE*, makes development easier and faster. The most visible part of an IDE is a program editor written to recognize the syntax of the target programming language. Such an editor can catch many, but not all, mistakes early in the process. The IDE also provides a mechanism for running the program directly from the editor. The most capable IDEs will include a mechanism for setting breakpoints and examining the state of variables. The developer marks a location in the program as a breakpoint and when the program is run, execution pauses when the breakpoint is reached. The developer can then examine and change the values of variables within the program. Execution can be resumed after the breakpoint or stopped to allow further program editing.

In addition to the IDE, all but the very smallest software development projects can benefit from a **version control system**. Such a system keeps track of every module in a system under development, tracks changes, and allows changes to be undone. It can even restore status to an earlier point in time. Examples of version control systems are SVN, which is centralized, and Git, which is distributed.

6.3 Operating Systems

In all but the very smallest microcontrollers there will be a layer of system software that supports the application software by providing an interface between the application and the hardware and managing the hardware resources of the system. The operating system also provides a user interface since the operating system manages the input and output devices. Thus, the operating system presents a **virtual machine** to both the application programs and the user. It provides resources and services not provided by the hardware alone.

The operating system provides several important functions. These include managing main memory and, in many cases, managing virtual memory.

Most operating systems provide for **multiprogramming**, that is, the ability to run two or more application programs concurrently. Many also provide for **multiprocessing**, the ability to effectively use two or more processors in a single computer system, or two or more processor cores. The operating system provides scheduling at several levels.

The operating system is responsible for managing files and handling input and output requests from application programs.

Bootstrapping

Starting the operating system is called bootstrapping[110], often shortened to booting. Firmware and the operating system cooperate to get the operating system started. For computers intended to run the Windows operating system, code called the Unified Extensible Firmware Interface (UEFI) is loaded from programmable read-only memory and run by the CPU. The code in the firmware looks for a bootstrap loader program, then loads and runs it. It is the responsibility of the bootstrap loader to locate, load, and run the operating system. Some bootstrap loaders allow selection of more than one operating system by the user.

Other computers such as mainframes use a similar process, starting with firmware that locates and loads the operating system.

6.3.1 Hardware Support and Privileged Instructions

A robust multiprogramming operating system must be able to deal with programs that are incorrect and possibly even malicious. To do so, the operating system needs three things from the hardware: **privileged instructions**, **protected memory**, and a **timer that can generate interrupts**.

Some machine instructions should be executed only by the operating system. For example, the operating system should handle all input and output to prevent conflicts. This is accomplished by designating certain instructions as "privileged." Privileged instructions include input and output operations, memory allocation and protection, and a few other categories like halting the processor. A mode bit indicates whether the operating system is running, called the **system state**, or an application program is running, called the **application state**. When a privileged instruction is sent to the CPU, the mode bit in the CPU is checked by the hardware to determine whether an application program or the operating system issued the instruction. If the instruction was issued by the operating system, it is executed. If it was issued by an application program, an "illegal instruction" trap is generated, and control passes to the operating system. The usual action of the operating system is to end the program that issued the privileged instruction.

If an erroneous or malicious application could read memory belonging to other applications or the operating system, it could get information it should not have. If it could write to memory belonging to other applications or the operating system, it could cause crashes or erratic behavior, and perhaps even execute unauthorized tasks. If memory is allocated only by the operating system and the hardware provides a way to prevent applications from reading or writing other than their own memory, those situations cannot occur. Memory management is discussed further in Section 6.3.4.

During ordinary operation of a computer system, the operating system gets control when-

---

110 The name comes from the phrase "pull yourself up by your own bootstraps."

ever an application requests a service provided by the operating system. Some mathematical computations might run for seconds or more without making an operating system request, and error or malice could put a program in an infinite loop that never makes an operating system request. To handle such conditions the hardware must include a timer that generates interrupts at regular intervals, perhaps 10 to 200 milliseconds.[111] These timer interrupts allow the operating system's scheduler to run other applications even when a very CPU-intensive application is part of the workload. Interrupts are discussed further in Section 6.3.2.

6.3.2 Concurrent Operation and Process Scheduling

In a multiprogramming system, several processes are in memory, running concurrently, and competing for CPU time and other resources. The operating system must schedule access to the CPU, memory, and other system resources according to the design objectives of the operating system.

Process ID
Pointer to parent process
Pointers to child processes
Process state
Program counter
Register save area
Memory pointers
Priority
Accounting data

Figure 6-2

A typical process control block.

A **process** is a program in binary form together with its data and other resources needed for execution. The process is the basic unit of work of the operating system. Each process has a process ID, a unique identifier for that process. Each process has a **context** that includes the program counter, the register contents, and any other information needed to allow the process to be interrupted and restarted. This information is stored in a **process control block**, also called a process table, maintained by the operating system. A typical process control block is shown in Figure 6-2.

Processes are created by a mechanism called forking or spawning. The process that creates another is called the parent process. The newly created process is called a child process of the parent.

The operating system schedules processes at several levels. The most interesting and probably the most important is dispatching, that is, determining which process will have access to a CPU next.

The operating system's dispatching process has several goals, some of which conflict. These include minimizing response time and maintaining response time consistency, maximizing CPU and other resource utilization, providing for graceful degradation under load, and making certain no process is starved of CPU time.

A process can be in one of three states, running, ready, or waiting. A process in the **running**

---

111 The interval chosen depends on the scheduling policy. A workstation for use by one person might choose an interval at the low end of the range to maximize responsiveness, while a server operating system might choose an interval at the upper end of the range to minimize context switching.

state is actively using a CPU and the CPU is executing instructions of that process. The number of processes in the running state is limited by the number of CPUs available. A process in the **ready state** is not waiting on any action by the operating system and could run if a CPU were available. A process in the **waiting state** is awaiting some action by the operating system, such as completion of an I/O request. The waiting state is also called the blocked state.

The operating system maintains a queue for each of the running, ready, and waiting states. When a process in the running state requests an I/O operation or other service of the operating system, it moves from the running state to the waiting state and the operating system schedules the service to be performed. The next program in the ready queue has its context loaded from its process control block and given control of the CPU. That moves the program from the ready state to the running state.

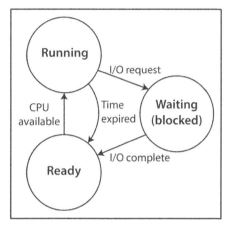

When the operating system completes an I/O operation or other service for a program in the waiting state, that program is moved from waiting to ready. It will run again when a CPU is available.

Figure 6-3
Running, ready, and waiting queues.

New processes are placed in the ready state by the operating system and will run when a CPU is available. Programs that terminate exit from the running state.

Priority scheduling

Most operating systems support the concept of priority, with higher priority processes getting access to a CPU before lower priority processes. One might assign a high priority to processes that accept user input and change the display, for example. That has the effect of making the system responsive to user input.

A problem with priority dispatching as that low priority process may face starvation; that is, may never get access to a CPU. One way to prevent starvation is to temporarily raise the priority of a low priority process each time it is passed over. When that process gets access to the CPU, its priority is returned to the original value.

Preemptive dispatching

Some processes could use the CPU for long periods without requesting services of the operating system. The timer discussed in Section 6.3.1 keeps that from happening. The timer generates interrupts every 10 to 200 milliseconds or so. That interrupt allows the operating system to gain control and select another process to run. The time between such interrupts is called the **time quantum** for a process. When the time quantum of a process expires, the process is moved to the ready queue and will run again when a CPU is available.

Threads

As discussed so far, a process has resources, including an address space in memory, and a single thread of execution, that is, a sequence of instructions that the process will execute when given access to a CPU. That was sufficient when computers had a single CPU. With multiple cores and multiple CPUs commonly available, it is now common to allow one process to have more than one thread of execution, or just **thread**. Each thread must have its own registers, program counter, and stack, but shares the address space and other resources of its parent process. On a system with multiple CPU cores, allowing one process to have multiple threads provides true parallel processing.

Allowing a process to have multiple threads also introduces substantial complexity into the operating system, complexity that is better handled in a course on operating systems than in a book on concepts.

Disk scheduling

The CPU is about six orders of magnitude faster than a magnetic disk, so it makes sense to spend some CPU time optimizing magnetic disk access.[112] The slowest operation for a magnetic disk is the process of seeking from one track to another. We immediately discard the idea of handling requests in order, or first-come, first served because that doesn't optimize seek time. Shortest distance first is also discarded because in a system under heavy load, a request with a long seek time could be postponed for an indefinite time.

Scheduling for magnetic disks uses an algorithm like that used by elevators in buildings and is in fact called the **elevator algorithm**. Elevators receive their input from floor buttons inside the car and call buttons on each floor. If an elevator starts on the ground floor it will go up until there are no more "up" requests, then change direction and serve only "down" requests. The same technique can be applied to disk scheduling. Disk requests are sorted into track order. If the disk heads are at the outermost track, they are moved toward the center until there are no more "in" requests, then change direction and handle "out" requests, also in order.

Using the elevator algorithm, the disk heads do not travel further than needed in either direction and move more or less smoothly inward and outward. The elevator algorithm usually serves the center tracks twice. Some operating systems locate frequently accessed files such as the virtual memory page file near the center of the disk for that reason.

---

112 Scheduling is much less important for solid state drives because there are no moving parts that correspond to the seek operation of a magnetic disk.

6.3.3 Disk Space and File Management

The file management component of an operating system is very visible to the computer user because the file management system provides the organizational structure for files and may impose limits such as limits on length and character set for file names.

A **file** is a named collection of data, usually in non-volatile storage, and occupying at least one allocation unit of storage.[113] Operating systems may maintain an association with the application program used for that file type. The Windows operating system uses the file extension and a separate table of associations, so double-clicking a .docx file starts Microsoft Word. Apple's macOS stores the association information in the file's metadata.

The file management system is a component of an operating system that provides a logical view of a file to users and application programs and hides much of the physical view.

The file management system communicates with the operating system's input/output control system (IOCS) and device drivers. Separating file management from input and output allows files to be on very different physical devices in a way that is transparent to the user. For example, in modern operating systems the user need not care whether a file is on a local magnetic disk, a solid-state drive, or on a network server.

File systems

On a magnetic disk or solid-state drive, a **file system** provides the mechanism for organizing and accessing data. A given operating system may support one or more file systems with one as a default. For example, the NTFS system is the default system for Windows and AFS is the default for Apple operating systems.

The physical properties of a storage device are often established when the device is manufactured. For example, a block is the physical unit of space on a magnetic disk drive, often 4 KiB. Allocation of space on solid state drives is more complex. The unit for reading and writing is the page, often also 4 KiB. However, a page can only be written to an empty area, and erasures must take place in blocks of many pages as described in Section 4.2.3. A physical device may be divided into multiple partitions, each of which can be treated as a separate device. For consistency, a partition is still present if the entire device is to be considered as one unit.

A file system provides a logical view of the storage medium it manages and usually allocates space in quantities larger than a block or page. The amount of storage allocated as one unit by the operating system is called a **cluster** or **allocation unit**. Clusters can be larger than the physical unit of space, but never smaller.

---

113 Microsoft's NTFS stores the data for very small files in the master file table, the directory data structure; very small files do not consume storage space other than the directory entry.

A file system is established on a storage device by formatting a partition, which could be the entire device. The file system type is determined when the device is formatted. For some file systems, the cluster size can be set during formatting. Formatting establishes the directory structure and adds all clusters in the file system to its structure of free space. Some operating systems offer a quick format option. After a quick format, any prior data is still present on the device, but is no longer accessible because the directory structure has been replaced by a new, empty directory. A full format, if available, scans the device for bad sectors, necessarily overwriting any data that may have been present. A quick format is likely to take a few seconds; a full format may take hours.

Free space can be managed with a bitmap or a linked list. With the bitmap mechanism, one bit is used for each cluster on the device. If the cluster is free, the corresponding bit will be a zero; if the cluster is in use, the bit will be a one. Large devices with many clusters necessarily require more space for such a bitmap.

The other alternative is a linked list. The operating system maintains a pointer to the first free cluster, and each cluster holds a pointer to the next free cluster.

The other major service provided by the operating system is maintaining a directory structure of files and sub directories. Some file systems, such as those available with Linux, maintain a single root directory.

Others, including Windows, have a root directory for each physical device. Directories may be tree structured. If the file system permits links, the structure will be a **directed acyclic graph**, or DAG.

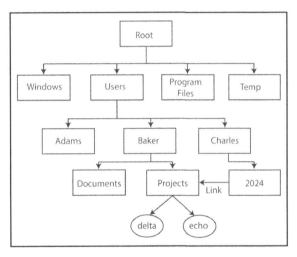

Figure 6-4

A directory structure. The link from "2024" to "Projects" makes this a directed acyclic graph rather than a tree.

File systems may provide several other facilities. File security may vary from none to full access control lists. Quotas set the maximum amount of file space that can be used on a per-user basis. Alternate data streams, also called forks, can be used to store two or more data items with a single file name. For example, macOS uses the data fork to hold the files' main contents and the resource fork to associate the file with an application to process that file. Snapshots provide a consistent view of an active file system for backups and similar purposes. Encryption can help protect the confidentiality of files. Compression reduces the amount of physical space a logical file requires. Some file systems provide for redundancy.

Accessing Files

Some operations, such as copying or moving a file, are performed on the file as a whole. And some application programs such as word processors read an entire file into memory and operate on it there. In other cases, an application program may view a file as a stream of bytes or as a collection of records. In the latter case the records may be of fixed length or separated by delimiters.

Opening a file causes the operating system to locate the file and allocate the resources, such as buffers and file's metadata, necessary to read and write the file. Opening a file causes the operating system to allocate a **file handle** and return it to the application. The file handle identifies the file and its resources to the operating system. Closing a file releases the operating system resources acquired when the file was opened and may do other things like flushing data from a memory buffer to the physical storage mechanism.

When a file is to be processed as a stream of bytes, there will be commands to open and close the file, and to mark it as a byte stream file. There will be a pointer that marks the current location within the file. An application program can read a specified number of bytes, which delivers the data and moves the file pointer. It is also possible to write a specified number of bytes to a byte stream file beginning at the location marked by the file pointer. There will be commands to move the file pointer to the beginning or end of the file or to an arbitrary location within the file.

When a file is to be processed as a collection of records, there will be commands to open and close the file, to retrieve a record, and to add a record at the end of the file. There may be commands to delete a record or to update a record. These commands are much more complex for variable length records than for fixed length records.

Files can be accessed sequentially and, on random access media like magnetic disks or solid-state drives, accessed randomly or through an index.

Sequential files are accessed in sequence from beginning to end, or until a specific value is found. Most files are accessed sequentially, including music and video files, program files in binary form, and most text or word processing files.

Files can be accessed randomly if the displacement of the desired record from the beginning of the file can be calculated. One common method for random access is hashing a key. A very simple example is that the name "Brown" is encoded with the UTF-8 values 66, 114, 111, 119, 110. The sum of those values is 520, and the record

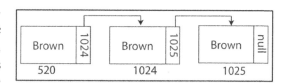

Figure 6-5

Hash collisions are resolved by linking to overflow blocks.

for Brown might be located at 520 times the length of each record, as shown in Figure 6-5. The problem, of course, is that all records with a key of "Brown" produce the same hash value. The condition of two or more records having the same hash value is called a **collision**. The problem of collisions is somewhat mitigated by longer key values and more sophisticated hashing algorithms. Unless the algorithm can guarantee there will be no collisions, there must be a way to handle them. The most common mechanism is linking. If a hash location already contains data, it also has a pointer to an overflow area where the second record with a given hash value should be stored. That record contains a pointer that is either null or points to the third area, and so on. Long overflow chains cause serious performance degradation. Random organization is uncommon except in database management systems.

Indexed file mechanisms have names like indexed sequential access method (ISAM) or something similar. Indexed access depends on two or more files. A "base file" contains the data and can be read sequentially, independent of the index files. One or more index files contain records with keys and pointers to the matching records in the base file. For example, an index file might contain the employee number 11505 and a pointer to that employee's record in the base file. Another index file might contain one record and pointer pair for each employee's family name. That would make it possible to search for all employees named "Brown." There may be multiple index files for different keys. When the number of records in the base file is very large, there may be multiple levels for one index.

6.3.4 Memory Management and Virtual Memory

In the earliest computers, memory was a scarce and expensive resource. Computers with 2K words were not uncommon. Programmers spent significant time making their programs fit into the available memory. Careful selection of algorithms and really tight coding helped, but sometimes a program was just too big to fit. In that case, programmers used overlays, the technique of dividing a program into pieces that were used at different times during the execution of the program.

Use of overlays

Consider an assembler program, the language translator that turns symbolic programs in assembly language into binary programs. Earlier we learned that assemblers make two passes through the source code. In the first pass the size of each item is determined, the location counter is stepped through the program, and

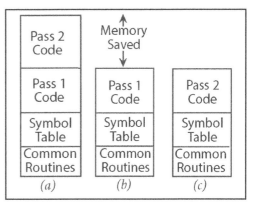

Figure 6-6

Hypothetical assembler program showing the use of overlays. A. The assembler without overlays. B Pass 1 code is loaded in memory but pass 2 is not C. Pass 2 code overlays pass 1

195

symbols and their locations are saved in a symbol table. On the second pass, binary values for instructions and data are generated and the addresses are looked up in the symbol table. Pass 2 generates the binary program.

The memory map of the assembler might look like the first part of Figure 6-6, with routines common to both passes, an area for the symbol table, and the code for the two passes. If that program were too big to fit in memory, the programmer might write it so that when it starts its memory map looks like the second part of the figure. The common routines, symbol table, and pass 1 code are in memory, but the pass 2 code is not. At the end of pass 1, when that code is no longer needed, the pass 2 code is loaded in its place. This technique is called overlaying. The third part of the figure shows the memory map after the pass 2 code overlays the pass 1 code.

Dividing a program into overlays and loading them was the responsibility of the programmer. It was a difficult and error-prone task. In 1961, a group of researchers at Manchester, England set out to find a way to automate the process of managing overlays.

The key idea of the Manchester group, and the idea that makes virtual memory possible, is to separate the concept of the address space from the physical memory locations.

Usable and unusable address spaces

To understand what that means, we must examine the way we think about address space and memory in a computer without virtual memory. Consider a computer capable of generating 64-bit addresses. Such a computer has an address space of 16 exbibytes,[114] more than eighteen quintillion bytes. However, it would be much more likely for the computer to have from four to perhaps 16 GiB of actual memory.

Figure 6-7 shows the address space of a computer with 64-bit addresses and 16 GiB of actual memory. The address space is still 16 exbibytes, but only 16 GiB of it is usable. If we have a program that requires more than 16 GiB, it can't be run on this computer unless we do something different. That something different is virtual memory.

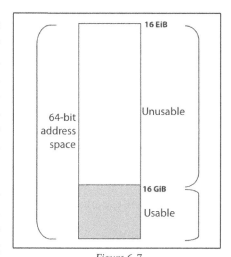

Figure 6-7

A computer with a 64-bit address space and 16 GiB of installed memory

---

114 An exbibyte is 2^{60} bytes. See Figure 1-2, Units for powers of two.

6.3.5 Virtual Memory

In a virtual memory system, the program and data are stored in secondary storage (disk) and only the parts in use at any given moment are brought into real memory. This works because of **locality of reference**. When we discussed cache systems, we described temporal locality of reference and spatial locality of reference. It is of the nature of von Neumann architecture computer systems that if a word from memory has been used recently, it is likely to be used again in the near future. Similarly, if a word has been used recently, words near it are likely to be used in the relatively near future.

Virtual memory is implemented by dividing the portion of the address space used by a program into fixed-size pieces called **pages**. The size of the pages is a power of two, typically from 512 bytes to about 64 K bytes. We will use a page size of 4 K in the example and discuss the trade-offs in selecting a page size later.

Real memory is divided into **page frames** which are the same size as the virtual pages. When a page is needed during the running of a program, it is copied into a page frame in real memory. The amount of real memory available is called the physical address space. The area available for the programmer to use (determined by the size of an address) is called the virtual address space.

The process of moving program pages to and from real memory is called **paging**. Paging is transparent to the writer of the program except that frequent paging can cause a program to run slowly.

We have skipped over some details up to now, and one of them is the need for address translation, or mapping. Address translation is made necessary by the following facts:

- Programs generate virtual addresses,
- The memory subsystem hardware only understands physical addresses, and
- Any page can go into any page frame.

Address translation is accomplished by a memory management unit, or MMU. The MMU may be a part of the CPU or a separate unit. The MMU and the operating system work together to implement virtual memory.

Consider an example of a computer with 32-bit logical addresses, one GiB of real memory, and a virtual memory system that uses 4 KiB pages. (We'll talk about larger address spaces and larger memories shortly.) The memory management process translates a 32-bit virtual address into a 30-bit physical address. This is done with the aid of a page table.

If there are 32 bits in an address, and a page is 4 KiB, there are 2^{20} or about one million pages in the virtual address space. These pages are represented by a page table with 2^{20} entries.

Each entry contains a valid bit that indicates whether the page is currently in main memory, a dirty bit indicating whether the page has been modified, and a frame number pointing to a page frame in real memory. There may be other bits indicating whether the page is executable, etc.

One GiB, the size of real memory, is 2^{30} bytes. Pages are four KiB or 2^{12} bytes. Since 30–12=18, the page frame numbers in the page table must be 18 bits wide.[115] The leftmost 18 bits of the 30-bit physical address will come from the page table. The rightmost 12 bits represent the displacement into the four KiB frame and are copied unchanged into the physical address.

Figure 6-8 shows that the CPU has generated a 32-bit address as shown in the upper right of the figure. As far as the CPU is concerned, this is just a 32-bit number. For purposes of address translation, it is useful to think of the address as a 20-bit page num-

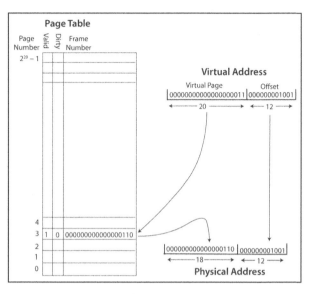

Figure 6-8

Translating a 32-bit virtual address to a 30-bit physical address

ber and a 12-bit displacement that identifies a cell within a page. We will think of a physical address as a page frame number and a displacement. Since the pages and page frames are the same size, the displacement from the virtual address can simply be copied into the displacement part of the physical address.

However, we have some work to do to translate the 20-bit page number into an 18-bit page frame number. In the example, the virtual page number is three. We look in entry three of the page table and find that the valid bit is a one, indicating that the page is already in real memory. We check the frame number from the page table and find that it is six. Virtual page three is stored in page frame six. The memory management unit copies this number into the frame part of the physical address, and the MMU has mapped a 32-bit virtual address onto a 30-bit physical address. The memory hardware can now retrieve the desired cell.

Remember, the idea that the Manchester researchers had was to separate the concepts of address space and physical memory. Virtual memory allows programmers to use the entire address space defined by the size of an address, regardless of the amount of physical memory present.

---

115 When numbers are represented as a power of a base, multiplication and division can be accomplished by adding or subtracting exponents provided all numbers have the same base.

In the example, we assumed that the page containing the needed cell was already in main memory. That doesn't always happen. A reference to a cell that's not in main memory is called a **page fault**.[116] In case of a page fault, the MMU would have signaled an interrupt upon finding a zero valid bit. The operating system would read the page from disk into a free page frame, update the page table, and restart the instruction that caused the page fault.

The process of reading pages in from disk only when they are needed is called **demand paging**. Pages are not loaded into page frames until there is a demand for them.

A program typically starts with none of its pages in real memory. The first reference causes a page fault. Soon, however, all the pages needed for a given part of the program are in memory. This set of pages is called the **working set**. The composition of the working set changes over time as the program runs.

The working set of a program is the amount of real memory necessary to satisfy the locality of the program at any given time.[117] If the working set of a program is smaller than the available physical memory, the program runs nearly as fast as it would if it had free access to enough real memory for the entire program. If there is not enough real memory to hold the working set, page faults occur frequently, and the CPU spends more time moving pages around than it does running the program. This condition is called **thrashing**. The solution to the problem of thrashing is to add more main memory or to reduce the degree of multiprogramming, the number of processes running concurrently, to reduce the demand for main memory.

When there's no free frame – page replacement policy

When a page fault occurs and there's no free page frame, the operating system must make room for the new page by replacing a page already in main memory. The designer of a virtual memory system must decide on a page replacement policy to determine which page will get evicted from its page frame when there's no free frame.

Least recently used (LRU) is not a suitable replacement policy for cache because of the amount of time consumed by bookkeeping. Cache operations happen very fast. In virtual memory, things happen more slowly, and it's possible we can afford the effort required for LRU.

An alternative is FIFO, or first-in first-out. The oldest page is evicted from its page frame, regardless of when it was last used. The advantage of FIFO is that bookkeeping must only happen when a new page is loaded, and not every time a page is referenced. However, in 1969, László Bélády demonstrated that increasing the number of page frames, *i.e.,* the size of main memory, could *increase* the number of page faults. The overhead of LRU may be worth it after all.

---

116 Despite its name, a page fault is not an error; page faults are a part of the routine operation of a virtual memory system.

117 This is different from many definitions found on the World Wide Web. This one is correct. The working set is how much memory a program *needs* to run normally, not how much the program currently has.

The "dirty bit" in the page table tells whether the page has been modified while in main memory. If it has, it must be written to disk before a new page can occupy that page frame. If, however, the page is unmodified, it already matches what's on the disk and can just be overwritten.

How big is a page?

Earlier we glossed over the problem of how big to make a page. No matter what we choose for a page size, most programs won't be an exact multiple of the page size. On average, half of the last page in a program will be wasted. Since the unused bytes in a page occupy space in a page frame when the page is loaded, we would like to minimize the waste, and this drives us toward smaller page sizes. Similarly, we find that the first and last pages in each part of the working set generate some waste, driving us to smaller pages. Smaller pages waste less main memory.

However, each page requires a page table entry. Smaller pages mean more pages, and so more page table entries. Further, larger pages use I/O more effectively than smaller pages. As with much of the rest of computer architecture, the designer is faced with a set of trade-offs.

Large address spaces and memories – multilevel page tables

In the example above, we need a one million entry page table. That's not entirely out of the question with a GiB of real memory, even though each process needs its own page table. For a processor that generates 64-bit addresses and uses four KiB pages, the page table would need 2^{52} entries, a very big number indeed.

The solution is to make page tables sparse, that is to have only the entries needed. That is done with multilevel page tables. Instead of a 20-bit virtual frame number and 12-bit offset, the 32-bit addresses in the example above could be divided into two ten-bit parts and a 12-bit offset. The first ten-bit part points to an entry in a top-level page table. The top-level page table would be 2^{10} or 1,024 entries long. Each entry in the top-level page table points to one of 2^{10} second-level page tables that contain the physical page frame number. The important part of this scheme is that not all second-level page tables are needed, and so not all of them will be in memory. Only the second-level entries for memory actually used by a program need to be present. A program that uses one GiB of virtual memory needs only the top-level page table and perhaps as few as eight second-level page tables, the exact number depending on how memory is used.

Most 64-bit operating systems of the 2020s use this technique with four or even five-level page tables. A few, such as some IBM operating systems, use another technique called an inverted page table. An inverted page table has one entry for each page frame in real memory rather than one for each possible virtual page. We will not consider inverted page tables further in this book.

Speeding up virtual memory – the translation lookaside buffer

The page tables themselves are held in virtual memory, so every memory access by a program requires two memory accesses, one for the item being read or written, and one for the page table. Even worse, it is possible to have a page fault trying to read the page table.

The solution is to take further advantage of locality of reference. Just as locality of reference means that only a few pages of a process generally need to be in main memory at any one time, locality of reference means that only a few of the pages in memory will be highly active. A **translation lookaside buffer** (TLB) that is generally a part of the memory management unit[118] holds a small number of page table entries for those very active pages. According to Tanenbaum (2001) there are rarely more than 64 entries in a TLB. When implemented as part of the MMU, the translation lookaside buffer is in associative memory. Associative memory means that all entries in the table can be searched in parallel. If the page table entry for the requested page is in the TLB, the MMU can return the page frame address directly and without a memory access. So, the *translation lookaside buffer serves as a specialized cache for the page table.*

Updating the TLB is very similar to updating the pages in real memory. If there is no hit on a requested page in the TLB, one entry is evicted and an entry is made for the page just accessed.

6.3.6 Management of Other Resources

The operating system can give exclusive control of some devices, like optical drives and communication ports to application programs. The screen, keyboard, and pointing device are necessarily shared in a multiprogramming system that uses a graphical user interface. Screen sharing is accomplished by assigning a *window* to an application program. The application program controls the contents of the window, but the operating system handles the placement of the window on the screen. The user can control how the windows are arranged by providing input to the operating system, usually by dragging and resizing windows.

The operating system controls the keyboard and pointing devices. Information is passed to an application program through the mechanism of a window having focus. Only one window at a time can have focus, and input from keyboard or pointing device is passed to the application program owning that window.

Spooling

Printing presents a special problem because it is reasonable for more than one application to produce printed output concurrently. Sending two or more concurrent streams of data to the same printer would produce unwanted results. This problem is solved by a process

---

118 Some RISC processors use software to manage the TLB.

called spooling[119]. The operating system intercepts the application program's printer output and saves the data to disk. Each application program has its own spool queue in which its printed output is stored. When the application program ends, or signals the end of printing, the operating system waits until the printer is free and sends data from the queue on disk to the printer. Operating systems can manage more than one physical printer, each with its own physical characteristics. Most operating systems provide controls to manage printing priority, distribute print jobs to multiple printers with the same capabilities, and to delete jobs from the print queue.

Deadlock

One resource allocation problem that operating systems must address is that of deadlock. Deadlock is the circumstance where each of two processes holds a resource needed by the other, and neither can continue execution. For example, two processes together consume all available memory. If each process then needs additional memory, neither can continue.

If the resource causing deadlock is preemptable, the operating system can preempt one of the processes, allow the other to run, and finally allow the preempted process to continue. In the example above, memory is a preemptable resource. The operating system can swap one process to disk allowing the other to continue, and later swap the preempted process in. Many resources, such as optical storage, cannot be preempted.

Operating systems can prevent deadlock by requiring each process to request all resources it will need before allocating any resources. This approach precludes processes from dynamically acquiring resources as needed.

Andrew Tanenbaum (2001) describes the "ostrich approach," namely allowing deadlocks to occur and requiring manual intervention to resolve them.

6.3.7 Tuning and Limits on Throughput

Throughput is the amount of work performed by a computer system in a given time. For transaction processing systems such as online banking systems, throughput is often measured in transactions per second, or TPS. Other systems might use other measures. Sometimes relatively minor changes, called **tuning**, can improve the throughput of a computer system. Most operating systems provide measurement tools that tell the percent of utilization for major resources such as the CPU and memory. Tuning should start with those resources at or near 100% utilization.

---

119 The name spooling likely comes from SPOOL, an acronym for Simultaneous Peripheral Operations On Line, an early form of multiprogramming from IBM in which an application program and a spooler program ran concurrently. The operating system could capture data destined for slow devices like printers or card punches and send it to magnetic tape. From there the spooler program could send the data to the printer while another application program ran. Spooling was also used to capture input data from slow devices like card readers so that application programs could read the data from magnetic tape.

Magnetic disks are a special case when tuning. They are usually the slowest storage devices attached to a computer, and the slowest operation for a magnetic disk is the seek operation, moving the disk heads from one track to another. If you have many applications using the disk, or one application that generates many disk operations, the disk could be a bottleneck. Replacing a magnetic disk with a solid-state disk can sometimes produce a dramatic improvement. If that isn't possible, installing an additional disk drive and moving some data to the second drive might be of help. For example, putting a database management system's data on one drive and the indices on another can improve performance by overlapping seek operations.

Virtual memory is a special consideration when tuning disk access. As we saw in Section 6.3.4, if the amount of available real memory is less than the sum of the working sets of the active applications, the system enters a state called thrashing when more time is spent moving data between memory and disk than in doing actual work. In that case, increasing the size of real memory might relieve a disk access problem.

In considering CPU-bound applications, it is important to take into account the number of cores in the CPU chip since each core is effectively a CPU. Unless an application is specifically written to take advantage of multiple cores, it will use only one. So, if you have an application that reports using 25% of the CPU on a four-core machine, it is likely that that application is CPU bound. A faster CPU might help, as might rewriting the application. Also remember the advice of Grace Murray Hopper: "In pioneer days they used oxen for heavy pulling, and when one ox couldn't budge a log, they didn't try to grow a larger ox." Instead, they used a team of oxen. If an application's workload can be divided among two or more computer systems that might be the most scalable way to address the bottleneck.

Although there is at least as much art as science in system tuning, one more bit of advice from Hopper is appropriate: "One accurate measurement is worth a thousand expert opinions."

6.4 Virtualization

Modern CPUs are very fast. Maximizing the use of the CPU means keeping it busy nearly all the time, but CPUs in server environments are frequently idle. The computing environment in industry is likely to consist of many computers doing different things, and even running different operating systems. Multiple computers increase expense and complexity with concomitant management difficulties.

In a computer system, the hardware and operating system together constitute a virtual machine because together they expose to application programs services not provided by the hardware alone. The same hardware with a different operating system exposes different services. This is easy to see when you consider running Windows or Linux on the same hardware. The services available to applications are very different depending on which operating system is chosen. We said in Chapter 0 that hardware and software are logically equivalent and repeated it again in this chapter. We can use this logical equivalence to expose more than one set of services at the same time to get multiple virtual machines on the same hardware and at the same time.

Virtualization allows running more than one operating system on a single computing platform. It can help accommodate the fact that different applications may need different operating systems or different operating system configurations. That reduces hardware expense and hardware complexity. It also reduces hardware operating cost, including the cost of space, cooling, and power. The penalty is increased software complexity and sometimes increased software expense.

In addition to allowing multiple and different operating systems on a single hardware platform, virtualization provides a safe platform for testing. In the event of difficulty, the virtual machine can simply be deleted. In a multi-client environment, giving each client a separate virtual machine may improve security.

6.4.1 Native and Hosted Virtualization

In this context, a **virtual machine** is a simulated physical computer, capable of running an operating system and application software. The software that allows for instantiation of multiple virtual machines with multiple operating systems is called the **hypervisor**[120] or

virtual machine manager, VMM. The term *physical machine* refers to the actual hardware. **Guest operating system** refers to an operating system running on a virtual machine, and **host operating system** refers to one running on the physical machine and supporting a hypervisor.

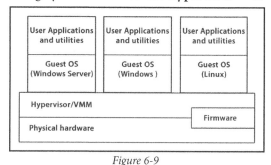

Figure 6-9

Type I, native virtualization

There are two main approaches to virtualization. In one approach, called type I or native virtualization, the hypervisor runs directly on the physical machine. Figure 6-9 shows type I virtualization with the hypervisor running directly on the hardware and with access to the firmware. The firmware is not visible to application programs, but is necessary for starting the system, and may include functions used by the operating system or hypervisor.

Native virtualization systems are typically used with servers, with the goal of improving the

---

120 Early operating systems were called supervisor programs. By extension the program that runs supervisors must be a hypervisor.

execution efficiency of the hardware. The efficiency comes from the fact that one fewer layers of software is needed. They are arguably also more secure, as they have fewer additional layers than the alternative hosted approach.

In type II, or hosted virtualization, the hypervisor runs as an application under an operating system that provides the interface to the hardware. The hypervisor, or VMM runs as an application on the host operating system. When most applications are for the host operating system, they can run without the overhead of virtualization. The same hardware can still support other operating systems and applications that require them. For example, a computer running Windows 11 may also need access to Linux or an older Windows version from time to time. Hosted virtualization systems are more common in client or single-user computer systems, where they run along with other applications on the host operating system and are used to support applications for alternate operating system versions or types. This may result in increased security concerns since the hypervisor has the same access as any other application on the computer. Further, the hypervisor is exposed to any security vulnerabilities in the host operating system. Hosted virtualization works best when the guest operating systems are used lightly or infrequently.

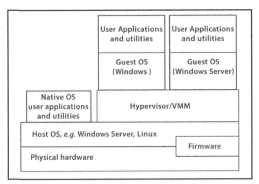

Figure 6-10
Type II, hosted virtualization.

In either type of virtualization, the virtual machine manager must share the resources of the hardware among the guest operating systems. Memory can be handled with separate virtual memory spaces and the CPU scheduled as with a single operating system. Disks can be physically partitioned, or each guest operating system can get a virtual disk that appears as a single large file to the underlying system. Network access can be handled with separate physical network devices for each guest operating system, or the hypervisor can provide virtual network devices. In the latter case, the hypervisor is responsible for routing packets among the virtual network adapters and to and from the physical adapter. Devices like optical drives are usually allocated to one guest operating system, with the allocation changes as needed.

6.4.2 Planning for Virtualization

Virtualization can reduce hardware complexity and operating cost, but if not implemented and managed carefully, can lead to out-of-control software complexity. Proper planning is the key to smooth implementation and operation.

Defining the goals of a virtualization project is the first step in planning. Are the goals maximizing hardware utilization, providing security by isolating multiple clients, providing a testing environment, being able to run infrequently used but necessary applications, or something else? There will likely be more than one goal but deciding on the important ones will drive the rest of the choices.

Once the goals are defined, it will be possible to list the host operating systems and applications that will be virtualized. Not everything that can be virtualized should be. For example, a particularly resource-intensive application might be better left on a server of its own. If virtualized, it is certain to run more slowly and bog down other applications on the same physical hardware. Similarly, applications that need specialized hardware, such as document scanning in volume, may not be good candidates for virtualization. Certain key services such as an Active Directory domain controller or a domain name system server may not be good candidates for virtualization because so many other services depend on them. There are programs that will not run at all in a virtual environment and others with license restrictions that may make virtualization uneconomical.

Are all applications supported in the selected virtual environment? Which ones are not?

The choice of virtualization software will drive many of the other decisions in implementing virtualization. The choice of guest operating systems and applications to be virtualized may influence the choice of virtualization software, so those two activities are somewhat iterative. There are many choices of virtualization software, both free and paid, and the choices change frequently.

Virtualization may streamline hardware configurations but is unlikely to decrease the hardware budget. The hypervisor adds a new layer of software complexity for which systems administration staff must be trained. Successful use of virtualization requires careful planning, training, and careful implementation.

6.5 Database Management Systems

Early business applications operated on data as files, collections of usually fixed-length fields organized into usually fixed-length records. Such files were stored on tabulating cards or magnetic tape, and later, on magnetic disk. Programs were closely coupled to the structure of the file, and changing the file structure meant changing every program that used that file. File processing systems often duplicated data, storing the same information in two or more places. Duplication provides an opportunity for inconsistency. For example, if an address field is stored in two different files, there's an opportunity for one but not the other to be updated. There is no longer one single answer to "what is this person's address?"

Database management systems attempt to make programs independent of data definitions, improve data sharing, reduce program maintenance costs, and enforce consistency. A **database** is an organized, self-defining collection of logically related data accessible both directly through a user interface and by application programs through an application program interface. Databases are self-defining because the definitional metadata are stored in the database along with the application data. The organization depends on the database model used.

One of the earliest database management systems was IBM's Information Management System, IMS. The original IMS design was to produce a bill of materials for a spacecraft. A bill of materials is inherently hierarchical, with the finished product, in this case a spacecraft, at the top of the hierarchy. Below are the sub-components, sub-sub-components, all the way down to individual nuts, bolts, and other parts. IMS worked very well in hierarchical applications but fit less well in other applications.

The other early database model was the network model, also called the graph model or CO-DASYL model. It was invented by Charles Bachman and adopted by the Conference of Data Systems Languages Database Task Group in 1969. The network model is more flexible than the hierarchical model but requires the database designer to specify connections between data items.

6.5.1 The Relational Database Model

Edgar F. (Ted) Codd applied the mathematics of set theory to the problem of data modeling and, in 1970 published "A Relational Model of Data for Large Shared Data Banks" in the *Communications of the ACM* (Codd, 1970). As a result of this work, the Association for Computing Machinery presented Codd with the Turing Award in 1981.

In the relational model, a data system is modeled as entities which are noun-like things such as department or employee, and the relationships[121] between them. Relationships can be one to one, one to many, or many to many. Each entity is represented in the database as a table of rows and columns. For each table, one or more columns comprise a unique **primary key** and the presence of the primary key makes each row unique.

In the data modeling stage, entities are changed to normal forms[122] which prevent anomalies by removing duplication of data. For example, if a table of employees included the department name for each employee, it would be necessary to change the rows for every employee in a department if the department name changes. It would also be possible to have different names for the same department, for example "IT" and "Information technology." That is referred to as an *update anomaly*.

With the table described above, deleting the last employee of a department makes the de-

---

121 Do not confuse *relationship* with *relation*. In the relational model a relation is represented as a table. Relationships are the connections between relations.

122 A normal form is a named step in the process of normalization of data, that is the process of removing anomalies. For example, a database in third normal form is free of most insertion, update, and deletion anomalies.

partment itself cease to exist. A deletion anomaly exists when deleting something also removes something that should not be deleted.

If orientation date is required for an employee row, one can't add an employee who has been hired but not yet assigned an orientation date. That's an *insertion anomaly.*

Continuing the example, we would remove the update and deletion anomalies by **normalization**. We would design the database with an employee table and a separate department table. The primary key of the employee table might be an employee number and the primary key of the department table might be a department number. Now the department name exists only in one place, in a row of the department table. Employees are assigned to departments by including the department number in the employee row. The department number in an employee row is called a **foreign key**. The insertion anomaly is resolved by allowing the orientation date to be null.

Normalizing the data in this way allows the database management system to enforce integrity constraints on the data. If department number is identified as a foreign key in the employee table, the database management system can prevent assigning an employee to a non-existent department. That is a referential integrity constraint.

A relational model database management system can do much more than you see in this brief description and comes with a solid mathematical foundation; we can prove things about a relational database design. The relational model comes with a non-procedural language for retrieval from the database, the Structured Query Language, or SQL.[123]

There is a cost trade-off, though. Continuing the example, producing a report of employees listing department names requires getting the department name from a separate table from the employee information. In the language of the relational model, that's called a **join**, and joins are relatively expensive in both CPU time and I/O operations. For that reason, the relational model was not widely adopted until the operation of Moore's Law increased computing power enough to make it practical.

The structured query language, SQL

Part of Codd's design of the relational model was a query language, SQL, to operate on relational databases. SQL has components for data definition, data manipulation, and data control. The data definition component provides mechanisms for creating databases and tables, modifying them, and deleting them. The data control mechanism provides for protecting databases, including setting limits on what operations a user is allowed to perform.

The largest part of SQL is the data manipulation component. It provides for adding, updating, deleting, and retrieving data from the tables that form a relational database. It includes

---

123 SQL is often pronounced "sequel." The language was originally named Structured English Query Language, SEQUEL, by IBM but the name was changed because of a trademark conflict.

four important SQL operations, INSERT, UPDATE, DELETE, and SELECT. The INSERT operation adds a row to a table. The UPDATE operation modifies an existing row, and the DELETE operation removes a row.

The SELECT operation implements queries; it retrieves data from a database. It is the most used and most complex of the SQL operations. A very simple example might be

```
select name, department from employees where class = 'faculty'
and rank = 'professor' order by family-name, given-name;
```

Such statement would select all faculty members with rank of professor and list them in alphabetical order by family name, then given name.

Much more complex applications of SELECT are possible and even usual. Continuing with the example above. The "employees" table would likely contain a department number, with the department name being in a table of departments. Using SELECT one could perform a join operation on the employees and departments tables to allow listing the department name rather than the number.

6.5.2 The ACID Properties

For many applications, database management systems must have four properties collectively called by the acronym ACID.

The A of ACID is **atomicity**. Some things we do with databases may require more than a single database operation. In a banking application processing a check might require removing $100 from Smith's account and adding $100 to Jones's account. Those two operations would be packaged as a transaction. Transactions are either *committed* if all operations succeed or *rolled back* if any operation fails. The property of atomicity guarantees that the operations in a transaction either succeed or fail as a whole, and if any operation in the transaction fails the state of the database is as it was before the transaction was attempted.

The second property is **consistency**. A transaction leaves the database in a consistent state, that is, one that satisfies all the constraints of its design.

The third property is **isolation**. A transaction must be isolated from other transactions until it is committed; it can neither interfere with other transactions nor be visible to them until committed. Specifically, isolation means that write operations made within a transaction are not visible outside the transaction until the transaction is committed. *Locking* prevents two concurrent transactions from operating on the same data.

The final property is **durability**. Once a transaction is committed it persists in the database and can be recovered if there is a database failure. Recovery is generally implemented by writing journal records, before and after images of the database, for each operation that changes the database. The journal records can then be applied to an earlier backup copy of the database. That process is called *forward recovery* and can recover the database to the exact point of failure.

The four ACID properties say that transactions are atomic, consistent, isolated, and durable.

Why are the ACID properties so important in some applications? It makes little or no difference that a Google query made in the United States does not retrieve a relevant page added to Google's database in Dublin, Ireland a few seconds earlier. It makes a huge difference if an airline's system does not immediately record the fact that the seat you are trying to reserve was sold to a customer in Dublin a few seconds earlier. Processing transactions in strict order is called **serializing** them, and it is something relational databases on mainframes do very well. Mainframe computers run airlines, banks and other financial institutions, and other businesses with both high transaction volumes and the need to serialize those transactions.

6.5.3 NoSQL Databases

Relational database management systems do several things very well at the cost of overhead in CPU time and I/O operations. As the number of rows in a database grows from hundreds of thousands to millions and then billions, that overhead becomes significant. Database management systems that optimize performance have emerged in the first decades of the 21st century. These are sometimes called NoSQL databases, that term being interpreted literally as no SQL, that is no relational properties, or "not only SQL."

There are four major classes of such databases, key-value databases, graph databases, document-oriented databases, and wide-column databases.

Of those, key-value databases may be the easiest to understand. A unique key identifies a value, and that value can be retrieved using the key. The value part is unstructured with respect to the database management system. It might be a web page, an image, a video, or a document like a book or article. It could also have an internal structure such as a JSON[124] array, but that structure isn't visible to the database management system.

The graph database is the network model database mentioned in the introduction of this chapter. In mathematics, a *graph* is a collection of nodes connected by edges. In the graph model database, the nodes hold the information we called entities earlier, and the edges that connect nodes model relationships. In the employee/department example earlier, there is

---

124 JavaScript Object Notation.

no direct[125] way to assign an employee to more than one department. In the graph model, employee and departments would be nodes, but a single employee could be connected to more than one department. The connections, the edges of the graph, are called relationships, and a single employee could be connected to multiple departments using multiple edges. The edges have direction, and in this case the direction is from employee to department. The relationship is "works in." Some graph databases allow the relationships to have numerical values. With such a database, we could say that a particular employee works 25% for marketing and 75% for sales.

In a document-oriented database, a document is a set of structured data such as a JSON object, but the different documents in the database need not have the same structure. Document-oriented databases provide for fast retrieval by eliminating the join operations of relational databases by denormalizing data. To continue the example, department name would be stored in the document for every employee. Enforcing consistency of department names becomes the responsibility of the application and changing a department name or other denormalized value requires updating each place it appears. For example, changing a department name from "Maintenance" to "Building Services" would require updating the record of every employee in the Maintenance department.

Wide column databases define tables of rows and columns, but the database is stored column wise on disk, not row wise.

6.6 Summary of Learning Objectives

*This section of the chapter tells you the things you should know about, but not **what** you should know about them. To test your knowledge, discuss the following concepts and topics with a study partner or in writing, ideally from memory.*

The general-purpose nature of computers requires software to adapt them to specific purposes.

There exist classes of problems that are either undecidable or intractable. Some intractable problems have heuristic solutions. We express the time or space complexity of a problem using Big-O notation.

Large software projects often have major problems. Software engineering seeks to mitigate those problems but lacks the foundations of classical engineering disciplines. High level and fourth generation languages address some, but not all, the difficulties of software development. Software projects may also benefit from specialized development environments and version control systems.

---

125 In the relational model, allowing one employee to work in more than one department generates a many-to-many relationship between the employee table and the department table. There can be many employees in one department, and an employee can work in many departments. This is accomplished with a helper table called an *associative entity*.

High level languages require translation. There are three major mechanisms for translation of computer languages.

Operating systems provide an abstraction layer between the hardware and application programs. A robust multiprogramming operating system places demands on the hardware and requires three specific features. Multiprogramming operating systems allow multiple applications to run concurrently, allocating machine resources to each project. Because magnetic disks are slower than the CPU, the operating system may also attempt to optimize disk operations.

The operating system provides mechanisms for allocating space on magnetic or solid-state drives, for managing free space, and for organizing data.

The operating system is responsible for managing memory and allocating memory to processes. Memory management often includes virtual memory. The operation of virtual memory depends on certain properties of von Neumann architecture computers. These properties allow definition of a working set as the amount of memory a program needs to function with minimal overhead. If the working set cannot be satisfied, a type of performance degradation with a specific name occurs. A virtual memory system keeps track of the contents of memory using special tables that may become large for large memories. A virtual memory system must choose an algorithm for page replacement and may employ a translation lookaside buffer.

The operating system manages activities like printing and other resources such as optical drives. Operating systems may attempt to avoid deadlock or handle deadlock conditions.

There exists software that will virtualize entire CPUs, allowing multiple operating systems and their applications to run on a single hardware system. Such software is of two basic types.

Database management software is separate from the operating system and provides a mechanism for managing complex datasets. A robust database management system provides four specific properties. Many database management systems depend on a particular design model, although systems for large databases often depart from that model. There is an important special-purpose language for use with databases.

6.7 References

Brooks. (1987). No Silver Bullet Essence and Accidents of Software Engineering. *Computer*, 20(4), 10–19. https://doi.org/10.1109/MC.1987.1663532

Codd, E. F. (1970). A relational model of data for large shared data banks. *Communications of the ACM*, 13(6), 377–387. https://doi.org/10.1145/362384.362685

IEEE Standard Glossary of Software Engineering Terminology. (1983). *ANSI/ IEEE Std 729-1983*, 1–40. https://doi.org/10.1109/IEEESTD.1983.7435207

Knuth, D. E. (1974). Structured Programming with go to Statements. *ACM Computing Surveys*, 6(4), 261–301. https://doi.org/10.1145/356635.356640

Parnas, D. L. (2021). Software Engineering: A Profession in Waiting. *Computer*, 54(5), 62–64. https://doi.org/10.1109/MC.2021.3057685

Schneider, G. Michael, G., Judith. (2013). *Invitation to Computer Science*. Cengate Learning.

Tanenbaum, A. S. (1990). *Structured Computer Organization* (3rd ed.). Prentice-Hall.

Tanenbaum, A. S. (2001). *Modern Operating Systems* (2nd ed.). Prentice-Hall.

Wirth, Niklaus. (1976). *Algorithms + Data Structures = Programs*. Prentice-Hall.

Chapter 7
Information Security

"The question to ask when you look at security is not whether this makes us safer, but whether it's worth the trade-off."

—Bruce Schneier

Not a day goes by without news of a computer security failure: data leaked or breached, files encrypted and held for ransom, financial or other credentials cracked. Most of these failures are, or should be, preventable.

Everyone who works in the information technology field or works with information technology to accomplish their jobs has some responsibility for security. In the United States and elsewhere, Federal and state laws may impose obligations with regard to information security. This chapter introduces the concepts, terminology, principles, and practices of information security. It will help prepare you for one or more courses in information security, or to understand the concepts as you use information technology.

The foundation of an information security program is an information security policy that describes which information assets are to be protected and the constraints on the use of those assets.

Figure 7-1
Blaise de Vigenère, French diplomat, cryptographer, and alchemist
© *Trustees of the British Museum*

7.1 What Does "Secure" Mean?

A system is **secure** if it "does what it is intended to do *and nothing else*" (Pfleeger & Pfleeger, 2006).[126]

That captures a big idea in a very few words. Every security failure is the result of a computer system doing something other than what was intended.

Through unpatched software and configuration errors, Kennesaw State University's Center for Election Systems allowed some 6.5 million voter records to be available on the Internet although the records were intended to be confidential.[127] (Torres, 2017)

Sometimes, failure of intentionality is more subtle. Microsoft designed the Windows Meta-

---

126 Simson Garfinkel and Eugene Spafford wrote much the same thing in *Practical UNIX Security* in 1991: "A computer is secure if you can depend on it and its software to behave as you expect."

127 The Center for Election Systems was formerly operated by KSU under a contract with the Georgia state government.

file graphics format to include executable code that was run when an image was viewed. That was for Windows 3.0, released in 1990, when there was little thought of connecting personal computers to the Internet. In late December, 2004, malicious actors discovered that they could execute arbitrary code on victims' computers if the victim simply viewed a specially-crafted image with a Web browser. Microsoft absolutely intended that displaying WMF images would cause code to be executed. What they did not intend was for malicious actors to exploit this capability to do damage.[128] The Windows Metafile example shows that the intended use of computer systems must be specified carefully and in depth. That is done through the establishment of security policies, as discussed below.

Often when people think of information security, they think of malicious actors, or "hackers." As the examples above show, security problems are at least as likely to occur from error. A well-designed information security program protects against error, environmental failure such as a power outage, and other inadvertent causes as well as malicious attack.

7.2 Properties of a Secure System

There are three principal properties of a secure information system: confidentiality, integrity, and availability. The essence of security is protecting these three properties. Of course, there's a lot more to security than three things, but the tools focus on protecting one or more of those three properties.

7.2.1 Confidentiality

Confidentiality is the condition that information is not revealed to unauthorized parties. An organization's information security policy must identify what information is confidential and who is authorized to have access to that information. **Disclosure** is the compromise of confidentiality.

Confidentiality and privacy

Privacy can mean freedom from surveillance or the right to control information about oneself. The first definition addresses things like license plate readers and facial recognition systems. The second definition addresses things like financial, student, or patient databases. It can also address the data collected by surveillance systems (Baase, 2008).

Organizations may have a legal, contractual, or moral duty to defend the privacy of those whose information they collect and store. This duty is fulfilled by maintaining the confidentiality of such information, but privacy itself is not addressed by information security. Privacy is addressed by law, contract, and moral obligation.

---

128 Microsoft released a patch for the vulnerability on January 6, 2005.

7.2.2 Integrity

Integrity is a measure of how much we can trust data, software, or systems. Since integrity is a measure of "how much," it is much harder to quantify than confidentiality.

Data integrity is the state that information agrees with the source from which it was derived and has not been altered or destroyed in an unauthorized matter. As with confidentiality, the information security policy describes how and by whom data may be changed or destroyed.

Origin integrity tells how much we trust that information came from the source it is supposed to have come from.

Program integrity tells how much we trust a computer program to do what is intended and how certain we are that it hasn't been modified in an unauthorized manner.

The compromise of integrity is called **alteration**.

7.2.3 Availability

Availability is the property that information systems are available to authorized users when and where needed. Availability is usually defined in terms of "quality of service," in which authorized users are expected to receive a specific level of service stated in terms of metrics like uptime and response time. The compromise of availability is **denial**.

7.2.4 Properties, States, and Controls: the McCumber Model

John McCumber (1991) proposed a model for information security that relates the three properties – confidentiality, integrity, and availability – to the states of information and the controls that can be applied to protect the three properties.[129] The premise of the McCumber Model is that to develop an effective information security program, one must consider the properties of a secure system, the states of information, and the controls available. The value of the McCumber model is that it prevents focus on one or a few items.

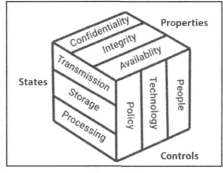

Figure 7-2
The McCumber Model

The states of information are transmission, storage, and processing. The McCumber Model shows that the properties of confidentiality, integrity, and availability must be protected for all three states of information.

---

129 The original illustration had a 3 × 3 grid on each visible face of the cube. "People" was labeled "Education, training, awareness," and the three sets of labels were on different faces than shown here.

On the last face of the cube are the types of controls available: policy, technology, and people. The McCumber Model shows that all three control types should be applied to all three properties. The McCumber Model helps us think about information security in three dimensions.

The "people" part to the controls dimension refers to those who use or are responsible for the organization's information assets. Assuring that everyone understands their responsibilities with respect to information security and also has the knowledge to fulfill them is an important part of an information security program.

7.2.5 Other "Properties"

Some authors discuss "properties" in addition to confidentiality, integrity, and availability. Among them are non-repudiation, authentication, and auditability.

Non-repudiation means that someone cannot effectively deny supplying data, sending a document, or taking an action. Non-repudiation is a consequence of high origin integrity. If one has high confidence in the origin of a document or other information, it is difficult or impossible to deny having supplied the document or information.

Authentication and auditability are controls rather than properties. An authentication mechanism requires a subject to prove identity before being granted privileges on a system. Auditability is a control on integrity. If a system maintains a secure record of all changes, it becomes possible to answer the question, "Was this changed, and if so, when and by whom?"

7.3 Goals of an Information Security Program

An information security program must have three goals: **prevention**, **detection**, and **response**.

The first goal of an information security program is to prevent disclosure, alteration, or denial of the information resources being secured.

News reports of information security failures often include information that an intrusion or other attack started months before it was discovered. We must accept that not all security incidents will be preventable. An effective program will have mechanisms in place to detect security failures as they occur or soon after.

Once a security incident has been detected, it is too late to plan a response. *Ad hoc* responses lead to mistakes. Instead, an effective information security program plans responses in advance of incidents occurring and tests the plans. An effective response plan covers recovery from the incident and return to normal operations.

The three goals are addressed through policy, technical controls, and procedures, as shown by the McCumber model. An effective program provides for **defense in depth**. That means multiple layers of defense, the failure of any one of which will not compromise the asset being protected. For example, firewalls and anti-malware software can be deployed to prevent files from being encrypted by ransomware. An effective and tested system of backups, stored where they are safe from infection, provides a recovery mechanism if prevention fails.

7.4 Policy, Controls, and Procedures

Every information security program must be grounded in an **information security policy** that describes the intended use of the system, including what information assets are to be protected and the constraints on the use of those assets. The *definition* of a secure system is one that does not violate the organization's security policy. That means the policy must fully and correctly capture the security requirements of the organization. The policy describes the "what" of information security and should be technology neutral.

For example, a policy might state, "Student grades are to be viewable by the student, by the student's parents or guardians if the student is under 18, and by university employees or agents with a legitimate educational purpose to have access to grades."[130]

Procedures describe how people should implement policies and might relate to how technical controls are implemented and used. Given the example above, those employees or agents who should have access to grades might have a value set in their university login records. There would be specific procedures for setting and removing that value. Procedures, along with technical controls, describe the "how" of information security.

Technical controls include things like access control mechanisms for logging in, firewalls, anti-malware software, and access control lists that provide fine-grained control of access to information technology assets.

Information security policy should be developed based on a risk assessment, as described in Section 7.5. Policies and technical controls can be developed from industry best practices and adjusted for the organization's own assessment of assets and risks. In evaluating best practices, it is important to be sure those adopted meet the requirements of the organization.

One of the best lists of requirements for procedures and controls was published over 50 years ago. (Saltzer & Schroeder, 1973) Here is their list, with brief comments by this author:

- *Economy of mechanism:* Simple controls and simple procedures work best.

---

130 This isn't enough for a comprehensive policy. The policy must also define "legitimate educational purpose," possibly by enumerating the roles that qualify, and describe who can record grades and who can change grades after they have been recorded.

- *Fail-safe defaults:* Policies, procedures and controls list those things that *should* be allowed, and controls must deny everything else. A mistake will cause access to fail, and the subject whose access fails will complain. Trying to list those things that should *not* be allowed is a recipe for disaster. Marcus Ranum called that "enumerating badness" (Ranum, 2005).[131]
- *Complete mediation:* Control mechanisms must check *every* access to an information asset.
- *Open design:* A protection mechanism must work even when an attacker knows the design of the mechanism. This was first stated as Kerckhoffs' Principle by Dutch cryptographer Auguste Kerckhoffs in the 19th century.[132] Depending on keeping the design of a security mechanism secret is called "security by obscurity" and it fails as soon as a malicious actor learns the mechanism.
- *Separation of privilege:* Access should not be granted on the basis of a single condition. A mechanism that requires two actions is safer than a mechanism requiring only one. This is a kind of defense in depth. An example is two-factor authentication, a login that requires both a password and a security key. Compromise of either one alone will not allow access.
- *Least privilege:* Users of information assets should have access to those resources required to do their jobs and nothing more.
- *Least common mechanism:* Mechanisms protecting assets should not be shared. Controls protecting multiple assets must meet the requirements of the asset needing the most protection. The implication is that assets needing different levels of protection should have separate, independent controls.
- *Psychological acceptability:* Protection controls should be so easy and so natural that they are routinely used correctly.

7.5 Assets, Risks, and Risk Management

The existence and use of information technology assets creates risks to those assets. Consider an automobile as an example. A car parked in a secure garage can be crushed and destroyed by a falling tree. It's rare, but it can and does happen. Driving the car increases the risk by exposing it to threats like collision. The same thing is true of information technology assets. An information security program involves identifying the organization's information technology assets and the threats to those assets, then managing the risks present.

---

131 Dr. Ferrol Sams described enumerating badness this way: "He's not a bad boy, he minds well; I just can't think of enough things to tell him not to do" (Sams, 1982).

132 Claude Shannon restated this in 1949 as "assume the enemy knows the system."

7.5.1 Identifying Assets and Threats

The threats to information assets are failures of the three properties of a secure system. **Disclosure** is the threat that compromises confidentiality, **alteration** compromises integrity, and **denial** compromises availability.

An organization's information technology assets can be broadly classified as hardware, software, data, documentation, people, and infrastructure.

People from all parts of the organization should be involved in building the list of assets because there are likely to be information assets unknown to the information technology department. The inventory of assets should be reviewed each time an information system is put into production or decommissioned and also at regular intervals.[133] Asset identification should include the asset name, use within the organization, and asset owner. The asset owner is the person or position in the organization authorized to set policy for the asset. Users of the asset must also be identified. If there is an asset custodian, often the information technology department, identify the custodian. Depending on the type of asset, one may need to collect things like manufacturer name and serial number.

When the asset list has been developed, and each time it is reviewed, a list of threats to the asset should be produced or updated. As with asset identification, this works best if people from throughout the organization participate.

7.5.2 Risk Management

A **risk** is the probability that a threat is realized and damages the asset. Risk management is the process of identifying and controlling the risks facing an organization. In the insurance industry, risks are characterized by **annualized loss expectation**, or ALE. The ALE is the cost if a threat is realized multiplied by the number of times the threat is expected to be realized each year. The multiplier will be a fraction for events expected to happen less frequently than once a year. To continue with the automobile example, your insurer does not know whether you will be in an accident next year, but they know to several decimal places how many people of similar age, sex, driving record, and type of car have been in accidents in the past. They know how much it cost to pay the resulting claims. They use that information to compute an ALE for you and use that to set the price of your insurance.

It is important to remember that the ALE is applicable only over large numbers of similar assets. For any single, specific asset, the annual cost is zero if a threat is not realized and is the full economic cost if a threat is realized.

It is seldom possible to be this precise in an information security program because there's

---

133 In an earlier career, the author conducted an annual asset review as part of the preparation for each year's financial audit.

not sufficient data. It may be necessary to characterize the probability of a risk being realized as low, medium or high. It is worthwhile to try to put a dollar range on the cost of a risk being realized.

Risks are classified along several dimensions:

- Direct or indirect risks[134]
- Risks to information
- Environmental risks
- Physical risks.

With risks classified, it is possible to design policies, technical controls, and people controls like procedures to reduce the risks.

Figure 7-3 provides guidance on which controls to design and implement first. One should address those risks with both a high probability of occurrence and a high cost if the threat is realized. However, Figure 7-3 does not account for the cost of controls. It may be advantageous to implement some less important controls early in the process if they are easy and cheap. It may also be necessary to forego some controls entirely if their cost or technical complexity

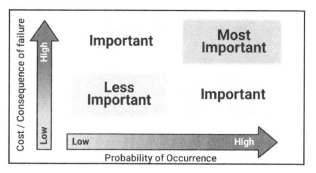

Figure 7-3
Priority of designing and implementing controls

exceeds what the organization can support. Such an analysis is called a **cost-benefit analysis**. Cost-benefit analysis compares the financial benefit of adding a control (itself determined by risk of loss) with the cost of proposed controls.

As controls are implemented, the level of risk will decrease, but it will never reach zero. The remaining risk is called **residual risk**. The purpose of an information security program is to reduce residual risk to a level compatible with the organization's resources and tolerance for risk.

7.6 Identification, Authentication, and Access Control

In this discussion, we use **principal** to refer to a unique entity, perhaps a person or an information system. An **identifier** specifies a principal with respect to an information system.

---

134 Direct risks compromise the asset itself if realized; indirect risks are things like business interruption, damage to reputation, and legal liability.

Each of you probably has several identifiers, things like logins to various systems. Your legal name is an identifier.

Depending on the security requirements of a system as expressed in policy, a process of **identity proofing** may be necessary. Identity proofing is assuring that the claimed identity of a principal is the true identity. The documents necessary to get a driver's license are a form of identity proofing.

Authentication is the binding of a principal to a specific identifier internal to the system. Authentication is crucial to security because all decisions on access to a system's resources must assume that the binding is correct.

A simple authentication example is a system with login based on user ID and password. The login prompt asks, "Who are you?" and the correct reply is an identifier, the user ID. Often the identifier is widely-known or easy to guess.[135] Then the system asks, "Prove it!" and the correct response is a password matching the identifier. In this scenario, the password is assumed to be known only to the principal and not able to be obtained or guessed by others. If the password is correct, the assumption for security decisions is that the principal associated with the identifier is the one using the system, and access decisions are based on that assumption.

A strong system of authentication and access control protects confidentiality by assuring that only those authorized by policy have access to data. It protects integrity by assuring that only those authorized by policy to change data can do so.

Authenticating factors

There are three[136] factors that can be used for authentication: something one knows, something one has, or something one is.

Something one knows: typically, this is a password, but might be a pattern traced on a touch screen or another challenge, like an algorithm. A simple example of a challenge might be that the system presents a random integer and the principal must add 27 to it.

Something one has: In the 21st century, this is often a security key like the YubiKey. It could be as simple as a metal key used to unlock doors or start automobiles. It could also be a mobile phone to which the system sends a text message that must be entered to complete the login.[137]

---

135 For many years my user ID at my university was "bbrown." It was also part of my email address.

136 Some authors place things like signatures and unlock patterns in their own category, *something one does*, and add *somewhere one is* for authentication by IP address, geolocation, etc.

137 If you are using a mobile phone in this way, a Web search for "SIM swapping" will be enlightening.

Something one is: This is properly called biometric authentication.[138] Typical mechanisms are recognition of faces or fingerprints, but there are systems based on other characteristics, including hand geometry and scans of iris or retina. A handwritten signature is a form of behavioral biometric authentication that can be validated automatically. (Rosso, Ospina, & Frery, 2016)

Each of these factors has strengths and weaknesses, a discussion of which is beyond the scope of this chapter.

Multi-factor authentication

For much of the history of remote access to information systems, the standard for identification and authentication was user ID and password. The problem is that people can't remember multiple strong passwords, so they choose weak passwords or reuse passwords across multiple systems, or both. Weak passwords are easily compromised. If passwords are reused, a compromised password on one system compromises all of them.

By requiring two or more of the factors – something you know, something you have, something you are – a compromise of only one of them will not be sufficient to gain access. This is another example of defense in depth.

Access control and auditability

Once authentication is complete, there exists a binding of the principal and the identifier, or user ID. Except for the very simplest systems, where authority on the system is all or nothing, further decisions are necessary to determine what the principal may do. This is called **authorization** or **access management.**

Many modern authorization systems use **access control lists** (ACLs). Each object, such as a file, has a list of those identifiers (principals) allowed to access the object, and what access is allowed. For example, the Windows operating system includes access permissions for reading, writing, modifying, and executing files. Other types of objects, like disks or printers, have different sets of permissions suitable to the kind of object being protected.

The UNIX operating system and its look-alike, Linux, use a different model in which there are three permissions: read, write, and execute, and three levels of access: owner, group, and everyone. It is possible to exercise very fine-grained control using the UNIX model. Extensions to UNIX and Linux provide for access control lists.

Designers of access control systems must remember Saltzer and Schroeder's principle of fail-safe defaults. Access should be denied unless explicitly granted. Those who administer

---

138 Not to be confused with biometric identification, a different and much harder problem. Biometric authentication asks "Does this face or fingerprint belong to Alice?" Biometric identification asks, "To whom does this face or fingerprint belong?"

access control systems must remember the principle of least privilege. Give each principal the rights necessary to perform that principal's permitted functions and no more.

Access control systems in both UNIX / Linux and Windows provide for logging of changes in access permissions and of access to objects. Enabling logging provides auditability; it is possible to know what happened, when it happened, and who did it. Auditability, in turn provides accountability for those who use the information system.

7.7 Security of Data Communications

A detailed look at the principles of security of data communications is beyond the scope of this book. However, the Covid-19 pandemic that began in the United States in 2020 forced far more remote work than was usual before the pandemic and created new challenges in securing data communications. It seems likely that increased remote work, and so increased demand for data communications and increased security challenges, will continue even though the pandemic has subsided. In some organizations, network security was focused on "protecting the perimeter" of the network using firewalls and intrusion detection devices and limiting the number of remote connections. That is no longer a viable strategy, although firewalls and intrusion detection remain an essential part of the communication security toolkit.

Communication security in the 21st century is becoming more focused on **endpoint protection**, that is, on protecting the devices that connect to a corporate network. Endpoint protection seeks to overcome the problem that a device such as a laptop can become infected with malicious software while not connected to the corporate network, then transfer the infection to machines within the network upon connection.

A **firewall** serves as a choke point on a network that determines which packets are allowed to pass and which will be dropped. The decision of whether to allow a packet is made according to configurable firewall rules. Such rules may consider the direction, incoming or outgoing, of the packet, source and destination port numbers, and source and destination addresses. Some firewalls engage in packet inspection. Shallow packet inspection involves checking the headers of higher level protocols, which are considered payload at the Internet Protocol level. Some firewalls look at the data portion of the payload. This is called deep packet inspection. Deep packet inspection is used to attempt to detect unauthorized data transfer or attempts at unauthorized entry (intrusion) into systems attached to the network.

An **intrusion detection system** is a combination of hardware and software that monitors traffic for packets that indicate malicious activity or violations of organizational policy. Intrusion detection systems work by checking packets for signature data that indicates malicious activity or analyzing network behavior to detect anomalies. Systems that can take action similar to a firewall to attempt to stop an intrusion are called **intrusion prevention systems**.

Modern networks present a challenge to deploying intrusion detection or prevention systems. Such a device must be able to observe network traffic in order to analyze it, but modern networks purposely segment traffic using switching and VLANs as described in Section 5.3.2.

A **virtual private network (VPN)** provides a secure connection either between networks such as main and branch offices, or between a network and an endpoint, such as a remote employee's laptop computer. The connection is secured from eavesdropping by encryption, and extends the facilities of the network to the branch office or endpoint, including access to DNS and directory services as well as to file and other servers. A VPN can be implemented as a split tunnel, in which requests for corporate services pass through the VPN and requests for other Internet resources do not. This conserves bandwidth at the corporate location at the expense of allowing Internet access that is not mediated by the protections provided by the corporate network.

In **end-to-end encryption**, packets are encrypted at the source device and not decrypted until they reach the destination device. This reduces the opportunity for adversaries to intercept data prior to encryption or after decryption. However, it also makes it impossible for firewalls and intrusion detection/protection systems to inspect the contents of the packets.

Transport layer security (TLS) provides a mechanism for encrypting data from endpoint to server and was originally intended to protect transactions on the World Wide Web. It now protects other kinds of traffic as well. TLS is discussed in Section 5.4.

7.8 Cryptography

Cryptography[139] refers to the use of ciphers[140] to obscure the meaning of text or other data by scrambling the bits of a document, message, or other data so that the content is impossible to read without reversing the encryption process. A cryptographic system consists of a long and random collection of bits called the key and algorithms for encrypting and decrypting. The algorithms are assumed to be known by an adversary. The key must be kept secret. The encrypting process combines the key with the data, called **plain text**, to produce encrypted data, called the **cipher text**. Encrypting data protects confidentiality.

Cryptography has been used to protect secrets since at least 1500 BCE. Around 1580, French cryptographer Blaise de Vigenère (Figure 7-1) improved an earlier cipher, now called the Vigenère cipher, and invented another. At the time, the Vigenère cipher was called *le chiffre indéchiffrable*.[141] The Vigenère cipher withstood attack for nearly 300 years. In 1863, Austrian military officer Friedrich Kasiski published a method of attacking the Vigenère cipher by deducing the length of the key.

---

139 From the Greek words for "hidden writing."

140 Codes operate at the level of meaning, *e.g.* "One if by land and two if by sea." Ciphers operate at the level of symbols or small groups of symbols, transform data using transposition, substitution, or both, and are reversible.

141 The undecipherable cipher.

Cryptographic techniques can be used to protect data integrity by revealing tampering and to protect origin integrity through digital signatures and cryptographic authentication.[142]

Effectively unbreakable cryptosystems exist, are available, and are well-documented. Attempting to use home-grown cryptosystems is very dangerous and should never be considered as part of an information security program. While it might seem very cool to design and implement your own cryptosystem, it turns out to be surprisingly hard to do right. Unless you have the equivalent of a Ph.D. in mathematics with an emphasis on cryptology and a dozen years' experience, it's an extremely bad idea to trust important information to home brewed crypto. Experiment all you want, but when you are serious about protecting information, use cryptosystems developed by experts, examined by other experts, and that have withstood the test of time.

7.8.1 Symmetric Key Cryptography

Symmetric key cryptography uses the same key for both encrypting and decrypting. It is an appropriate tool for protecting the confidentiality of data in storage. Even if encrypted data are compromised, they are of no use to an attacker without the key. The encryption key must be protected, but that may be easier than protecting a large store of data. A suitably strong key will be 128 or 256 bits, 16 or 32 bytes, and can be stored off line until data in storage must be decrypted. Care must be taken in the handling of data that has been decrypted.

Symmetric key cryptography is less useful for data being processed because the key must be available. That might mean that a compromise of the data also results in a compromise of the key.

Symmetric key cryptography is not generally useful by itself for data in transmission because both sender and receiver must have a copy of the key. The problem of how to transmit a key securely over an unsecure channel is called the **key exchange problem**. Key exchange is addressed by key exchange algorithms and asymmetric key cryptography, both of which are discussed below.

There are several symmetric key algorithms that are effectively unbreakable. One of them is AES, the Advanced Encryption Standard, established by the National Institute of Standards and Technology in the United States in 2001.

The **one-time pad** is a symmetric key algorithm that is provably unbreakable. The key must be randomly generated and as long as the message. Each key must be used only once, hence the name. Although provably unbreakable, the one-time pad is impractical because of the difficulties of generating and distributing many long, random keys.

---

142 The Certified Information Systems Security Professional (CISSP) Common Body of Knowledge says cryptography also protects availability. That is something of a stretch to say the least.

7.8.2 Asymmetric Key Cryptography and Key Exchange

In the mid-1970s, four groups of researchers[143] independently invented a mechanism that uses two different keys with the same data, one to encrypt and one to decrypt. The key usually used for encrypting is called the **public key**, and the key usually used for decrypting is called the **private key**. Data encrypted with a particular public key can only be decrypted using the corresponding private key. You can give the public key to anyone, and they will not be able to decrypt messages that others may have encrypted with the same public key. Such a system is called **asymmetric key cryptography**, or public key cryptography.

This eliminates the key exchange problem because it is no longer necessary to exchange keys. One looks up the public key of a recipient – it's available publicly – and encrypts. The recipient decrypts using the corresponding private key.

The problem with asymmetric key cryptography is that it is computationally intensive. Keys are thousands of bits long and encryption requires exponentiation using those long keys. Encrypting or decrypting a message with the RSA[144] algorithm can take 10,000 times as long as encryption with a modern and secure symmetric key algorithm.

Key exchange algorithms and hybrid cryptography

It is possible to obtain the benefits of public key cryptography while paying only a part of the computational penalty. Instead of using asymmetric key cryptography to encrypt an entire message for transmission, it is used to solve the key exchange problem. The sender generates a random number 128 or 256 bits long and encrypts the random number using asymmetric key cryptography. Since the random number is perhaps 16 or 32 bytes, encryption is fast even with a computationally intensive algorithm. Using the random number as the key, the sender uses a symmetric key algorithm like AES to encrypt the message. The key, encrypted with an asymmetric key algorithm, and the message, encrypted with a symmetric key algorithm, are sent to the recipient together. The recipient first uses the recipient's private key of the asymmetric key pair to decrypt the generated key, then uses that key to decrypt the message. Such a scheme is called hybrid cryptography. This mechanism is effective only if the private key used to encrypt the session key remains secure.

Forward secrecy

If a public key is used to encrypt a session key and the corresponding private key is compromised,[145] the adversary can decrypt the session key and with that, decrypt the com-

---

143 Three of these groups published their work at the time. The work of the fourth was classified by the military of the United Kingdom and not declassified until 1997.

144 Named for its inventors, L.M. Adleman, R.L. Rivest and A. Shamir.

145 A private key can be compromised by carelessness, but in the United States and elsewhere, it may also be possible to compel production of a private key with a court order or other legal process.

munications. All future communications using the same public/private key pair are also compromised. If past communications have been captured and stored, they, too, can be decrypted.[146]

There are key exchange algorithms that cannot be used to encrypt messages but that can enable two parties to negotiate a shared secret key over an unsecure channel. One such algorithm is the elliptic curve Diffie-Hellman key exchange algorithm. If asymmetric key cryptography is used to validate the identities of parties as described below, but a key exchange algorithm that doesn't depend on the security of the channel is used to generate a shared symmetric key, compromise of the private key no longer compromises the communication itself. Such a mechanism is called **forward secrecy** or sometimes, optimistically, perfect forward secrecy. It is possible to break forward secrecy by breaking the elliptic curve Diffie-Hellman algorithm, thought to be very difficult, but compromise of a private key, whether through carelessness, malice, or legal process, will not compromise the content of the messages.

Quantum-resistant asymmetric key cryptography

Quantum computers apply a fundamentally different approach to computation. It would take decades for the fastest von Neumann architecture computers to find the prime factors of a 2,048-bit number if it were possible at all. A quantum computer and Shor's Algorithm could find the prime factors in a few seconds or less. That isn't an immediate concern because no quantum computer capable of running Shor's Algorithm on such large numbers currently exists. Experts estimate that it will be 2030 or later before current public key cryptography algorithms can be successfully attacked with quantum computers.

However, the year 2030 is not that far in the future. In 2016, the U.S. National Institute of Standards and Technology announced a contest that would select quantum-resistant cryptography algorithms for standardization. In 2019, NIST narrowed the field of entries to 26 possible candidates. The four were selected as candidates for standardization in 2022. NIST plans to publish a final draft by 2024.

7.8.3 Cryptographic Hashes and Digital Signatures

Part of defense in depth of the integrity of information is to be able to detect tampering. This is accomplished using a cryptographic hash[147] algorithm. A cryptographic hash algorithm takes variable-length data as its input and produces a small, fixed-size output. For SHA-256, the output is 256 bits, or 32 bytes. The output of such a hash algorithm is called a **digest**.

An effective cryptographic hash algorithm has two important properties. First, even a sin-

---

146 The U.S. National Security Agency has built a data center near Bluffton, Utah to store encrypted communications for possible future decryption. The data center was completed in May, 2019.

147 It's called a "hash" because the output has no intrinsic meaning.

gle bit difference in inputs will produce very different hash values. Second, it should be impossible to construct two inputs so that both produce the same hash value. That's called a **collision**, and a hash algorithm that allows collisions can't produce a unique "fingerprint" of its input.

It is not possible to determine the original input given only the hash value. However, for small inputs like passwords, it may be possible to mount a **brute force attack** in which many or all possible values are used as inputs to the hash algorithm to see whether any results in the same hash value as the one under attack.

Cryptographic hashes can be used to detect changes in data. To do so, create a hash digest of the data when it is a known-good state. The digest must be stored separately and securely. The integrity of the data can then be tested by re-computing the digest and comparing it with the original. If they're equal, the assumption is that no tampering has occurred. The strength of that assumption depends on the resistance to collisions of the chosen hash algorithm and the security of the initial digest value.

It is important to know that there are different kinds of hashing algorithms for different purposes. Hash algorithms for integrity checking or digital signatures, like SHA-256, are designed to be fast. Hash algorithms for storing passwords, like BCRYPT or SCRYPT, are specifically designed to be slow to make brute force attacks time-consuming. There are also cryptographic hash functions, like MD5, that were once thought to be secure but have since been found to have flaws.

Digital signatures

Some asymmetric key cryptography algorithms have the property that the public and private keys are cryptographic inverses of one another. Data encrypted with a given public key can only be decrypted using the corresponding private key. However, data or a message encrypted using the private key can be decrypted using the public key. Such a message is not confidential because anyone can decrypt it using the public key. However, there is a strong assumption that it could only have been encrypted by the owner of the corresponding private key. It has been digitally signed. How strong is the assumption? As strong as our knowledge or belief that the holder of the private key has kept it private. If the private key has been compromised, the digital signature is no longer reliable.

Rather than encrypting an entire message using the sender's private key, which would be very slow, digital signatures are implemented by first computing a hash digest of the data to be signed, then encrypting the digest with the signer's private key.

To validate a digital signature, compute a digest of the signed data using the same algorithm used to sign the data. Decrypt the signature using the signer's public key, then compare the decrypted signature, really a message digest, to the digest just computed. If they're equal, one can conclude that the data were signed using the signer's private key, *and also* that the data haven't been tampered with or corrupted. If the data had been changed, even though the digital signature was correct, the computed digest would be different.

Digital certificates

Suppose Bill wants to send a confidential message to Alice, with whom his only method of contact is email. Bill looks up Alice's public key, perhaps on the OpenPGP key server. But Bill has a problem, namely, how to be certain he really has Alice's public key. If evil Eve the eavesdropper had somehow compromised the key server and substituted her own public key for Alice's, Eve would be able to decrypt and read any messages she could intercept.

The solution to Bill's problem is a digital certificate. The purpose of a digital certificate is to bind an identity, in this case Alice's, to a public key. Figure 7-4 is a simplified diagram of a digital certificate. The identifier (Alice's email address), the public key, and the other information, including a certificate version number and expiration date, are the body of the certificate. They're all in plain text; anyone can read them with no deciphering necessary.

Identifer	alice@example.com
Alice's public key	mQENBFFho2kBCAC2 YKYuIBMDT4osUNfJqw HNLmaKFp8c0xiSg0JD
Other information	Version: 1.0 Expires: 2038-01-01
Signature	charlie@example.com **FaBIG+cHww4yYnzS0 6fuT01OCU1tDkHpH**
Signature	donna@example.com **R2d2uwWJ0ZqV8VjBf c3po1OCU1tDkHp5R**

Figure 7-4
Simplified diagram of a digital certificate.

The certificate in Figure 7-4 has two signatures, by Charlie and Donna. The important parts are the identifiers, in this case email addresses, and a cryptographic hash digest of the body of the certificate, encrypted with the signer's private key. By signing, Charlie and Donna attest that the public key in the body of the certificate is really Alice's.[148]

To verify a signature, Bill computes his own digest over the body of the certificate. He then uses Charlie's or Donna's public key, obtained separately, to decrypt the signature. If the decrypted digest matches the digest Bill computed, Bill can trust that he has Alice's true public key because Alice has been "introduced" by Charlie or Donna. The amount of trust depends upon how much Bill trusts Charlie or Donna.

If Bill doesn't know, or doesn't trust, Charlie or Donna, he can look at who has signed their public keys. Bill's asymmetric key software will expand the search automatically, looking for someone whom Bill has marked as a trusted introducer. This concept is called the **web of trust**, in which parties vouch for one another.

---

148 Keys are often exchanged in person at "key signing parties." Perhaps you and friends or classmates want to organize a key signing party. You can find detailed instructions on the Web.

Certificate authorities and the public key infrastructure

Another kind of digital certificate, an X.509 certificate, usually has only one signature, that of a certificate authority. A certificate authority is a company, a non-profit, or in some countries, a government agency, that takes on the task of verifying that public keys belong to the named principal. The certificate authority acts as a *trusted third party*. Certificates issued in this way are used by TLS[149] to encrypt traffic between browsers and servers and to provide a measure of assurance that a person who wants to connect to, *e.g.*, apple.com has actually reached Apple's servers.

Such an arrangement is not without problems of its own. Not all certificate authorities are both equally careful and equally trustworthy. There have been a few instances of certificate authorities issuing fraudulent certificates. A big threat is that a certificate authority's "signing key" – the private key used to sign digital certificates – becomes compromised. There are ways to mitigate these problems, but they are beyond the scope of this chapter.

7.9 Summary of Learning Objectives

> *This section of the chapter tells you the things you should know about, but not **what** you should know about them. To test your knowledge, discuss the following concepts and topics with a study partner or in writing, ideally from memory.*

Security problems can be caused by malicious actors, but they can also arise from error or environmental failure.

The three properties of a secure information system are confidentiality, integrity, and availability. The threats to information assets are disclosure, alteration, and denial.

Every information security program must be grounded in an information security policy that describes the intended use of the system, including what information assets are to be protected and the constraints on the use of those assets. An information security program is a risk management program that manages risks to the organization's information assets.

A principal is a unique entity that may attempt access to an information system. The authentication process binds a principal to the internal representation of that principal. Authentication is crucial to security because all decisions on access to a system's resources must assume that the binding is correct. Once a principal has been authenticated, it is possible to make authorization decisions about what the principal is allowed to do.

Cryptography is the use of ciphers to obscure information until the encryption is reversed by decryption. Cryptography can protect the confidentiality and integrity of information. Classes of cryptographic systems are symmetric key cryptography, asymmetric (public) key

---

149 Transport Layer Security, the facility used to encrypt traffic on the World Wide Web.

cryptography, and cryptographic hash functions. Digital signatures and digital certificates protect the integrity of information, including cryptographic keys.

7.10 References

Baase, Sarah. (2008). *A Gift of Fire* (3rd ed.). Pearson Education.

McCumber, J. (1991). Information Systems Security: A Comprehensive Model. *Proceedings of the 14th National Computer Security Conference: "Information Systems Security: Requirements & Practices,"* 739–739. National Institute of Standards and Technology. https://doi.org/10/01/proceedings-14th-national-computer-security-confer/Final

Pfleeger, C. P., & Pfleeger, S. L. (2003). *Security in Computing*. Prentice-Hall Professional.

Pfleeger, C.P., & Pfleeger, S. L. (2006). *Security in Computing* (4th ed.). Prentice-Hall Professional.

Ranum, Marcus. (2005, September 1). The Six Dumbest Ideas in Computer Security. https://www.ranum.com/security/computer_security/editorials/dumb/

Rosso, O. A., Ospina, R., & Frery, A. C. (2016). Classification and Verification of Handwritten Signatures with Time Causal Information Theory Quantifiers. *PLOS ONE*, 11(12), e0166868. https://doi.org/10.1371/journal.pone.0166868

Saltzer, J. H. (1973). Protection and control of information sharing in multics. *Proceedings of the Fourth ACM Symposium on Operating System Principles,* 119. https://doi.org/10.1145/800009.808059

Sams, F. (1982). *Run with the Horesmen*. Peachtree Press.

Torres, K. (2017, July 14). Georgia to shift elections work in-house, away from Kennesaw State. *Atlanta Journal-Constitution*. https://www.ajc.com/news/state--regional-govt--politics/georgia-shift-elections-work-house-away-from-kennesaw-state/JAazLxUB-0SODnPMqEGNWdJ

Appendix A
Programming LMC / TBC

TBC, the Tiny Binary Computer, is, as the name says, a *binary* computer, but designed to be at least mostly compatible with Stuart Madnick's Little Man Computer, which is a decimal computer. The purpose is to allow students to see the differences between decimal and binary computers. The difference is important because all modern general purpose digital computers are binary computers.

A.1 Format of Assembly Language Statements

Assembly language statements for TBC are of the form:

```
[label] op code [address] [comments]
```

The label, if present, must begin at the left, with no preceding white space. The operation code must be preceded by white space regardless of whether a label is present. (This is different from LMC, which allows operation codes to begin at the left.)

Labels, operation codes, and symbolic addresses are case-insensitive. Labels and symbolic addresses are not length limited. For valid operation codes, see A.2 Operation Codes and A.3 Extended Operation Codes

Addresses may be symbolic addresses, which correspond to labels defined elsewhere in the source program, or numeric addresses. Numeric addresses may be expressed as decimal numbers or hexadecimal numbers. Hexadecimal numbers must be prefixed with "0x," the digit zero followed by the letter x. Example: 0x5A or 0x5a. Addresses are limited to the range 0-127 or 0x0 to 0x7f. Anything following the address, or for operation codes that do not take an address, anything following the operation code, is treated as a comment.

By default, the assembler generates object code beginning at location zero. The address where a sequence of instructions will be loaded can be changed using the ORG (origin) assembler directive, which takes a numeric address as an operand. The address can be decimal or hexadecimal. Example:

```
org   0x50
add   const1  // The "add" will be at address 0x50
brp   done    // BRP will be at 0x51, etc.
```

The first executable instruction must be at location zero, as it will be by default.

The DAT assembler directive reserves storage for a 12-bit numeric constant and optionally initializes its value. The constant may be a signed or unsigned decimal number or a hexa-decimal number. To express a negative number in hexadecimal, use the two's complement of the unsigned value. Because TBC uses 12-bit words in two's complement format, con-stants are limited to the range -2048 to +2047. If no operand is given, DAT reserves space but does not initialize it. Example:

```
const1      dat   1
minus1      dat   0xfff
minus1      dat   -1
datum       dat             // one word not initialized
```

A.2 Operation Codes

The first nine operation codes are identical to Madnick's LMC. (Operation code 4 is not used.) The remaining operation codes are extensions for TBC.

Op Code	Mnemonic	Meaning
0xx	HLT <addr>	**Halt.** Instruction execution stops. Operating the "reset" switch will restart the program from location zero. The mnemonic COB is accepted as a synonym for HLT. The address field is ignored.
1xx	ADD <addr>	**Add.** The contents of memory at address <addr> are added to the accumulator. An *Overflow* machine check[150] occurs if the result is greater than 2047 or less than -2048; the truncated result is stored in the accumulator.
2xx	SUB <addr>	**Subtract.** The contents of memory at address <addr> are subtracted from the accumulator. An *Overflow* machine-check occurs if the result is greater than 2047 or less than -2048; the truncated result is stored in the accumulator.
3xx	STO <addr>	**Store accumulator.** The contents of the accumulator are stored in memory at address <addr>; the previous contents of memory at <addr> are lost. The mnemonic STA is accepted as a synonym for STO.
4xx		Not used

---

150 A machine check is an unrecoverable error. The processor halts and the program must be corrected.

Op Code	Mnemonic	Meaning
5xx	LDA <addr>	**Load accumulator.** The contents of memory at address <addr> are loaded into the accumulator; the previous contents of the accumulator are lost. The contents of <addr> are unchanged.
6xx	BR <addr>	**Branch unconditionally.** The value of <addr> is stored in the program counter, causing the next instruction to be fetched from that location. The mnemonic BRA is accepted as a synonym for BR.
7xx	BRZ <addr>	**Branch if zero.** If the accumulator holds the value zero, the value of <addr> is stored in the program counter, causing the next instruction to be fetched from that location. If the accumulator is non-zero, the program counter is not modified and the next instruction will be fetched in sequence. The accumulator is not modified.
8xx	BRP <addr>	**Branch if positive.** If the sign bit of the accumulator is zero, the value of <addr> is stored in the program counter, causing the next instruction to be fetched from that location. If the sign bit is one, the program counter is not modified and the next instruction will be fetched in sequence. The accumulator is not modified. Note that a value of zero in the accumulator will cause the branch to be taken because the sign bit of the number zero is zero.
901	IN	**Input.** A number is requested from the input subsystem and stored in the accumulator. The previous contents of the accumulator are lost. The input subsystem will not deliver values greater than 2047 nor less than -2048. The mnemonic INP is accepted as a synonym for IN.
902	OUT	**Output.** The contents of the accumulator are copied to the output subsystem as a decimal value, followed by the newline character. The accumulator is not changed.

A.3 Extended Operation Codes

The operation codes below are not part of the Little Man Computer's instruction set. They have been added to the Tiny Binary Computer to expose to students how a stack can be used for subprogram calls and how programmed I/O is performed.

Op Code	Mnemonic	Meaning
Axx	CALL <addr>	**Subprogram call.** The number at the highest memory address is decremented, the program counter is stored at the address pointed by the contents of the highest memory address, and the <addr> portion of the instruction is placed in the program counter. In other words, the highest memory address is used as a stack pointer for a stack that grows downward from high memory. Resetting the machine or loading a program stores the address of the highest memory location in that location. For a machine with 128 words of storage, the value 0x7F is stored at location 0x7F.
Bxx	RET <addr>	**Return from subprogram.** The memory location pointed by the contents of the highest memory address is loaded into the program counter and the value at the highest memory address is incremented. Only the rightmost seven bits of the value on the stack are used. The address field of the instruction is not used and is reserved.
Cxx	OUTN <addr>	**Output with No newline.** Identical to OUT except that sending the newline character is suppressed.
Dxx	OUTC <addr>	**Output Character.** The rightmost seven bits of the accumulator are sent to the output subsystem, to be interpreted as an ASCII character rather than a number. No newline character is sent.

Op Code	Mnemonic	Meaning
Fxx	PIO	**Programmed Input/Output.** TBC uses the three highest possible memory addresses, 0xfd, 0xfe, and 0xff as registers for I/O. The programmer must store a device address in 0xfd; the input device is 0x000 and the output device is 0x001. For output, the data word to be written must be stored at address 0xff. For input, the value read will be placed in address 0xff. After the registers are set up, the program issues the PIO instruction. The program must then loop, testing address 0xfe until it becomes one, indicating the completion of the I/O operation. Any input or output operation attempted before 0xfe becomes one will cause a machine check.
	DAT "<STR>"	**Character data pseudo-instruction.** The characters in <str>, which must be enclosed in double-quotes, are stored in the rightmost eight bits of consecutive words. Example: DAT "Hello, world!" Escaped characters are not allowed. A newline character may be stored by coding DAT 0x00A. If 0x00A is processed by an OUT instruction, it will be rendered as 10. If it is processed by OUTC, it will be rendered as newline.

A.4 Operation

TBC source and object programs are stored in the browser's local storage. That implies a constraint of working on one specific machine, something that may not be possible in a lab environment. The solution is to save source programs using a text editor like Notepad++. The source code can be pasted into the left pane of the assembler screen and assembled.

One can also load a program stored on the local machine in the browser's local storage using the pull-down selector and *Load* button.

Clicking the *Assemble* button assembles the program and produces an assembly listing. The object program is stored in the browser's local storage for execution using the Virtual Machine tab.

Loading and Running a Program

An assembled program can be loaded into the virtual machine by selecting its name in the drop-down and clicking "Load." The program is loaded into memory, the program counter (PC) is set to zero, and the highest memory location is loaded with its own address so that it can be used as a stack pointer.

When a program has been loaded, clicking "Run" starts the simulated clock running, and the program runs at a speed proportional to the clock speed. Clicking "Step" executes a single instruction from the location pointed by the program counter. Note that executing a single instruction may take up to six clock cycles.

The "Pause" button stops execution at the end of the current instruction. Because each instruction takes several clock cycles, Pause does not necessarily take effect instantly.

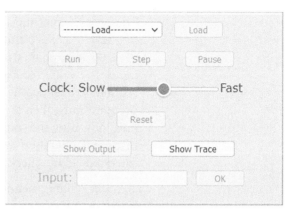

Figure A-1
The simulated control panel for the TBC

Clock Speed

Clock speed is set by a range control (slider.) The speed is variable from a few seconds per pulse to about 50ms. per pulse. Speed changes take effect only at the end of the current instruction, and not immediately.

Reset

The *Reset* button sets the program counter to zero and loads the highest memory location with its own address. Using Reset allows a program to be restarted without re-loading it. Reset is valid only when the clock is stopped.

Show Output and Show Trace

The default is that the green screen area shows the output of the running program. The virtual machine also keeps a record of every instruction that is executed, a trace of the running program. The "Show output" and "Show trace" buttons toggle the output area the program output and program trace. The initial default is to show the output.

Input Area

The input area is active only when an input instruction is being executed. The clock stops while input is pending and resumes with the input value in the accumulator. Three kinds of input are accepted:

- A decimal number in the range -2,048 to +2,047 The plus sign is not required for non-negative numbers.
- A hexadecimal number, prefixed with "0x" in the range 0x0 to 0xfff. Any value over 0x7ff is interpreted as a negative number in two's complement format.
- A single printable character; the eight bits of the character's ASCII code are stored in the rightmost eight bits of the accumulator.

Pressing the enter key terminates the input operation.

Register and Memory Contents

While a program is running on the virtual machine, you can place the mouse cursor over a register or memory cell to see the values in binary or decimal and, for memory cells, how the cell would be interpreted as an instruction. It takes a about a second for the tool-tip to appear.

Breakpoints

Clicking in a memory cell will set a breakpoint at that location. When it is about to be loaded as an instruction, the clock will stop so that you can inspect the contents of memory and registers. Click "Run" or "Step" to continue. You cannot set a breakpoint on a cell used for data because it is never loaded for execution.

Saving the Output

Click the "select all" icon on the lower right out the output screen, or click in the output screen and press control-A. Press control-C to copy the selected text to the clipboard; the text may then be pasted into another program such as an editor.

Appendix B
Architecture of the Tiny Binary Computer

The Tiny Binary Computer is entirely a creature of software emulation, but we wanted to show that it is possible to build hardware that will execute the TBC instruction set. With the exception of input and output, the student who applied himself could, in theory, grundle over to the digital logic lab and build a TBC from logic gates, a clock source, and a power supply. If twelve switches were used for input and twelve LEDs for output, it would be possible to realize all of TBC in hardware, but you would get only one input operation per program run without substantial extra work.

There are some details left out, such as the fan-out of the gates used and the way loading registers from the C-bus on the rising edge of the clock is implemented. These are engineering details, and the fact that they are omitted does not diminish the practicality of the general design.

Early computers and today's simple computers all follow the pattern of registers, an ALU, two input buses and an output bus. The size of the registers and buses and the design of the ALU depend on the instruction set of the computer. The microprogrammed implementation described here is patterned after an implementation described in Andrew Tanenbaum's *Structured Computer Organization, Third Edition* (1989.)

B.1 Memory

The Little Man Computer, with which which TBC is backward-compatible, could hold three-digit integers. In twos complement binary, that needs eleven bits, which is a distinctly odd size for a computer word. TBC was designed with a twelve-bit word. That may seem like an odd size as well, but the very successful DEC PDP-8 had twelve-bit words. Data words use twelve-bit two's complement notation, giving TBC an integer range of -2,048 to +2,047. Instruction words have four bits of operation code and eight bits of address. The eight-bit address gives TBC a theoretic capacity of 256 words of memory. Like many real computers, TBC is not "maxed out" with memory; only 128 words are "installed" in the simulated computer.

Memory is connected to the CPU by two buses and three control lines. The memory address bus is a unidirectional bus connected to the CPU's memory address register (MAR). The MAR specifies the address in memory to be accessed during a read or write. The memory data bus is a bidirectional bus connected to the memory data register (MDR). The MDR holds data to be written to memory on a write and receives data from memory on a read.

The three control signals are *read*, *write*, and *presence detect*. A read signal commands memory to deliver the contents from the address in the MAR to the memory data bus, and so the

the MDR. A write signal commands memory to accept data from the MDR and write it to the location specified by the MAR.

The presence detect (PD) signal causes the memory system to indicate the memory size by placing the highest usable memory address on the memory data bus; it will be available at the memory data register (MDR) in the next clock cycle. In a real computer, presence detect returns detailed information about the memory subsystem, including memory size, on a separate serial connection from the memory module. That information is used by the firmware and operating system. TBC uses presence detect to get the address of the stack pointer. In a real computer, the stack pointer is initialized as part of starting a process. Some computers have a stack pointer register to speed up access to the stack pointer.

Except for presence detect, memory operations require two clock cycles. Memory timing is discussed below.

B.2 Data Path: Registers and Buses

The data path of TBC is shown in Figure B-1. The data path of a computer is the arithmetic and logic unit (ALU), the registers, and the buses that connect them. The instruction decoder (I-decoder) / control unit is also shown in the figure. It is discussed in a later section.

TBC has five registers. The memory address register (MAR) holds one memory address to be used in a memory read or write operation. The MAR is an eight-bit register, allowing TBC to address 256 words of memory. It can be loaded from the C-bus and is connected continuously to the memory subsystem. The memory subsystem only uses this address when commanded to read or write.

The memory data register (MDR) is the same size as the TBC's word size: twelve bits. It can be loaded from the C-bus or driven onto the A-bus. It can also send data to memory on a memory write or be loaded with data from memory on a memory read.

The accumulator receives the results of

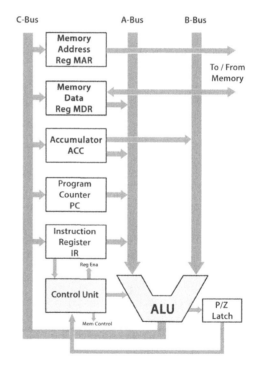

Figure B-1
The datapath of the Tiny Binary Computer

arithmetic or logical operations. It is a twelve-bit register. It can drive the A- or B-bus and can be loaded from the C-bus.

The program counter holds the address of the next instruction to be executed. It is an eight-bit register that can be loaded from the C-bus and enabled onto the A-bus.

The instruction register holds the instruction currently being executed. It is a twelve-bit register that receives twelve-bit quantities when loaded from the C-bus. When the instruction register is enabled to the A-bus, only the rightmost eight bits are transmitted; the high-order four bits are filled with zeros. The leftmost four bits of the instruction register, corresponding to the operation code of a TBC instruction word, are connected continuously to the I-decoder and control unit.

All three main buses are twelve bits wide. The C-bus can load more than one register simultaneously, although that capability is not used in TBC. Only one register can be enabled to the A-bus and only one to the B-bus during any cycle.

B.3 Arithmetic / Logic Unit

The instructions of TBC can be executed with only four ALU functions:

Add: The addends are enabled on the A- and B-buses; the sum is returned on the C-bus.

Subtract: The subtrahend (in MDR) is enabled on the A-bus and the minuend (in Acc) is enabled on the B-bus. The difference is returned on the C-bus.

Copy: The value on the A-bus is copied unchanged to the C-bus.

Increment: The value on the A-bus is incremented and the new value is returned on the C-bus.

An ALU to compute those functions can be formed from one full adder per bit with three extra gates (two AND gates and an EXCLUSIVE OR gate) that provide for control inputs. One bit slice of such an ALU is shown in Figure 3-6. The Ena A (enable A) control input causes the value on the A bus to be passed to the ALU and adder. The Inv A (invert A) control input causes the value on the A-bus to be inverted before being passed to the full adder. The Ena B (enable B) determines whether the value from the B-bus is passed to the ALU and adder.

The final ALU is composed of twelve instances of the circuit of Figure 3-6. A fourth control signal, increment, is connected to the carry-in bit of the rightmost bit slice. A four-bit configuration of such an ALU is shown in Figure 3-7.

The four required functions of the ALU are produced with the control signals. In addition, the ALU can emit constants zero, one, and minus one, also shown.

Addition is straightforward; A is enabled, not inverted, and B is enabled. For subtraction, the bits of the A-bus, which must be the subtrahend, are inverted by the Inv A control. The Increment control provides for the addition of one to form the two's complement of the value on the A bus, which is added to the minuend on the B-bus. If only A is enabled, the value on the A-bus is copied unchanged to the C-bus. If Enable A and Increment are enabled, the value on the A-bus is incremented (by one) and the result is passed to the C-bus.

If none of the four controls is enabled, the output is constant zero. If only Increment is enabled, the output is constant one. If only Invert A is enabled, the output is all ones, a two's complement minus one.

The V (overflow) signal is asserted when the carry into the leftmost bit is different from the carry out of the leftmost bit. An overflow condition causes a machine check and halts the program. The P (positive) signal is the inverse of the leftmost bit, which is the sign bit of a two's complement number. So, P is asserted when the value produced by the ALU is non-negative. The Z (zero) signal is asserted when all bits of the ALU result are zero.

B.4 P/Z Latch

The arithmetic and logic unit produces a P (positive) signal that is the inverse of the sign bit of the ALU output, so it is a one when the ALU output is non-negative and a zero when the output is negative. It also produces a Z (zero) signal that is the NOR of all 12 result bits, and so is a one when the output of the ALU is zero. These signals are input to the P/Z latch. The P/Z Latch is enabled to write concurrently with the accumulator register, so the P and Z outputs always reflect the state of the accumulator contents. The output of the P/Z latch is input to the I-decoder and control unit, providing a mechanism to test the state of the accumulator without requiring an additional data path cycle.

B.5 Control Unit

TBC's control unit is microprogrammed. The instruction decoder and control unit must generate 17 control signals, as shown in the table. In addition, we need two bits to control branching in the microprogram, one bit to control use of the op code as a branch target, and eight bits of address for microprogram jumps. Each microprogram word is 30 bits; for simplicity, we would use a ROM with 32-bit words because these are likely to be commercially available. The layout of the microprogram requires 256 words of ROM, although not all of them are used. The control signals that must be generated are these:

The P and Z bits cause the control unit to test the bits pf the P/Z latch, which reflect the current contents of the accumulator. The associated micro-operation is only executed if the specified bit is true.

Data Path Control Signals		
ALU	4	Enable A (EnaA); Invert A (InvA); Enable B (EnaB); Increment (Inc)
Memory	3	Read, write, PD (presence detect)
A-bus	4	Select one of four registers to enable onto the A-bus
B-bus	1	Indicates that Acc is to be enabled onto B-bus.
C-bus	5	Selects any of five registers for write from the C-bus
Microprogram Controls		
Op Code	1	If 1, the operation code from the instruction register, shifted left 4, is used as branch target
Jump	2	00=no jump; 11=unconditional jump; others reserved
P	1	Microinstruction executed only if the P bit is set
Z	1	Microinstruction executed only if the Z bit is set
Next Addr	8	If *jump* is non-zero, the address of the next microinstruction

The two tables below show the ADD and BRP instructions using register transfer language, and with the actual bits of the microprogram.

For ADD, op code 1

Operation	Loc	EnaA	InvA	EnaB	Inc	Read	Write	PD	A:MDR	A:Acc	A:PC	A:IR	B:Acc	C:MAR	C:MDR	C:Acc	C:PC	C:IR	Op Cd	Jmp	P	Z	Next Addr
MAR←PC; read	00	•				•					•			•									
PC←PC+1	01	•			•						•						•						
IR←MDR; op code	02	•							•									•	•	• •			
MAR←IR[addr]; read	10	•				•						•		•									
wait	11																						
Acc←MDR+Acc	12	•		•					•				•			•				• •			00

For BRP, op code 8

Operation	Loc	EnaA	InvA	EnaB	Inc	Read	Write	PD	A:MDR	A:Acc	A:PC	A:IR	B:Acc	C:MAR	C:MDR	C:Acc	C:PC	C:IR	Op Cd	Jmp	P	Z	Next Addr
MAR←PC;read	00	•				•					•			•									
PC←PC+1	01	•			•						•						•						
IR←MDR; opcode	02	•							•									•	•	• •			
IFP; PC←IR[addr]	80	•										•					•			• •	•		00

The LOC column of the tables shows the address in the microcode read-only storage. It is a hexadecimal number. Each machine instruction starts at location 00 in the microprogram. The code there, `MAR←PC; read` copies the program counter to the memory address register and sends a read signal to the memory subsystem. That causes memory to start a read of the address in the program counter, which holds the address of the next instruction. This starts the fetch part of the fetch-decode-execute instruction cycle.

The next microinstruction, PC←PC+1 increments the program counter so that it points to the instruction following the current one, probably the next instruction. Memory is slower than the CPU, so the read started at location 00 is not yet complete.

ALU	Memory	A-Bus	B-Bus	C-Bus	Op Code	Jump	P	Z	Next Address	Not Used
4	3	4	1	5	1	2	1	1	8	2

Figure B-2

Format of a TBC microprogram word

By the time the program counter has been incremented, the memory read has been completed and the instruction word is in the memory data register, completing the fetch part of the instruction cycle.

The instruction IR←MDR; op code copies the memory data register to the instruction register. The "op code" modifier bit commands the control unit to shift the operation code, a one, left four bits to produce hex 10 and load the next microinstruction from that address. That is the "decode" part of the instruction cycle.

The execute part of the instruction cycle begins with MAR←IR[addr]; read. The square brackets indicate that only the address part of the instruction register will be copied to the MAR. The "read" modifier starts a memory read to load the operand, the value to be added, into the MDR.

The memory read takes two cycle times and there is no useful work to be done while waiting for memory, so the next instruction, at location hex 11, is "wait." There are no microcode bits set, so a data path cycle takes place, but nothing is changed. At the end of the cycle, the value to be added will be in the MDR.

The last part of the execute phase, after the memory read is complete is, ACC←MDR+ACC. The value from the MDR is added to the accumulator and the result is placed in the accumulator. The "Jump" bits are 1,1, an unconditional jump, and the next address is 00. That will start the fetch of the following instruction.

The BRP, branch on positive, instruction is more interesting because it performs a conditional branch. The first three microinstructions are the fetch and decode parts of the instruction cycle and are the same for all instructions. They were discussed above. Notice that the program counter was incremented during the fetch phase, so it points to the instruction immediately following the current one.

Any time a value is stored in the accumulator, the P (positive) and Z (zero) bits are set in the P/Z latch. The execute part of the cycle starts at address hex 80 with IFP; PC←IR[addr]. The "ifp" modifier commands the controller to execute the rest of the microinstruction only if the P (positive) flag is set. If the P flag is set, the address part of the instruction register is copied into the program counter; otherwise, the program counter remains pointing to the instruction immediately following this one. The "Jump" bits are 1,1, an unconditional jump, and the next address is 00. That will start the fetch of the following instruction, from the branch target if P was set, or the next sequential address if not.

Operation code zero (HLT) is handled with digital logic as a special case. A zero in the operation code field is detected using a four-input NOR. The output is ANDed with the Op Code bit of the control word. A result of true stops the processor clock and so stops execution of the microprogram.

Figure B-2 shows the layout of a control word in TBC's microprogram control store. The bits are shown in the order they were discussed above. Tanenbaum (1989) pointed out that they would probably be arranged in a way that minimized crossing of conductors when the CPU was laid out for a semiconductor die. That's an engineering detail that need not concern us while we are working at the level of logical design.

B.6 Stack

An extension to the LMC instruction set provides for a stack that grows downward from the highest memory address. The highest memory address is used as a stack pointer. It is initialized with its own location when a program is loaded or the machine is reset. That is, address 0x7F is loaded with the value 0x7F. The call instruction decrements SP and stores the program counter at the location pointed by SP. The RET (return) instruction places the value at location SP into the program counter and increments SP. If a TBC with 256 words were implemented, location 0xFC would be the top of usable memory and top of the stack because the top three addresses are used for programmable I/O.

The location at the highest memory address can be used for program storage provided the CALL and RET instructions are not used in such a program.

B.7 Timing

The most important thing about understanding timing in TBC (and real computers) is that things do not happen instantly. Computation with digital logic introduces gate delays, and even sending a signal from one part of the CPU to another isn't instantaneous because the signals travel no faster than the speed of light. The purpose of a CPU's clock is to allow enough time for signals to travel through the gates and buses to perform the desired computations. For real computers, clock speeds are measured in gigahertz: billions of pulses per second. Using the TBC simulator, one can adjust the clock speed from a pulse every couple of seconds to several pulses per second. The idea is to make TBC's clock slow enough for you to observe what is happening.

Instruction Timing

The fetch/decode/execute cycle of the von Neumann architecture means that each instruction consists of some number of individual steps. In TBC, each step is accomplished in one data path cycle.

Data path Timing

The data path of a computer comprises the registers, the ALU, and the buses that connect them. TBC completes one data path cycle with every cycle of the computer's clock. Each instruction takes multiple data path cycles, so each data path cycle does part of the work of one instruction.

TBC uses an asymmetric clock; that means one part of the cycle, in this case clock-low, is longer than the other part, the clock-high part of the cycle. The clock-low part of the cycle must be long enough for generation of control signals, propagation of data on the buses, and computation by the ALU. By contrast,

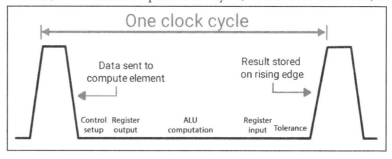

Figure B-3

Operations that take place during one clock cycle

the clock-high part of the cycle need be only long enough for the registers to be loaded from the C-bus.

The diagram in Figure B-3 is similar to that in Figure 2-18. A clock cycle starts on the falling edge of the clock. The falling edge triggers the instruction decoder and control unit to set up the necessary signals. That takes a certain amount of time, shown as "control setup" in Figure B-3.

The control signals include register-enable signals for those registers that are to put their contents on the A- and B- buses. The time for the registers to send their contents to the A- and B-buses, and for the signals to reach the ALU is shown as "register output."

The arithmetic-logic unit is combinational logic; it is computing continuously. Its outputs change in response to changes in the inputs. However, the output of the ALU is not valid until it has valid inputs, and for a time after that equal to the gate delay through the ALU. That time is shown as "ALU computation" in the figure. It then take time, shown as "register input," for the output of the ALU to travel along the C-bus and be available at the inputs of the registers.

The last time interval in the figure is labeled "tolerance." Because of manufacturing variation, electronic devices manufactured identically will still be slightly different. The allowance for tolerance means that an instance of this CPU that happens to be slightly slower than the design specification will still work correctly.

By the end of the clock-low portion of the cycle, the result of the current computation has propagated through the C-bus and is available at the inputs of the registers. One or more registers will be selected by the "register enable" signals from the control unit to receive the results, and the results will be stored in those registers on the rising edge of the clock. (Usually, a result is stored in only one register, but it is possible to store the same result in more than one.)

Notice that no signals are necessary to trigger operations between the falling edge of the clock and the next rising edge. It is only necessary to hold the clock in the low state for long enough to allow propagation of signals through the buses and the ALU, then back to the register inputs.

Memory Timing

In a real computer, memory is many times slower than the CPU. For a computer with a four GHz clock and 15 ns memory, memory is about 60 times slower; the clock will pulse 60 times before memory delivers a result. To compensate, real computers implement cache memory. Most memory requests can be satisfied from a small, fast cache memory that is only about two to ten times slower than the CPU.

To show that the CPU must often wait on memory, but to keep the waiting time from being so long that the simulation is useless, TBC requires two clock cycles for a memory access. That is, if a memory read is commanded in clock cycle one, the result is not available in the memory data register until the beginning of clock cycle three. Whenever possible, the control unit does useful work while waiting for memory. For example, the program counter is incremented while waiting for memory to deliver an instruction in the "fetch" part of the cycle. Otherwise, the control unit executes a no-operation cycle while waiting on memory.

B.8 Input and Output

The IN and OUT instructions are executed "behind the scenes" by the simulator. The OUT instruction completes in four cycles; the explanation might be that the I/O subsystem always has a buffer ready for output and can accept in one clock cycle. The clock is stopped while the instruction executes. No detail of the I/O process is exposed by the simulator when the LMC I/O instructions are used.

TBC can also do memory mapped I/O, which exposes programmed I/O with busy waiting to the simulated program. TBC uses the three highest possible memory addresses, 0xfd,

0xfe, and 0xff as registers for I/O. Address 0xfd is the I/O address register, 0xfe is the I/O status register and address 0xff is the I/O data register.

The programmer must store a device address in 0xfd; the input device is 0x000 and the output device is 0x001. For output, the data word to be written must be stored at address 0xff. For input, the value read will be placed in address 0xff. After the registers are set up, the programmer issues the PIO instruction. The program must then loop, testing address 0xfe until it becomes one, indicating the completion of the I/O operation. Any input or output operation attempted before 0xfe becomes one will cause a machine check.

B.9 References

Tanenbaum, Andrew (1989). *Structured Computer Organization, Third Edition.* Upper Saddle River, NJ, Prentice-Hall.

Tanenbaum, Andrew (2006). *Structured Computer Organization, Fifth Edition.* Upper Saddle River, NJ, Prentice-Hall.

Index

Made in the USA
Las Vegas, NV
04 October 2024

96287587R00155